Not
So Simple

D0927365

Not So Simple

The "Simple" Stories by Langston Hughes

Donna Akiba Sullivan Harper

University of Missouri Press

COLUMBIA AND LONDON

Copyright © 1995 by
The Curators of the University of Missouri
University of Missouri Press, Columbia, Missouri 65201
Printed and bound in the United States of America
All rights reserved
5 4 3 2   99 98 97 96 95

Library of Congress Cataloging-in-Publication Data
Harper, Donna Sullivan.
  Not so simple : the "Simple" stories by Langston Hughes / Donna
  Akiba Sullivan Harper.
    p. cm.
  Includes bibliographical references and index.
  ISBN 0-8262-0980-7
  1. Afro-American men in literature.   2. Afro-Americans in literature.
  3. Simple (Fictitious character)   I. Hughes, Langston, 1902–1967.
  II. Title.
  PS3515.U274Z645   1995
  813'.52—dc20   94-47195
                                                              CIP

⊗This paper meets the requirements of the American National Standard
for Permanence of Paper for Printed Library Materials, Z39.48, 1984.

Text Design: Elizabeth K. Fett
Jacket Design: Stephanie Foley
Typesetter: Bookcomp
Printer and binder: Thomson-Shore, Inc.
Typefaces: ITC Garamond Book

For permission to reprint copyrighted material, see the last printed page
of the book.

With gratitude and love
to my wonderful parents,
Edwin Charles Sullivan, D.D.S.,
and the late Iva Reid Sullivan

As the greatest only are,
In his simplicity sublime.

—ALFRED, LORD TENNYSON,
"Ode on the Death of the Duke of Wellington"

Contents

Acknowledgments

WHO WOULD EVER HAVE IMAGINED that a student would take a required assignment for Freshman Composition and turn it into a career? That was my experience, thanks to the inspired teaching of Jessie Lemon Brown of Hampton Institute—now professor emeritus of Hampton University. All acknowledgments for my own writing about Langston Hughes must start with her. Of course, I also thank Langston Hughes for writing such magnificent, rich, and endlessly entertaining works.

I am also grateful to my teachers and my students at Oberlin College, where I tested my first theories on Hughes and aesthetics. I am especially grateful to my mentor and now colleague, Calvin C. Hernton, and to the students who were brave enough to enroll in my "Langston Hughes and the Black Aesthetic" course. Of those students, special thanks go to Sylvia Gaston Hamilton for her sociological considerations of Hughes's works.

I am indebted to the meticulous readings of my doctoral dissertation by my committee, Robert Wheeler, Elizabeth Stevenson, and particularly Peter Dowell. Their suggestions and criticisms led to further investigations. My colleague and friend Robert Higgins also helped my work, and he introduced me to Griffith J. Davis, who was an angel on my shoulder during the lengthy process of completing the dissertation. Our friend Griff has now passed on, but my thanks go to Bob for that crucial introduction.

The networking of professional life includes many persons who have played a role in helping to take me from a finished doctoral dissertation to a finished book. Ron Baxter Miller introduced me to his editor, Beverly Jarrett. That connection was vital. Ron has continued to encourage and nurture my scholarship. Beverly has been marvelously patient with me and has never wavered in her support for the merit of this study. Arnold Rampersad has been a scholar and a friend, assisting both personally and professionally, with everything from his brilliant biography of Hughes to his kind support, recommendations, and advice. The book would never have happened without these three people. Thank you.

I would probably never have met Arnold, had not Henry Morgan and Henry Harder of Missouri Southern College planned and hosted the first Langston Hughes Study Conference in Joplin, Missouri, March 13–14, 1981. Thanks to the Danforth Foundation, I was permitted to convert a dissertation stipend into a travel grant, which enabled me to sit at the feet of the giants in Hughes scholarship: the late Richard Barksdale, the late Therman B. O'Daniel, the late George H. Bass, and living legend Arnold Rampersad. Established scholars, budding scholars, college professors, public school teachers, performing artists, and insightful laypeople all converged—some on program, others in the audience. I shall always be indebted to the Danforth Foundation and to Henry Harder and Henry Morgan for creating that landmark conference. The reverberations continue and—I hope—will never cease.

My students at Spelman College, who have kindly subjected themselves to *The Best of Simple* in many of my classes, have opened my eyes to wonderful new insights. Particular thanks to the students who took the "Langston Hughes Seminar," and, among those, special thanks to Tayari Jones, Laura Pearl Morrison, Tacita Mikel, and Gina King. My book discussion group, consisting of women from Hillside Presbyterian Church and Temple Sinai, also shared ideas and allowed me to test my theories. Thank you Tish Wilson, Lelia Crawford, Joanne Nurss, Ava Johnson, Roz Hosenball, Barbara Katinsky, Susan Golden, Millie Bailey, and Fran Zuspan, Emma Stanford, Elsie Heyman, and Barbara Schaffer. Another church member who reads avidly but does not attend our book discussions, Al Pride Jr., brought to my attention the new Jesse B. Semple in the Derrick Bell allegory and has offered support and encouragement. Thank you, Al.

For the actual research I am deeply grateful, first of all, to the Faculty Resource Network at New York University, whose summer scholar in residence opportunity in 1991 restored my confidence in my own intellect. (Teaching full-time can do funny things to a person's brain.) The Faculty Resource Network certainly recharged my mental battery and gave me new confidence in my ability to seclude myself for a while and concentrate in June 1991. Particular thanks to James W. Tuttleton, my faculty host, and to the staff in the English Department. I want Leslie Berlowitz and staff to know how valuable their program is. I would like to thank Spelman's former provost, Ruth Simmons, for hearing my anguish and for providing relief. My thanks, also, to all parties connected with that program.

In the summer of 1992, a grant from the Coca-Cola Foundation provided funds for me to return to Yale University for a full month of research in the excellent James Weldon Johnson Collection in the Beinecke Rare Book and Manuscript Library. The staff in the Beinecke are cheerful, knowledgeable, patient, and helpful. This book absolutely depended upon that collection and that staff. What a joy to have dependable and pleasant staff to make that research as easy and convenient as possible. Yale University is also very generous in its support of computer-aided scholarship. My fingers would never have survived a month of research without the use of the laptop (usually no. 5) in the Beinecke and then the facilities in Yale's Computer Center. If only all universities supported scholarship so graciously. My thanks to Yale. I am grateful to Coca-Cola for financing that month of study. I would like to thank Spelman's current provost, Glenda Price, and her assistant, Virginia "Flo" Roberts, for keeping me informed of these opportunities and for supporting me.

The people of New Haven, Connecticut—in particular my adopted church home of Bethel—helped to make my visits there quite pleasant. My landlady and friend, Sheila Brent, provided a room for rent, but she also provided hospitality. My thanks to John Hanna, for alerting me to Sheila and to Bethel. Thanks also go to Tisch Jones, for introducing me to John Hanna and for her lasting friendship and encouragement.

My Spelman College family has been tremendously understanding, supportive, and helpful. Thanks to President Johnnetta B. Cole, former provost Ruth Simmons, current provost Glenda Price, former chairperson June Aldridge and current chairperson Anne B. Warner, and to all my colleagues who covered the classes while I was granted a year of release from teaching in 1992–1993 so that I could devote attention to this work. I would like to thank my colleagues in other departments who have been tremendously nurturing and enthusiastic as I journeyed through this writing process. Particular thanks to Harry LeFever, who provided me with texts concerning participant observation—a specific aspect of sociology that had grown rusty since I studied at Oberlin with Kiyoshi Ikeda. Blessings and gratitude to my Spelman family for prayer support during the illnesses and deaths in my family while the writing and revisions continued. Particular thanks to Lois Moreland, Zadie Long, Yvette Williams Higgins, Candace Raven, Jane Najmuddin Smith, Geneva H. Baxter, Pushpa Parekh, Tina and Clarence Johnson, Delores Stephens, Sharifa Saa, Ray Grant, Rhoda Martin Hendrickson, Madeline Picciotto, Kris McDermott, Shirley Toland, Gloria Wade-Gayles, Jean Billinglea-Brown, Beverly Guy-Sheftall, Marika Visvesvara, Siga Jagne, Judy Gebre-Hiwet, Dalila de Sousa Sheppard, Ada Jackson, Gwen Billingslea, Cynthia Spence, and Tina Sizemore.

My friends and colleagues, most notably Sandra Govan, Dolan Hubbard, James Trotman, Jacqueline Rouse, Violet Harris, Carolyn Denard, Trudier Harris, and Eloise McKinney Johnson, have offered vital encouragement.

For giving me my own personal copies of all the Simple volumes, I must thank several people: for *Simple Speaks His Mind,* Arnold Rampersad; for *Simple Takes a Wife,* Charles Blockson; for *Simple Stakes a Claim* and *Simple's Uncle Sam,* my other "mommy," Margaret Williams Reid; for *The Best of Simple,* my parents, Edwin C. Sullivan and the late Iva Reid Sullivan. I have been richly blessed to have friends and family who knew of my passion for Simple and who gave to me these personal copies, without which this analysis would have been terribly troublesome.

The many speaking engagements that have allowed me to share my theories have been extremely important to my work. Special thanks to Raymond Patterson of City College of New York (and my sister poet, Mari Evans, who graciously relinquished her place in the program to accommodate my participation in 1988); Louis Suggs, who invited me to Clemson University; Emery Wimbish of Lincoln University, Pennsylvania, for the excellent three-day conference in which I was privileged to participate in 1992; Dennis Wiseman, who included me as consultant and *The Best of Simple* as text in the NEH summer seminar at Wofford College in Spartanburg, S.C., in 1992; Sundiata Cha-Jua, then of the University of Missouri–Columbia, who kindly included me in the birthday symposium on Langston Hughes in 1994; and to Henry Morgan and Henry Harder, of Missouri Southern College, and Randy Brown and Patsy Robinson, of the City of Joplin, for including me in the second annual Langston Hughes Celebration in 1994, which was a truly memorable experience. My colleagues in the Association for the Study of Afro-American Life and History, the College Language Association, the Middle Atlantic Writers Association, and the Modern Language Association have kindly included me in their annual programs from time to time, and I appreciate those opportunities. Last, but not least, I thank my hometown folks in Suffolk, Virginia, who have allowed me to babble about Langston Hughes and Simple in the First Baptist Church on Mahan Street, at Suffolk High School, and at John F. Kennedy High School.

I have mentioned the helpful documents and staff at the Beinecke Library at Yale. Let me also note the helpful resources and staff at the Schomburg Center for Research in Black Culture at the New York Public Library (where I serendipitously met Jean Blackwell Hutson, thanks to Larry Greene). I also acknowledge the help I received from the materials and staff at the libraries of Hampton University, University of Georgia, Atlanta University Center, and Emory University.

For their help in reading drafts of the manuscript, I am grateful to several people. Arnold Rampersad and Leslie Sanders provided essential comments to help me enrich my discussions. I fear I have not developed all the wonderful ideas they suggested, but I deeply appreciate the guidance. Indeed, the chapters are richer thanks to their insights. My student assistant, Atuanya Cheatham, has rendered marvelous help with the many tasks linked to revision and typescript preparation. My thoughtful copyeditor, Gloria Thomas, has surely rendered this text more sensible to readers new to Simple. I am indebted to her and to the entire staff at the University of Missouri Press.

My family has been patient and encouraging in the long years leading to this work. Always their love has enriched my life. I am especially grateful to my parents and to my family, including Blass W. Gatling Sr., Lonnie T. Reid, Margaret Williams Reid, Flora Walden Chase, Patricia J. Sullivan, Laverne Hunter Maurant, Laura R. Shell, Jarvis and Iva G. Brown, and the late Edith Reid Gatling and Mae Mandy Sullivan. Special blessings to my husband, Jerome Harper, and to my daughter, Selena Harper.

My supporters, helpers, and advisors have been wonderful. However, any errors of judgment or errors of fact must be attributed to me.

A theme in all these bits of gratitude is that somehow I was in the right places at the right times. I do not call that auspicious placement luck or coincidence. I call it a blessing from God. For all these financial, personal, and intangible blessings that have led to this book, I thank God, from whom ALL blessings flow.

Abbreviations

BECAUSE *THE BEST OF SIMPLE* and the recently published *The Return of Simple* offer the most convenient means by which the general reader may access the Simple stories, whenever possible all page references will be to these volumes rather than to the earlier volume under discussion. When the Simple stories under discussion do not appear in either of these two collections, they will be cited as they appear in other published volumes, and any episodes not collected in any book will be cited according to their newspaper publication.

The following editions and abbreviations were used in citations throughout the book:

Collections of Simple stories by Langston Hughes:

Mind *Simple Speaks His Mind.* New York: Simon and Schuster, 1950
Wife *Simple Takes a Wife.* New York: Simon and Schuster, 1953
Claim *Simple Stakes a Claim.* New York: Rinehart, 1957
Best *The Best of Simple.* New York: Hill and Wang, 1961
Sam *Simple's Uncle Sam.* New York: Hill and Wang, 1965
Return *The Return of Simple,* ed. Akiba Sullivan Harper. New York: Hill and Wang, 1994

Frequently named publications:
CD *Chicago Defender*
Post *New York Post*

Repository for papers, manuscripts, and correspondence of Hughes and other terms used in association:
JWJ The Langston Hughes Papers, James Weldon Johnson Collection, Beinecke Rare Book and Manuscript Library, Yale University

MS   Manuscript
MSS   Manuscripts
LH   Langston Hughes

Not
So Simple

_____

"Day-after-Day Heroism"

THE WORDS *SIMPLE* AND *SIMPLICITY* recur in analyses of Langston Hughes's works. A disturbing consequence of this trend has been an exclusion of Hughes's works as texts for modern criticism, a dismissal of Hughes as being too simple to merit literary analysis.[1] While several critics have focused on Hughes, only Ron Baxter Miller has devoted an entire book to a complex analysis of Hughes's poetry in terms of the most recent critical strategies. What Miller and other devoted Hughes scholars know is that Hughes's works possess the illusion of simplicity—a sleight that hides a depth of complex uses of language, psychology, sociology, and history. With his literary illusion, Hughes demonstrates what Richard Wright considered to be a desirable "complex simplicity."[2]

A primary example of Hughes's deceptive simplicity is the character whose name and history represent the illusion of being simple. Thoughtful reflection upon the stage of Hughes's career during which he launched the character, upon the historical period that shaped the character, and upon the stages of the character's development will begin an appropriate consideration of why Jesse B. Semple, "Simple," was really *not* so simple.

During the 1940s, the decade of the second world war, Langston Hughes was in his forties and had achieved a significant measure of success. He was well educated, honored, active in many areas of writing, and had published thirteen books in different genres. A bio-bibliographical note in *What the Negro Wants,* published in 1944, included the following details about him:

1. For example, many recent critical works by Henry Louis Gates Jr. barely mention Hughes, if they mention him at all.
2. Wright, "Blueprint for Negro Writing," 60.

He studied one year at Columbia and was graduated from Lincoln
University [Pennsylvania] in 1929. His alma mater conferred upon
him the degree of Litt. D. in 1943. He is a member of The Authors'
Guild, the Dramatists' Guild, ASCAP, the Advisory Council of the
Writers' War Board, the Music War Committee, and the board of
the magazine *Common Ground*. Mr. Hughes has contributed to the
*Saturday Evening Post, Survey Graphic, Esquire, New Yorker, Nation,
New Republic, Crisis, Opportunity, Theatre Arts, Poetry,* and *Common
Ground.* He wrote in collaboration with Clarence Muse the scenario
for "Way Down South." His play, "Mulatto," ran for a year at the
Vanderbilt Theatre, New York. "Don't You Want to be Free?" gave 135
performances at the Harlem Suitcase Theatre. His historical pageant,
"For This We Fight," was presented at Madison Square Garden, June
7, 1943. His works, all published by Knopf, are *The Weary Blues, The
Dream Keeper, Shakespeare in Harlem, The Ways of White Folks, Not
Without Laughter* and his autobiography, *The Big Sea.*[3]

This list omits *Fine Clothes to the Jew,* his second volume of poetry,
which was out of print at that time and which had drawn nasty criticism and even condemnation. In addition, the list omits six slim and
mostly topical volumes of poems published with several small firms
before 1944. Even with its gaps, however, this biographical statement
indicates those achievements of which Hughes felt proudest at the
beginning of the 1940s and reveals the variety of genres in which
he had already been published—poetry, short stories, novels, song
lyrics, and drama. Despite his versatility, he was best known then
and remains best known now as a poet. However, his poetry in the
1940s received little praise and was found to be cynical, sad, and—at
best—a subtle blending of tragedy and comedy.[4]

The 1940s, however, gave Hughes a new area of fame and achievement. Viewing the decade retrospectively in the headnote about
Hughes in their anthology, James A. Emanuel and Theodore L. Gross
praise the creation of Jesse B. Semple as a major accomplishment in
Hughes's career:

None of these books of the 1940's, and none of the awards or positions
that came to Hughes then—the thousand-dollar grant from the American

---

3. Rayford Logan, ed., *What the Negro Wants,* 348.
4. Edward J. Mullen, ed., *Critical Essays on Langston Hughes,* 12-13.

Academy of Arts and Letters in 1946, the posts as poet-in-residence at Atlanta University in 1947 and as "resource teacher" at the Laboratory School of the University of Chicago in 1949—distinguish the decade so much as the one night that the author spent at a Harlem bar near his St. Nicholas Avenue address. That night in 1942, the one great fictional character that Hughes was to conceive, Harlemite Jesse B. Semple, was born when the poet heard "Simple's" prototype tell a girlfriend about his job making cranks in a New Jersey war plant.[5]

Without question, Simple was "the one great fictional character" Hughes offered to the literary world. The note goes on to compare Simple to other notable creations: "Soon his vividness on paper had a wholeness and a reality that would rank him with Huck Finn, Mr. Dooley, and Uncle Remus." This praise reflects the critical consensus about the Simple stories, which feature humorous dialogues between Jesse B. Semple (pronounced Jessie B. Sample) and a usually unnamed straight man, or foil.

Literary critics, scholars, and Hughes's fellow artists have praised Jesse B. Semple as "the most famous character in black fiction" and the Simple stories as "Langston Hughes's greatest contribution to American culture." For example, Arthur P. Davis, the pioneer in criticism of Simple, summarizes in his 1974 book, "Most critics feel that the Simple series is Hughes's best work in fiction and that Simple is his greatest single creation."[6]

What makes Simple such a notable creation? The dozens of critical assessments echo the opinion that Jesse B. Semple represents the Negro[7] everyman—the average Harlem citizen—and most of them elaborate upon the value of such a characterization. Simple is an ordinary working black man representative of the masses of black folks

5. Emanuel and Gross, eds., *Dark Symphony: Negro Literature in America,* 195–96.

6. Roger Rosenblatt, *Black Fiction,* 103; Eugenia Collier, "A Pain in His Soul: Simple as Epic Hero," in Therman B. O'Daniel, ed., *Langston Hughes: Black Genius,* 131; Davis, *From the Dark Tower: Afro-American Writers, 1900 to 1960,* 69.

7. Throughout this book, the terms *Negro, black,* and *African American* will be used interchangeably. While political implications would place different connotations on those racial designations, in this text, the reader should regard them as synonyms for Americans of African heritage.

in the 1940s. Like many other blacks, he has migrated to Harlem from the South. He therefore vividly remembers the racism he experienced in Dixie and celebrates the opportunities for African Americans in the North.

In the same way that racism shadows even the new economic and political freedom Simple finds in the North, his troublesome romantic past inhibits his new love life. He has left but not divorced an exploitative and unloving wife, and therefore he cannot satisfy the requests of his highly respectable lady-friend, Joyce, to marry her. Joyce aspires toward culture and home-ownership, and she eschews the nightly beer outings Simple enjoys. The corner bar offers Simple more than beer, however. The relaxation there compensates for his daily routine of hard work for minimal pay, and he is also able to exchange ideas in the bar, where he discourses at length in his own straightforward way about the world, the nation, and his own life. Through his narrations Simple introduces a large (and heavily female) supporting cast: guardian Aunt Lucy, estranged wife Isabel, best girl Joyce, good-time girl Zarita, landlady Madam Butler, society lady Mrs. Sadie Maxwell-Reeves, early love interests Mabel and Cherie, and cousins F. D., Minnie, and Lynn Clarisse. Simple also finds a way to include a reference to race in almost every conversation, much to the dismay of the foil.

Ananias Boyd, as the foil eventually came to be known, is a college-educated man who remains in the neighborhood bar late into the night "observing life for literary purposes" (*Best*, 12). He is articulate, moderate, and generally in better financial shape than Simple. He has never lived in the South, and he does not speak often about his job or his love life. He usually just listens to Simple and questions him, but on some topics he argues with him in an effort to help his outspoken friend appreciate the broader view of whatever topic he is addressing. Every so often, however, Simple's point of view is inarguable, so the foil ends up agreeing with him, thereby emphasizing the wisdom of Simple's point.

Hughes began the Simple columns having conversations himself with his fictional Simple Minded Friend. Gradually his own college-educated, widely traveled persona was transferred to Simple's bar buddy/foil, and as Hughes became more careful in crafting his Simple stories, he more and more consistently created for the bar buddy a distinct personality and distinct language marked by a refined, occasionally stuffy diction. Confusion sometimes arises over whether the bar buddy should be called "Boyd," since Hughes did not call him that in most of the Simple columns but eventually gave him that name for dramatic purposes when he produced his Simple play, *Simply Heavenly,* in 1957. The confusion is intensified by the fact that Simple mentions in some of the early stories a fellow roomer named Ezra Boyd; the Boyd in the play is Ananias Boyd. In his last collection of Simple stories, *Simple's Uncle Sam,* Hughes ended up calling the foil by the name Boyd.

An important note about Boyd is that his college education does not alienate him from the masses. Whereas Sterling Brown notes that Hughes sharply satirizes Aunt Tempy in *Not without Laughter* as a high-tone striver and does not treat her with sympathy,[8] Boyd, who because of his college education and elevated language could be suspected of being a striver, is likeable, although he remains far less rounded than Simple. The characterization of alienated, high-and-mighty strivers in the Simple saga is restricted to a minor figure in the play *Simply Heavenly,* a character known only as "Character." Even the society-minded Joyce and the ultimate society lady, Mrs. Sadie Maxwell-Reeves, gain some sympathy in their portrayal as strivers in the stories, but Character, described as "a snob," or "that character trying to make people think he's educated," elicits ridicule and scorn from the other people in the bar Simple frequents in the play. Speaking with an affected dialect, he asks for "a thimble of Scawtch," as Bodiddly mocks, which is a drink order "like the English," the bartender announces. Miss Mamie proudly contrasts Character with Boyd: "One thing I like about Boyd here, even if he is a writer, he ain't always trying to impress folks. Also he speaks when he comes in a public place."[9] Simple not only tolerates the foil's education, he draws upon it. On the other hand, he feels comfortable reprimanding his bar buddy when he perceives an exaggerated erudition or any other offensive air surfacing. The foil, then, emerges as a sympathetically presented upwardly mobile, college-educated persona.

8. Brown, *The Negro in American Fiction* (Washington: The Associates in Negro Folk Education, 1937).
9. LH, *Five Plays by Langston Hughes,* 123–24.

Simple's intimate interaction with the foil—a very different sort of person from himself—becomes an important factor in Simple's genuine humanity and in the reader's ability to appreciate it. When Boyd and Simple converse in "that poor man's club that is a bar," the beer equalizes them. Thus, we have an environment that creates a "suspension of hierarchial precedence" in some ways similar to the "Carnival" period M. M. Bakhtin discusses. In the local bar, Simple and Boyd experience what Bakhtin finds in the carnival atmosphere: "a special form of free and familiar contact . . . among people who were usually divided by the barriers of caste, property, profession, and age." With these and the barriers of education and geographic origins broken down, the corner bar creates an atmosphere "for new, purely human relations. These truly human relations were not only a fruit of imagination or abstract thought; they were experienced." With the foil and Simple in the bar, equality was not merely imagined, it was truly experienced. The intrusion of "Character" talking about "stereotypes" in the bar in *Simply Heavenly* illustrates that Boyd was an equal, a peer, in the bar.[10]

This formula of "free and familiar" dialogue and interchange between these significantly different men began on February 13, 1943, when the *Chicago Defender* published Hughes's first dialogue with his "Simple Minded Friend." This "very happy creation" was an experiment in Hughes's weekly editorial column, "Here to Yonder."[11] Favorable response from readers and encouragement from John Sengstacke, publisher and editor of the *Defender,* led Hughes to continue to develop this Simple character. Within three years, he sought to publish his first book-length collection of the Simple episodes, which proved to be anything but simple. Nevertheless, Hughes persevered.

He revised and condensed the columns. He improved characterization and enhanced the distinctions between the vernacular language of Simple and the measured and educated diction of the Hughes persona/foil/Boyd. The result of his years of improvement and design

10. "Simple's Long Trek to Broadway," in "Simply Heavenly MSS," JWJ; Bakhtin, *Rabelais and His World,* trans. Helene Iswolsky (Bloomington: Indiana University Press, 1984), 10.

11. Arna Bontemps praised the Simple Minded Friend as a "very happy creation" in a letter to LH, February 22, 1943, in Charles H. Nichols, ed., *Arna Bontemps–Langston Hughes Letters, 1925–1967,* 121.

was *Simple Speaks His Mind,* published in 1950, the first of six books and one play to collect as literature the ideas originating in the popular columns recording the conversations of Simple and the foil. The success of that first book led to the publication of others: *Simple Takes a Wife,* in 1953; *Simple Stakes a Claim,* in 1957; the play *Simply Heavenly,* in 1957; *The Best of Simple,* featuring selections from the three earlier volumes, in 1961; and *Simple's Uncle Sam,* in 1965. These works have been anthologized and performed extensively in the United States and have enjoyed numerous translations.

The premise of the Simple stories appeals as the primary step in the human quest for peace, understanding, and common ground: two men from different educational and cultural backgrounds meet on an equal plane, exchange ideas, develop a friendship, and bridge the gap between them. Each society has its own barriers, whether they be barriers of education, gender, class, sexual preference, or physical ability. By observing Simple and Boyd, readers vicariously experience themselves overcoming the barriers in their own world, reaching out to someone different, and finding in that person a friend.

Significantly, though, Hughes broke through these barriers while remaining within the Afrocentric sphere he had claimed as his preferred medium. Despite their differences, the foil and Simple are both black in a racially unbalanced society. Thus, one barrier is broken, but the larger one remains. In a way, the Simple premise renders permanent the chasm between the races. The two main characters seldom encounter whites. They exist in a world within a world: Harlem, the separate black community in New York City. Perhaps a celebration of the longevity of the Simple stories sadly witnesses the continuity of American race prejudice. Contemporary readers of the Simple tales repeatedly affirm that they know someone like Simple. How can a Simple still exist in the 1990s—so many years after all the laws were passed to permit the vote, to end the poll tax, to end the restrictive covenant in housing, to end discrimination in military service, education, and employment? Why do so many readers in the 1990s still recognize in Simple someone they know? Could the racial oppression against which Simple railed continue to exist? Yes, racism remains in full force, proclaims the public outcry about the 1992 acquittal of four white Los Angeles policemen who had been videotaped beating Rodney King, a black man they pulled over on the highway.

On the other hand, recognizing someone "exactly like Simple" may not necessarily mean recognizing a working-class African American suffering from racial oppression. Fans of Simple range far beyond the African American residents of Harlem. They span the globe. Therefore, Simple's appeal can be termed universal. Readers can see in Simple's racial oppression the same kinds of forces that oppress people sexually, economically, ethnically, or because of physical limitations. Perhaps the humor in Simple's tales allows us to laugh at the continuing hypocrisy of American proclamations of "liberty and justice for all," even in the face of vehement objections to President Bill Clinton's earliest efforts to allow openly gay people to serve in the U.S. armed forces. Perhaps we hope for common ground with Simple, projecting from his desire to see a black general pinning medals on a white soldier ("Simple on Military Integration," *Best*, 81) a gay American's dream to see an openly gay general pinning medals on a straight soldier. Whether fifty years have left new black faces in the same old racially oppressed places or whether the name of the oppression has changed for some readers, the publication history of Simple tells us that Langston Hughes succeeded with his creation. Whether readers focus on the sameness of the race of Simple and Boyd or not, somehow, because these two different men become allies, their side of the racial barrier becomes a more humane and more appealing place to be. This study will examine Hughes's success from both a race-centered and a universal vantage point.

The extensive success in translation and the endurance in publication of the Simples stories become all the more astonishing when we take into account Simple's origins: the Negro press. Unlike any other significant fictional creation, Jesse B. Semple originated as an occasional feature in a weekly column that Hughes wrote for the *Chicago Defender,* a medium that served average African Americans. New York City publishers became involved later in the process, but Simple's origins rested with average African American readers in cities and in rural areas throughout the country, and even serving in the nation's armed forces abroad. One might assume that a character crafted to suit such a narrow audience would be too provincial, too ethnic, or otherwise too limited to appeal to a broader audience. However, the opposite has proven true. As Hughes himself commented, "A fictional character can be ever so ethnic, ever so local and regional, and still be universal in terms of humanity." As early as 1949, G. Lewis Chandler called Hughes a synecdochist because he could use the racial as a means to achieve the universal.[12]

A major part of Simple's "humanity" stems from his ordinariness. He was then and remains the kind of person many of us recognize. Hughes not only captured Simple's ordinary qualities, but he also imbued them with dignity, humor, and goodness. He was able to bring these qualities to the creation of Simple because he maintained his own racial pride and his sense of humor. Moreover, he enjoyed the ordinary black folks he met on his many lecture tours, as well as those among whom he made his home in Harlem. As Arna Bontemps wrote in 1952, "Few people have enjoyed being Negro as much as Langston Hughes." In his more politically charged analysis, Richard Wright links Hughes's upbringing and job history to his appreciation for ordinary African Americans: "Unlike the sons and daughters of Negro 'society,' Hughes was not ashamed of those of his race who had to scuffle for their bread. The jerky transitions of his own life did not admit of his remaining in one place long enough to become a slave of prevailing Negro middle-class prejudices." Because he loved, respected, and identified with ordinary African Americans, Hughes was able to represent faithfully the attitudes and the speech patterns of the Negro everyman, an ordinary Harlem resident. Blyden Jackson thoroughly praises Simple's ordinariness, claiming, "Whether or not [Simple] is truly like most ordinary Negroes, he is certainly, in both form and substance, what many ordinary Negroes were at least once prepared to concede without rancor that they thought they were. At least, to that extent, Simple must be accounted a folk Negro's concept of the folk Negro."[13]

Jackson finds Simple's ordinariness praiseworthy because "at the very heart of American racism there seems to be an assumption of the most dangerous import: to wit, that there are no Negroes who are average people." In Jackson's analysis, this dangerous racist view assumes that blacks are either *exceptional* (e.g., Ralph Bunche or Marian Anderson) or—especially in fiction—*grotesque:*

12. LH, "Simple Again"; Chandler, "Selfsameness and a Promise."
13. Bontemps, "Black and Bubbling," in Mullen, ed., *Critical Essays,* 80; Wright, "Forerunner and Ambassador," review of *The Big Sea,* in Michel Fabre, *Richard Wright Books and Writers* (Jackson, Miss.: University Press of Mississippi, 1990), 214; Jackson, "A Word about Simple," 111.

people whose distinctive stigma is failure, so that the prevailing
conclusion to a Negro's tale of Negro life is catastrophe—Bigger Thomas
awaiting execution; Lutie Johnson, Ann Petry's heroine in *The Street,*
fleeing the corpse of the would-be seducer she has just murdered; Bob
Jones, in *If He Hollers Let Him Go,* on his way to enforced military
service; the Invisible Man submerged, and lost, in his hole in the
ground.

In contrast to those exceptionally good and talented Negroes and
those plagued with failure, Jackson finds Simple to be "an ordinary
person who is a Negro."[14]

In the final volume of Simple stories, Simple himself elucidates
the distinctions between such people as Ralph Bunche, Thurgood
Marshall, Martin Luther King Jr., and himself:

> "I am proud to be represented by such men, if you say they represent
> me. But all them men you name are *way* up there, and they do not
> drink beer in my bar. I have never seen a single one of them mens on
> Lenox Avenue in my natural life. So far as I know, they do not even
> live in Harlem. I cannot find them in the telephone book. They all got
> private numbers. . . . And I bet they have not been to the Apollo since
> Jackie Mabley cracked the first joke." ("Coffee Break," *Return,* 102–3)

Simple, of course, enjoys "Moms" Mabley and Lenox Avenue. By all
accounts, he is an ordinary Harlem resident. The especially fascinating
thing about Simple, however, is that he always masters his circum-
stances. He may not be able to change his racist countrymen or create
better employment opportunities for himself, but he refuses to be
defeated by oppression. The victorious attitude of this ordinary man
clearly exceeds any racial or national boundaries, thereby proving
useful as inspirational literature in many cultures. As Hans Ostrom
points out, when Hughes created Simple he was "deconstructing
other typical images of the African-American male, as [Blyden] Jackson
suggests. So if Hughes was holding up a mirror to urban, working-
class African-American men, he was also smashing the false images
of 'the Negro' which white society had created."[15] Hughes wanted
to show heroism and greatness, and he saw such greatness among

14. Jackson, "A Word," 115–17.
15. Ostrom, *Langston Hughes: A Study of the Short Fiction,* 44.

the common people. More significantly, he saw such heroism as a tool for survival rather than as some final blaze of bravado before ultimate death and destruction. Instead of a Claude McKay "If We Must Die" heroism, his Simple demonstrates a Langston Hughes "Still Here" heroic achievement.

> I've been scarred and battered.
> My hopes the wind done scattered.
> Snow has friz me, sun has baked me.
> > Looks like between 'em
> > They done tried to make me
> Stop laughin', stop lovin', stop livin'—
> > But I don't care!
> > *I'm still here!*[16]

Hard work and exposure to the elements could scar or batter or freeze a person, but when that person could envision a better future for his or her offspring, somehow the hardships had to be endured. In Hughes's opinion, such endurance constituted a kind of "day-after-day heroism of work and struggle and the facing of drudgery and insult that some son or daughter might get through school and acquire the knowledge that leads to a better life where opportunities are brighter and work is less drab, less humiliating, and less hard." George E. Kent considers these survivors of daily drudgery to be typical of Hughes's vision, which emphasizes "a lifesmanship that preserves and celebrates humanity in the face of impossible odds."[17]

Besides capturing daily living, such portrayals could also inspire daily living. In his 1937 "Blueprint for Negro Writing," Richard Wright lambasted educated Negroes who had never considered that the creative works of their writers should have been guides for their daily living. Because black readers failed to expect inspiration from literature, African American writers produced works that became either "hallmark[s] of 'achievement'" or pleas to "white America for justice." Wright found that "rarely was the best of this writing addressed to the Negro himself." Instead, African American instruction emerged from the black church or black folklore, either of which produced "racial

16. "Still Here," *Selected Poems of Langston Hughes,* 123.
17. LH, "The Need for Heroes," 206; Kent, *Blackness and the Adventure of Western Culture,* 56–57.

wisdom" that was transmitted orally from one person to the next. Consequently, "two separate cultures sprang up: one for the Negro masses, unwritten and unrecognized; and the other for the sons and daughters of a rising Negro bourgeoisie, parasitic and mannered." With his genuine and ordinary hero, Simple, and with his oral or folk structure embedded within the "self-conscious" literary structure, Hughes ended that split and combined the two traditions. Oluropo Sekoni, a specialist in African and African American literary and cultural semiotics, finds that Hughes employed a "post-representational imagination" with which he was able to reconcile the contradictions between two aesthetic traditions—the folk tradition, represented by Simple, and the middle-class tradition, voiced by the foil. As Susan L. Blake points out, the Simple stories allowed Hughes to enhance the folk tradition, converting the telling of the tale into a written document that becomes a unifying tool for social change. The literature, universal and critically acclaimed, represented the voices and values of the Negro masses and channeled them into a victorious, self-controlled instrument.[18]

Langston Hughes deliberately created in Simple an African American who was victorious over the major oppression of racism and the many indignities of his life because he had become self-conscious about his role as a writer and about the historical impact of his characters. Hughes had articulated what he championed as "The Need for Heroes" in the *Crisis* a little over a year before he began writing his weekly column for the *Chicago Defender*. In the article, he declared:

> The written word is the only record we will have of this our present, or our past, to leave behind for future generations. It would be a shame if that written word in its creative form were to consist largely of defeat and death. Suppose *Native Son*'s Bigger Thomas (excellently drawn as he is) was the sole survivor on the bookshelves of tomorrow? Or my own play, *Mulatto,* whose end consists of murder, madness, and suicide? If the best of our writers continue to pour their talent into the tragedies of frustration and weakness, tomorrow will probably say, on

---

18. Wright, "Blueprint," 53–56; Sekoni, "Africanisms and the Post-Modernist Dimension of the Harlem Renaissance"; Blake, "Old John in Harlem: The Urban Folktales of Langston Hughes," in Mullen, ed., *Critical Essays,* 168, 175.

the basis of available literary evidence, "No wonder the Negroes never amounted to anything. There were no heroes among them."[19]

Blyden Jackson's praise of Simple certainly complements Hughes's own assessment that literary heroes were needed. Jackson found that, in *Not without Laughter,* in the Simple stories, and in most of his other writing, "Hughes never succumbed to the monstrous error of arguing that, because race prejudice is itself monstrous, it has made Negroes monsters."[20] To the contrary, Simple remained quite attractively human. He merely complained about his troubles— personal, national, and racial. As Simple describes himself, "I am no dangerous man. I am what folks calls an ordinary citizen. Me, I work, pay my rent, and taxes, and try to get along" ("American Dilemma," *Return,* 75).

It is worth noting that Simple—like many other ordinary African Americans—did not limit his negative evaluations to white people or to white racism. As one critic points out, "When Simple is not exposing the folly and injustice of the white world, he is unveiling the foolish social climbing, moral hypocrisy, and spiritual emptiness . . . of . . . blacks."[21] Thus, Simple remains victorious without becoming blind to the problems surrounding him.

How could such a problem-conscious character have such universal appeal over the years? Richard K. Barksdale credits Hughes's perception of humor as the attribute that permitted the author to present such a well-balanced character:

> Hughes was more than a poetic dramatist; he had a comic vision that enabled him to cover the pain and suffering of black urban existence with protective layers of wit, humor, and sympathetic understanding. The characters he presented . . . are error-ridden, often fearful, and yet filled with a good-humored acceptance of their own frailties. So in their small, unheroic ways they negotiate the complicated systems and bureaucracies burdening the black citizen in the biggest ghetto in America's largest city. This they do with a certain amount of bravado, a certain amount of humility, and a certain amount of good humor.[22]

19. "Need for Heroes," 184.
20. Jackson, "A Word," 118.
21. Charles A. Watkins, "Simple: The Alter Ego of Langston Hughes," 21.
22. Barksdale, *Langston Hughes: The Poet and His Critics,* 86.

The points being made in these various critical assessments are that Simple is both ordinary and black, and that he survives with his racial integrity despite racism. He is "a MAN, strong and unafraid, who did not die a suicide, or a mob-victim, or a subject for execution, or a defeated humble beaten-down human being."[23] Hughes's literary achievement is the creation of a character—very much a composite of real ordinary black men—who displays a well-rounded personality despite the negative impact of prejudice. Critical acclaim for this achievement persists fifty years after Simple's creation. This study should amplify the reasons for appreciating Hughes's accomplishment with Simple.

One aspect of that accomplishment has been virtually absent from public scrutiny, however. That hidden achievement is the actual translation of the character from one who sparkled in the *Chicago Defender* to one who retains his effervescence in book form. First finding a publisher willing to bring out the tales and then polishing Simple's character to satisfy editors for that publisher proved to be lengthy and arduous tasks for Hughes.

By learning about the original columns as they appeared in the newspaper, readers can correct the false impression so easily gained from scholarly references that indicate that readers followed Simple "week after week in the columns of the *Defender*."[24] Simple did not appear every week in the column, much to the dismay of his most ardent fans. Hughes wrote mostly nonfiction editorials, only adding Simple as a feature to help him reach readers who might hold views strongly opposed to his own. By examining the early versions of Simple, along with the different types of columns Hughes wrote at the same time, we can better evaluate how Simple fit into Hughes's plan for communicating with the readers of the *Defender*. The initial impetus for publication of the stories in book form was enthusiastic fans and an interested publisher. Based on their enthusiasm, Hughes began in 1945 to envision his dialogues as material for a book. This vision led him to increase Simple's appearances in the *Chicago Defender* from eleven in 1943 to twenty-three in 1949—one nearly every other week.

23. LH, "Need for Heroes," 184.
24. Jackson, "A Word," 111.

When we recognize in the newspaper those episodes that have been collected into one of the five volumes of Simple stories, we can also correct another false impression. Some writers, in explaining briefly that the Simple columns were later collected into books, may give the false impression that all the columns were merely copied from the newspaper and then lumped together for the Simple books. Hughes certainly attempted that easy method. With dozens of writing projects occurring simultaneously, he wanted nothing more than to staple and mail his existing columns and call that sheaf of paper a new book. Indeed, when he began to envision the Simple stories as a book in 1945, he advised his literary agent to distribute the manuscript, which was merely a collection of unrevised columns. However, publishers wisely refused to grant him the luxury of presenting those journalistic gems as book-length literature.

Instead, Hughes was compelled to select carefully the episodes he would include. A comparison of the original columns and the episodes preserved in books shows that many of the columns were omitted from the collected editions. Moreover, the collected versions reflect substantial editing and revising. In addition, to enhance story line and character development, Hughes wrote some entirely new episodes specifically for his first collection of Simple stories. When we fail to appreciate the effort and attention required to produce the enduring collections of Simple stories, we diminish our understanding of the craft that resulted in the creation of the Simple books. Hughes did not churn out Simple columns week after week, nor did his columns transfer directly from newspaper to book. Failure to examine the columns accurately and thoroughly has resulted in decreased appreciation for Hughes's political commentary and for his artistic abilities.

Another consequence of the critical focus upon the book-length collections of Simple stories is that scholars have neglected to analyze the pragmatic and artistic concerns that led Hughes to transform topical columns into enduring fiction. While he dealt with actual events of the 1940s and addressed the racially homogeneous audience of the black press when he created Simple, Hughes later revised his creation so that Simple could communicate effectively outside of that context of time and audience. These revisions offer literary scholars a significant means for evaluating the craft of Langston Hughes, and the history of the revision process soundly refutes any mistaken impressions that the Simple stories were hastily or carelessly assembled. In some instances, particular stories deserve a reexamination in light of the original dialogues published in the *Defender*. Additionally, each published volume ultimately represents a stage in a process, not just a fixed piece of literature.

To evaluate the revision process, this study takes advantage of the *Chicago Defender* and *New York Post* versions of Simple—which have always been available to critics—and it provides information from manuscripts, drafts, and editorial suggestions housed in the extensive James Weldon Johnson Collection at Yale University and unavailable to most scholars until the 1980s. The identity of the foil, the distinctive speech patterns of Simple and the foil, Simple's name, and the specific details of Simple's background and day-to-day life were not evident in the earliest days of the column, but they later crystallized in the books. Comparisons of the same episodes taken from column to book will reveal many of the creative innovations Hughes employed to insure that Simple could break away from the weekly newspaper setting. The lengthy processes of negotiating for the initial book contract and the arduous work of revising the manuscript for publication reveal the extent to which Hughes blended his artistic integrity with the suggestions of his agent and his editors to craft a work of fiction richly deserving of the critical acclaim it has received.

The Simple stories have not been unanimously celebrated, however. From the earliest days of his appearance in the *Chicago Defender* to the present, Hughes's Simple has gained both detractors and fans. Hughes remains best known as a poet, and many who love his poetry find the Simple tales excessively earthy, obvious, or prone to perpetuate stereotypes with demeaning dialect and unattractive behavior. Such readers wonder why Hughes ever put the character into print, and wonder even more why publishers have continued to reproduce the error Hughes made. Other fans of Hughes may not dislike the character, but they remain oblivious to Simple. For example, actor Danny Glover in 1992 read from Hughes's poetry for a one-hour program. When asked by an audience member whether he ever included the Simple stories in his readings, he replied that he was not familiar with Simple.[25] How has a creation so highly acclaimed

25. Questions and response from Glover's reading at Georgia State University, Wednesday, May 27, 1992. Since February 1994, Glover has included Simple in his Hughes readings.

failed to gain greater significance in the common public perception of Hughes's reputation?

Among readers acquainted with Simple, not all relish his perpetual focus on race or his use of black vernacular. For example, some readers enjoy or identify with the style of the dialogues or even the focus upon a humble common man, comparing the Simple episodes with other stories they know and have enjoyed, such as Sholem Aleichem's *Tevye the Dairyman and The Railroad Stories*, Garrison Keillor's stories, or Leo Rosten's *The Education of Hyman Kaplan*. Such readers appreciate the craft and the universality of the creation, although they may not always enjoy the subject matter or the dialect.

However, as long ago as the 1940s, Simple has attracted ardent fans and promoters who promised that he would become a classic, an immortal fixture in literature. Langston Hughes may have begun to believe these zealous prophesies by the time he died in 1967, since by then his Simple Minded Friend had grown to fill five published books, a musical play, and a comedy play without music, and had been translated and performed in dozens of languages throughout the world. The even more remarkable achievement is the continued vitality of this character. *The Best of Simple* remains in print, *The Return of Simple* has recently been published, and *Simply Heavenly* continues to be performed. These accomplishments confirm the universality of the Harlem everyman as Hughes carefully portrayed him. Moreover, these accomplishments testify to the perseverance and resilience of the author, who contended with several publishers, waged numerous battles over "rights," and weathered countless theatrical obstacles to achieve this list of publication and literary endurance for Simple.

While the germ that sprouted into the first Simple column may have appeared to Hughes rather easily when he conversed with a fellow in the neighborhood bar, the actual saga of Simple shows that the translation of folk characters and vernacular narration into universally celebrated fiction required both talent and tenacity on the part of the author.

Besides unraveling the process through which Simple evolved, this study will show readers that they may love only the tip of the Hughesian literary iceberg. The shelf life of books being what it is, the general public in the 1990s tends to know Jesse B. Semple as he is preserved in *The Best of Simple* or as he is presented on stage in *Simply Heavenly*. These vehicles offer likeable presentations of both

Simple and the lively supporting cast; however, episodes from *Simple Takes a Wife* and *Simple's Uncle Sam* that were not included in *The Best of Simple* provide several powerful and unmatched presentations of female characters. Other episodes from the newspaper columns never reached permanence in any book form; these columns, too, offer other important dimensions of Simple and his supporting cast.[26]

The Best of Simple, which is still in print, continues to reach generations of readers further and further removed from the climate of racial segregation from which Simple sprang. How then do current generations of readers view Simple? Does this character continue to teach, to amuse, and to entertain readers? Do the Simple episodes capture African American culture and American life in ways that will lead future generations of readers to enjoy them, making Simple immortal like Shakespeare's Romeo or Dickens's Scrooge? What qualities have already sustained readership for decades after the author's death?

This examination of Jesse B. Semple traces the initial appearance of the character within the weekly column Hughes wrote for the *Chicago Defender.* We follow the character to a manuscript form that is rejected by several publishers until it gains a warm and benevolent reception from the editors at Simon and Schuster. This publisher gives the world the first two book-length collections of Simple stories. We then follow Simple to Rinehart for a third volume and to Hill and Wang for the final two volumes Hughes compiled. We see Simple expand from his birthplace in the *Chicago Defender* to publication in a "white" paper, the *New York Post,* and into syndication in a variety of newspapers. We also note Simple's appearance on stage—even on Broadway—and on television. The summary comes easily, but the actual publication and production history was anything but "simple."

Beyond the historical tracking, this examination also delves into the characterization of Jesse B. Semple and the foil, as well as the women in Simple's life and his cousins. By exposing the less common

26. Hill and Wang published *The Return of Simple,* a new collection of sixty-two Simple episodes, in July 1994. In this new book, episodes include some from previously published books, but none that were published in *Best.* Twenty-five of the stories have never before been included within a book-length collection. This new collection should ameliorate readers' lack of acquaintance with those episodes.

episodes, we will uncover a complexity and a depth that belie the surface appearance of simplicity.

The exploration of characterization will inevitably lead to an evaluation of Hughes's use of language, humor, and social history in these tales. To demonstrate the amount of time and talent Hughes invested, a few scenes will be followed through several drafts to their published form.

Finally, critical reception of the Simple episodes will be interspersed throughout this discussion. Both the formal criticism from scholars such as Arthur Paul Davis and the informal criticism from hundreds of fan letters preserved in Yale University's James Weldon Johnson Collection and the New York Public Library's Schomburg Center for Research in Black Culture will highlight the popular and the insulting messages that the Simple tales communicated.

Readers already familiar with Simple should return to him filled with a new appreciation for his history and his depth. Readers not yet acquainted with him should find him required reading after learning how carefully he has been drawn and how attractive he has been since 1943 to readers all over the world.

1

The Simple Setting: The 1940s in the *Chicago Defender*

MERELY PICKING UP A BOOK of Simple stories, especially *The Best of Simple,* a reader misses vital information about the character's origins. Even the headnotes in anthologies take for granted that readers will gain sufficient information from the mere statement of fact that Jesse B. Semple, nicknamed "Simple," originated in a weekly column that Langston Hughes wrote for the Negro newspaper the *Chicago Defender.*[1] But there is a broader background that a reader needs to see to place Simple into the rich context in which Hughes created him. For example, Simple is an advocate for African American rights; he is what blacks in the first half of the twentieth century called a "race man"—a black man who observes the endless inequities of racial injustice and relentlessly demands redress. But without scholarly attention to the specific time and conditions during which the Simple stories were created, current and future generations of readers may neglect or distort the significance of Simple's preoccupation with race. In 1943, when the Simple Minded Friend first appeared in Hughes's weekly column, "Here to Yonder," all the folks who read it understood exactly why Simple hesitated about fighting the Nazi forces. But contemporary readers, possibly more familiar with the horrors of Nazi Germany than with the agonies and indignities of American racism, might not understand why Simple felt that a segregated army was no place to battle the advocates of Aryan superiority. To such

1. See, for example, Arthur P. Davis and J. Saunders Redding, eds., *Cavalcade: Negro American Writing from 1760 to the Present* (1971), 302; and Davis, Redding, and Joyce Ann Joyce, eds., *The New Cavalcade: African American Writing from 1760 to the Present* (1991), vol. 1, 554.

readers, Simple might seem stubborn, provincial, and prejudiced—like television characters Archie Bunker, Fred Sanford, and George Jefferson, to whom some 1980s and 1990s high school and college students have compared him.[2] These students' comparisons reveal that the humor and distinct individuality of Simple's characterization have been retained since 1943, but they also indicate that the conditions of segregation to which Simple responds in his dialogues may now appear to be fictitious or exaggerated, or at least that the details of these conditions are unknown to many students today. In fact, one student reading Simple for the first time asked, "What is Jim Crow?" His question illustrates the need to reintroduce Simple so that current and subsequent generations of readers can more fully appreciate the content and the craft of the Simple stories. If these readers enjoy Simple merely as a humorous character, they may think that he illogically lingers on the issue of race. The separation of race and racism from Simple's humor enervates the stories of their value for teaching survival in the face of oppression.

The most recent generations—born and educated in the America molded by the insistent demands for equal rights and by the infusion of African-American studies into all levels of education—take for granted rights and opportunities denied during the era of segregation. A writer for a popular magazine targeting a black audience wrote in 1985 that "we are in the unusual position of having to teach young people what things were like only a few years back—we can't assume they know." David Evans, who was then a senior

2. Twenty-three high school students in Jacqueline Roberts Scott's classes (John F. Kennedy High School, Suffolk, Virginia) reading and hearing Simple for the first time in April 1985 were asked to describe Simple and to compare him to someone with whom they were familiar—either fictional or real. Students compared Simple to Fred G. Sanford (portrayed on television's *Sanford & Son* by Redd Foxx) and George Jefferson (Sherman Hemsley's character on *The Jeffersons*). Some students found Simple "a chronic complainer" like Archie Bunker (Carroll O'Connor's character on *All in the Family* and *Archie's Place*) and Garfield the cat (a cartoon), while others highlighted Simple's egocentrism and compared him to Mel Sharpels (Vic Taymore's character on *Alice*), Dr. Winchester (on *M.A.S.H.*, played by David Ogden Stiers), and, again, Archie Bunker. More recently, in April 1994, thirty-six Spelman College upperclasswomen who read *Best* were asked to make the same comparison. Several students again named George Jefferson.

admissions officer at Harvard, is quoted in the same article: "We have an upper middle class that has never lived in a predominantly, or even a significant Black setting."[3] This study of the Simple stories will begin by providing the historical and cultural context of Simple's creation and development—details that could once be assumed but must now be taught.

Simple emerged during the 1940s, a period of both turbulence and success for Americans. Most memorable of the events that shaped the decade, and crucial to Simple's birth, is World War II. The war presented special challenges to African Americans, especially after they heard about the goal of the Four Freedoms that President Franklin D. Roosevelt announced in January 1941: freedom of speech, freedom of worship, freedom from want, and freedom from fear. Black Americans understood that these freedoms were goals for the postwar future rather than for the wartime present, but they wondered if these freedoms would apply to them at home in the United States.

As Langston Hughes saw the relationship between the war and the Negro's status, a terrible contradiction had emerged: "In the midst of a war ostensibly for the preservation of freedom and democracy, it is absurd to proclaim the Four Freedoms as a world-ideal and deny those same freedoms by force to a large portion of our own population."[4] World War II prominently affected domestic and international issues in the 1940s, determining such mundane matters as which foods were readily available and such major concerns as the direction of the national economy. Following the leadership of the National Association for the Advancement of Colored People, blacks ranked patriotism and national loyalty as a priority over domestic racial negotiations. Nevertheless, racism within the United States continued to influence their lives. So, led by the Negro press, blacks fought *first* for democracy abroad and victory over Hitler and the other Axis powers, but they continued to battle *also* for democratic victory at home, including the full rights of citizenship. Seeking those two victories, blacks called their program "the double-V campaign": victory abroad and at home. Thus, Simple began his dialogues during the years when African

3. Errol T. Louis, "The Life and Times of a College Buppie [Black Urban Professional]," 52, 102.
4. LH, "The Future of Black America," 3.

Americans struggled with their own mixed feelings about the United States and its hypocrisy regarding democracy.

The war affected African Americans positively and irreversibly: they served as loyal soldiers and support troops in the war zone, as civilian workers in defense industries, and as patriotic citizens lending moral support. At home the need for wartime labor resulted in blacks working in more skilled jobs than ever before. Particularly helpful in this regard were the jobs in the defense industry, but they were not secured without mass protest from blacks. Once desegregation was achieved in the defense industry, they agitated for desegregation of the armed forces. African Americans sensed the bitter contradiction, which Hughes pointed out, between fighting Hitler's fascism and enduring the racism and tyranny of the segregated American armed forces.

Unfortunately, segregation was only part of the demoralizing treatment black soldiers endured. Soldiers frequently received basic training at camps in the South, and for northern blacks, the Jim Crow laws were brutally offensive. Southern blacks loathed Jim Crow treatment, too, but Dixie truly shocked the northern blacks. As a result of this harsh treatment, the families and supporters of black GIs endured more than the usual concern of the "folks back home" about casualties during the war. The families also paid special attention to black soldiers' racial harassment, thereby growing angry and frustrated about their poor treatment. Such civilian frustration is considered to be a major cause of several race riots that erupted in 1943. This frustration, and the increased awareness brought on by the riots, led to an outburst of political interest in 1944. Legal and illegal restrictions prevented southern blacks from voting, but northern and midwestern blacks elected congressional representatives for the first time. Among those elected was the fiery and influential Adam Clayton Powell Jr., representing Harlem. Blacks seemed determined to force changes— although they never abandoned their loyal fight against the Axis powers. From this climate of acute race consciousness sprang Simple.

After the war, black and white Americans continued to experience life in two separate worlds. In the military, black soldiers were retained longer, restraining them from civilian employment. Back at home, African American civilians with defense jobs were fired sooner than their white counterparts, again depriving blacks of the employment that had been for them the most highly skilled and the most lucrative in United States history. In the face of this double-edged employment discrimination, blacks once again rallied to preserve or to gain financial stability. The Fair Employment Practices Committee, which had helped to secure black employment during the war, seemed unattractive to the peacetime Congress, and the campaign for a postwar FEPC led to lively protests by Congress and to vigorous debate and campaigning by blacks who sought to represent their own interests.

Other domestic restrictions seemed even more offensive after World War II than they had before wartime opportunities opened the eyes of African Americans. Educational opportunities remained limited for blacks, and housing restrictions created both psychological frustration and health problems linked to poor sanitation. Daily reminders of racism in segregated trains and buses in the South, coupled with both the limits and the victories for blacks in entertainment and sports, demanded that black Americans maintain racial consciousness. Thus, the 1940s, the period that gave birth to Simple, heightened racial awareness and conflict for African Americans. Simple's preoccupation with race genuinely reflected the attitudes of blacks embroiled in legal petitions, economic sanctions, and editorial campaigns to achieve permanent change in the political, economic, educational, and social systems.

Considering the politically charged climate of the 1940s, Jesse B. Semple might not have emerged as the likable, average fellow audiences have grown to love were it not for the place in which he first appeared: the Negro press. About a year before Hughes began writing his column for the *Chicago Defender,* he had praised the Negro press in general and the *Defender* in particular for accomplishing what "literary" black writers had not yet done: recording the narratives of contemporary black heroes. Urging his readers to seek the records of black heroes, he said, "Don't look for [heroism of] today in books because our few writers haven't gotten around to putting it down yet—but look in the back files of the Negro press: *The Chicago Defender* in the riot days of 1919 in that tough and amazing city."[5] Hughes admired the content and the impact of the *Defender,* and he recognized the special role of the black press.

5. LH, "Need for Heroes," 184.

As a part of the Negro press, the *Defender* performed specialized functions in segregated America: (1) protesting injustices to black Americans and helping to fight their battles; (2) stimulating black achievement by publicizing Negro success stories; and (3) providing information about events affecting the personal interests of blacks.[6] The function of protesting often led northern black newspapers such as the *Defender* to address issues pertaining to southern blacks. Covert pressure and outright terrorism sometimes inhibited the editors of southern black papers from speaking forthrightly. Northern black newspapers could protest southern injustices without recrimination because the Negro press—like the Negro church and the Negro school—was seldom seen by whites.

For news of general interest, African Americans read the major daily papers and listened to their radios, as did whites. In those general news sources, however, blacks in the 1940s found little about themselves. "Since the Negro has been essentially ignored in the white press except for crime or 'freak' celebrities, the Negro has been forced to establish his own press on society news for his own cultural needs." Moreover, the black press "recognizes that the majority of Negroes read the large white daily newspapers for the news, so the Negro newspaper is regarded as an *additional newspaper*."[7]

A comparison of the coverage of a major news item in 1941 by a Negro weekly and by two white daily papers will illustrate the treatment of black issues in the white press. Labor leader A. Philip Randolph rallied forces to pressure President Roosevelt to issue an executive order that would compel defense industries to give Negroes employment. A significant component of Randolph's pressure was the threat of a march on Washington. While the president did listen to reason, he finally succumbed only to the pressure of the promised march, which would have been terribly embarrassing to the United States in wartime. To prevent the march, Roosevelt issued Executive Order No. 8802 on June 25, 1941. The order declared

6. Jessie Parkhurst Guzman, ed., *Negro Year Book: A Review of Events Affecting Negro Life, 1941-1946,* 383, 385, quoting P. L. Prattis, executive editor of the *Pittsburgh Courier,* and Robert S. Abbott, founder of the *CD.* Also see James Walter Dees Jr. and James S. Hadley, *Jim Crow,* chap. 8, "Jim Crow in the News," 128.

7. Dees and Hadley, *Jim Crow,* 128.

a new United States policy "that there shall be no discrimination
in the employment of workers in defense industries or government
because of race, creed, color or national origin, and . . . that it is the
duty of employers and of labor organizations to provide for the full
and equitable participation of all workers in defense industries."[8] The
Chicago Defender considered Executive Order No. 8802 to be "one
of the most significant pronouncements that has been made in the
interests of the Negro for more than a century" and gave it front-page
banner headlines, a news story continued on two pages, and editorial
comment. By contrast, the *Atlanta Journal* failed to mention this
news item at all, and the *New York Times,* which, according to its
motto, provides "all the news that's fit to print," covered the executive
order in one sentence buried in a tiny article on page 10:

> WASHINGTON, June 25—President Roosevelt signed bills authorizing
> $50,000,000 for construction of bases for small naval craft, extending
> jurisdiction of American prize courts to cover captured aircraft;
> authorizing the Navy to use vessels stricken from its register as targets,
> and clarifying the rights of the Navy to require fewer than four years
> of training for aviation cadets. He issued an executive order instructing
> executive agencies to take steps to eliminate discrimination against
> Negroes and others in defense jobs.

Even an attentive reader could have overlooked that sentence about
the executive order. What a difference from the coverage received in
the black press. On the flip side of that coin, to illustrate what kind
of news about Negroes the *Times did* consider worthy of coverage,
notice that in the same week, the entertainment page of the *New York
Times* offered a three-inch article detailing a concert by Paul Robeson,
an example of what Blyden Jackson calls an "exceptional Negro" or
what Dees and Hadley call a "freak celebrity" worthy of white press
coverage.[9] No one would argue that newspapers should have ignored
Robeson's concert, but African Americans would certainly argue that

8. *Code of Federal Regulations,* Title 3—The President, 1938-1943 Com-
pilation (Washington, D.C.: U.S. Government Printing Office, 1968), 957. The
order also appears in "Full Text of Executive Order," *CD,* July 5, 1941, 1.

9. See "The Day in Washington," *New York Times,* June 26, 1941, 10, and
"Robeson Soloist at the Stadium; 14,000 Hear Baritone with the Philharmonic
Orchestra Under Hugh Ross; Spirituals on Program: 'Water Boy' Offered as

his concert was far less important than President Roosevelt's Executive Order 8802. Without the Negro press, African Americans would have known which songs Paul Robeson sang, but they would have lacked adequate coverage and celebration of this monumental event in their political and economic history.

The *Defender* occasionally pointed out the discrepancies in white press coverage, as in the cartoon and accompanying editorial in the March 17, 1945, issue. The cartoon showed a black patron at a newsstand that sold four or five different white daily papers, all of which proclaimed in banner headlines, "92nd RETREATS!" The black patron used a magnifying glass, however, to examine the Want Ad Section, where he read, "negro tank units trap 20,000 Nazis." The editorial explained:

> When the all-Negro 92nd Division in Italy retreated last month in the face of strong Nazi counter-attacks, virtually every leading metropolitan newspaper in America carried daily accounts of the action. Several magazines even [claimed] Negro troops are unsuited for combat.
>
> Last week a Negro tank battalion was in the vanguard of an American spearhead that joined with the Canadian First Army near the Rhine and trapped some 20,000 Nazis.
>
> Only one news agency, the International News Service, carried the story. And even INS credited the story to the British Reuters news agency. In the few papers in which the item appeared, it was played down as a one-paragraph story.[10]

The editorial went on to point out that not only had the "big daily metropolitan papers . . . done a sorry, slovenly job of covering Negro servicemen," but the War and Navy Departments also had "done very little." In fact, the editorial found that these executive departments too often made "a military secret" of "anything which tells of the achievements of Negro troops." Such omission in the daily papers would have been terribly demoralizing if the Negro press had not provided alternative coverage. Therefore, without apology and with good reason, "all news in the *Defender* is 'race-angled'" and "in

---

a Final Encore—Lawrence Brown Appears at the Piano," *New York Times,* June 24, 1941, 16. Jackson, "A Word," 116; Dees and Hadley, *Jim Crow,* 128.
    10. See "Conscience Pains for White Editors," *CD,* March 17, 1945, 10. The cartoon, on the same page, is called "White (or Yellow) Journalism."

general, the Negro Press is interested in news that touches the Negro, and rarely, if ever, pays any attention to news that has no racial significance."[11] Because the white press either ignored the average Negro or treated him unfavorably, blacks needed another medium through which to obtain relevant news about themselves.

The compelling and disturbing news articles and photographs of the times kept readers aware of the horrors of racial prejudice and the thrill of legislative improvements for civil rights. These areas formed the core of front-page news and often became the subjects of invigorating editorials and thought-provoking cartoons. The *Defender* had earned a reputation for bold political activism, and its presentation of news, editorials, and cartoons often encouraged readers to become politically active in order to rectify injustices. The paper also urged readers to reward people and agencies that made improvements in the quality of life for black Americans. These serious concerns were balanced by pleasant photographs of leggy brown beauties and popular black entertainers. Society news celebrated the academic achievements and romantic involvements of black Americans—both famous and ordinary. Gossip columns, advertisements, and war news all focused on Negroes. However, as with any weekly newspaper, most of the "news" was several days old by the time it hit the street. Consequently, "editorials, columns, and other non-news items [were] given a proportionately larger space than in an ordinary daily newspaper."[12] Therefore, Simple's initial appearance in the *Defender* meant not only that he had an audience of black people interested in news and commentary about black folks, but also that he had an audience that paid special attention to weekly columns, cartoons, and photographs. The black press offered Negroes stimulating material on which to build a reading habit. The regular features acquired loyal readers eager to see each week's new edition.

Appearing in the midst of these articles and features, Simple never needed to defend his anger about the travesties of American "justice" or to explain his excitement about Lena Horne and Nat King Cole.

11. St. Clair Drake and Horace R. Cayton, *Black Metropolis,* vol. 2, 401; Vishnu V. Oak, *The Negro Newspaper,* 36.
12. Myrdal, *An American Dilemma: The Negro Problem and Modern Democracy,* 916–17.

Hughes knew that in the *Defender* he was free to select topics and use language—including slang—that he surely would not have chosen for a predominantly white audience. He was able to enter the thoughts of a wide spectrum of literate blacks who regularly read the *Chicago Defender,* the third most widely read Negro newspaper of the 1940s and the oldest and most widely read of five Chicago weekly newspapers that targeted the African American audience.[13]

Not only did Langston Hughes respect the goals and accomplishments of the Negro press, but he also respected and courted its African American audience. Hughes had heralded a "black is beautiful" message in his works from his first published poem, "The Negro Speaks of Rivers." Therefore, the black press provided a perfectly suited outlet for his celebrations of black achievements and his encouragements for black stamina. The Negro press's focus on black people harmonized with his declarations as an author; throughout his career he forthrightly affirmed his intentions to focus upon black people in order to sustain his career as a writer:

> I did not want to write for the pulps, or turn out fake "true" stories to sell under anonymous names as Wallace Thurman did. I did not want to bat out slick non-Negro short stories in competition with a thousand other commercial writers trying to make *The Saturday Evening Post.* I wanted to write seriously and as well as I knew how about the Negro people, and make *that* kind of writing earn for me a living.[14]

His early ambition, as expressed in this statement, was to be a *black* professional writer—compromising neither his own ethnicity nor the black characters in his writings for the sake of publication. In the *Defender* column itself, Hughes explained that black people were a chosen subject for his writing: "Being colored myself, I find us terrific subjects for all kinds of writing, full of drama and humor and power and entertainment and evil and love and all sorts of things. . . . For instance, what more dramatic material could anybody want for books or poems than the plight of the Negro soldier right now fighting in

---

13. Statistics regarding the popularity of the *Chicago Defender* pervade numerous studies of the Negro press. See, for example, Guzman, ed., *Negro Year Book, 1941–1946,* 389, 399, and Drake and Cayton, *Black Metropolis,* vol. 2, 399–400.

14. LH, *I Wonder as I Wander: An Autobiographical Journey,* 5.

Europe for a dream as yet unrealized in Alabama?" ("The Power of Poetry"). Inspired by such "drama and humor and power," Hughes retained his commitment to black-centered material throughout his life. However, he admitted that, by dedicating himself to his race, he had left himself open to restrictions in publication:

> I am, of course, as everyone knows, primarily a—I guess you might even say a propaganda writer; my main material is the race problem— and I have found it most exciting and interesting and intriguing to deal with it in writing, and I haven't found the problem of being a Negro in any sense a hindrance to putting words on paper. It may be a hindrance sometimes to selling them; the material that one uses, the fact that one uses . . . problem material, or material that is often likely to excite discussion or disagreement, in some cases prevents its quick sale.[15]

In this comment, Hughes distinguishes between his own responses and the responses of publishers and readers, who are obviously important to any writer determining to earn his living through his works. He repeatedly criticized the barriers to publication that greeted black writers—denials of opportunity in film screenplays, in lecturing, and in publishing. Yet the difficulties of sustaining his career never discouraged him from being a professional writer. Moreover, the difficulties imposed upon him and his primary subject matter—the restrictions of race—never persuaded him to minimize his own racial identity or the racial pride of his characters.

Gwendolyn Brooks, poet laureate of Illinois since 1968 and a former consultant in poetry to the Library of Congress, wrote of Hughes, "His point of departure was always a clear pride in his race. Race pride may be craft, art, or a music that combines the best of jazz and hymn. Langston frolicked and chanted to the measure of his own race-reverence."[16] Arnold Rampersad, an award-winning biographer of Langston Hughes, found Hughes's affinity for racial subject matter a deeper force than race pride:

15. LH, "The Negro in American Culture," discussion transcript, WABI-FM, New York, 1961, in C. W. E. Bigsby, ed., *The Black American Writer,* vol. 1, 82.

16. Gwendolyn Brooks, *Report from Part One* (Detroit: Broadside, 1972), 70.

At thirteen, Hughes probably already viewed the black world both as an insider and, far more importantly, an outsider. The view from the outside did not lead to clinical objectivity, much less alienation. Once outside, every intimate force in Hughes would drive him back toward seeking the love and approval of the race, which would become the grand obsession of his life. Already he had begun to identify not his family but the poorest and most despised blacks as the object of his ultimate desire to please. He would *need* the race, and would need to appease the race, to an extent felt by few other blacks, and by no other important black writer. This psychological craving was a quality far more rare than race pride or a merely defensive antagonism against whites; it originated in an equally rare combination of a sense of racial destiny with a keen knowledge of childhood hurt.[17]

Thus, whether he "frolicked and chanted to the measure of his own race-reverence," as Brooks described it, or pursued "the grand obsession of his life," as Rampersad saw it, Hughes staked his career on race-centered material. Reflecting on the possibility of his own death, Hughes wrote playfully in his *New York Post* column, "If or when I die, should it happen, most of my work being deeply concerned with the problems of black folks, I would not object at all to a headline saying, 'Negro Writer Passes On'—because if ever there was a Negro writer, I am one."[18] Hughes gladly and unshakably chose to write ethnically, and in the *Defender* he could address his own people in their own vernacular—without fear that such colloquial diction, or such "problem material," would prevent the sale of the paper. Indeed, the Hughes column helped boost circulation. Therefore, by removing even the smallest fear that his choice of topic, tone, or vocabulary might inhibit publication, the *Defender* offered Hughes great freedom to focus exclusively upon the subject and audience he loved best: African American people. This freedom, this audience, and the need to meet a weekly deadline combined to create the conditions that spawned Simple.

The publication history between Hughes and the *Defender* commenced in 1942, when Editor-in-Chief Metz Lochard wired Hughes to

17. Arnold Rampersad, *The Life of Langston Hughes*, vol. 1: *1902–1941: I, Too, Sing America,* 22.
18. LH, "Obits and Race," *Post,* October 1, 1965.

seek an article, to be completed within nine days. He requested an article on Negro writers and the war for the *Defender*'s special Victory Edition. Hughes called the resulting article a "rush" job and thought it was "probably not very good, but best I could do with a cold—and in a hurry—in answer to Lochard's wire." This "rushed" product, "Klan or Gestapo? Why Take Either?" appeared in the September 26, 1942, Victory Edition, which the *Defender* promoted as "the biggest venture of its kind ever undertaken by the Negro press."[19]

Hughes's article appeared in a feature section that included contributions from Franklin and Eleanor Roosevelt; W. E. B. Du Bois; Wendell L. Willkie, the Republican candidate whom Roosevelt had defeated in the presidential election of 1940; Supreme Court Justice Hugo L. Black; Pearl Buck, author of *The Good Earth;* labor leader A. Philip Randolph; literary scholar Alain Locke; H. G. Wells, author of *The Time Machine;* and NAACP executive Walter White, among others. According to the *Defender*'s "To Our Readers" statement, each of these articles endeavored to "hasten the removal of the misgivings and misunderstandings that impair race relations."

In his article, Hughes concentrated on the attitudes and responsibilities he felt black writers should assume during that crucial time of war. He carefully distinguished between journalists, who wrote for almost entirely black audiences, and creative writers, who published in general magazines. He proposed three duties for journalists. First, they should point out that Hitler, Mussolini, and Hirohito were dangerous "devils" who must not be admired, despite the inadvertent benefits for Negroes that their actions may have caused. Second, they should point out that Negroes would err by thinking of World War II exclusively in terms of race. Third, they should

> reveal the international aspects of our problem at home, to show
> how these problems are merely a part of the great problem of world
> freedom everywhere, to show how our local fascists are blood brothers
> of the Japanese fascists. . . . to show how on the great battle front of
> the world we must join hands with the crushed common people of
> Europe, the Soviet Union, the Chinese, and unite our efforts—else we

19. Metz Lochard to LH, August 17, 1942, *CD* correspondence, JWJ; LH to Bontemps, undated, in Nichols, ed., *Letters,* 110; "To Our Readers," *CD,* September 26, 1942, 4.

who are American Negroes will have not only the Klan on our necks in intensified fashion, but the Gestapo, as well.

Hughes praised Negro journalists because they had "pleaded, cajoled, explained, and demanded democracy for the fourteen million sub-citizens of this country week by week." Nevertheless, since those pleas were "read exclusively by Negroes," the creative writers, who had whites in their audience, had "a task before them of great positive value to carry out": "to explain to our white American brothers why it is urgently necessary that we now and immediately take steps in this country—for all our sakes—to wipe out all forms of public discrimination against minorities within our borders." Noting that "fear and discrimination" may prevent southern Negroes from expressing their feelings, Hughes asserted that "it is the duty of our writers to express what these voiceless people cannot say, and to relate their longings for decency and fairness to the world aims of the President's Four Freedoms for everybody."

Hughes had addressed both black and white audiences, and he was careful in his own writing to deliver appropriate messages to each. Peter Bruck highlights the significance of audience for African American prose, and he singles out Hughes for having achieved wide audiences in both white and black publications:

> Hughes was published by such noted magazines as *Scribner's, The American Mercury,* and *Esquire,* thus gaining a non-parochial platform and a primarily white audience. His first published collection, *The Ways of White Folks* (1934), contains the first genuine satirical short fiction pieces by a black writer which received favorable reviews and sold fairly well. Needing no longer to succumb to the racially preconceived notions of a white reading public, he became the first black writer whose statements of the new ethnic pride and self-assertion were accepted. . . . Hughes was not only the first to gain a large white audience; he also became the first to gain a genuine black audience outside the popular taste of the *Crisis-Opportunity* readers.[20]

Hughes's works in *Crisis* and *Opportunity* spoke to relatively small black audiences, because these publications circulated to the more

20. Peter Bruck, "Black American Short Fiction in the Twentieth Century: Problems of Audience, and the Evolution of Artistic Stances and Themes," 8-9.

highly educated and more civic minded blacks who had joined the NAACP or the National Urban League. They did not reach the wide cross section of African American readers that the Negro press reached. On the other hand, in the widely read *Saturday Evening Post, Esquire, New Yorker, Nation, New Republic, Theatre Arts, Poetry,* and *Common Ground,* he addressed mostly whites. He knew that the serious business of the double-V campaign required the cooperation of blacks and whites, so he suggested different roles for writers, depending upon their audiences, and he went on to fill both roles himself.

Hughes could not have known that with his assignment of duties for black writers in "Klan or Gestapo? Why Take Either?" he was also outlining his own column in the *Chicago Defender.* Editorial and public response to Hughes's article must have been quite favorable. On October 2, 1942, only days after the Victory Edition hit the streets, Lochard telegraphed Hughes with a long-term offer to write a weekly column for the paper. Aware of the audience and the visibility that weekly exposure could give his name, his works, and his opinions, Hughes gladly received the offer, but despite his eagerness, he did not readily accept it. He had to protect his own interests. On October 4, he wired his response to Lochard: "Delighted to do column for you but have recently had same request from Am[sterdam] News [New York] so please let me know your terms." After giving the matter more thought, Hughes elaborated his concerns in a letter to Lochard, this time asking for specific information about payment, subject matter for the column, and secretarial help in answering letters. He was obviously attracted by Lochard's offer, but he needed to compare it to the one made by another black newspaper known for outstanding features.

As Rampersad's two-volume biography of Hughes shows, money remained a concern for the author. Clearly, then, he would need some specifics on payment for his services as a columnist before making the commitment. The subject matter would be African American issues, of course. Hughes was a great fan of the Negro press, so he knew this would be the case. However, he had experienced some restrictions upon his freedom as a writer, and such interference with his creative autonomy had always run contrary to his artistic integrity. As a very young man Hughes had declared, "An artist must be free to choose what he does, certainly, but he must also never be afraid to do what he might choose."[21] Thus, he needed to clarify his liberty to write what he chose to write, should he agree to contribute a weekly column to the *Defender*.

The question about help answering letters may surprise some people, but Hughes was dedicated to his readers and wanted to know how his fan mail would be handled. Fans were vital to him. As he would later state in his column, he felt that his fans and readers had sustained his will to write during the frequent intervals when his publications offered no income. In gratitude, he resolved to answer each correspondent at least once. That resolution was no minor commitment, because Hughes attracted many correspondents. In one month in 1947 he received 313 letters, and more than half of those were from strangers.[22]

Happily, Lochard planned to pay reasonably well, had no intention of limiting Hughes's selection of topics, and arranged to assist with correspondence. On October 26, 1942, he wrote a lengthy and enthusiastic reply to Hughes:

> I should be most happy to have you associated with us. You can do a damn good column a la Heywood Broun. Such a column, however, would carry more weight if it dealt with specific incidents and stories rather than abstract generalizations. Your magnificent piece in our Victory Edition provides an adequate pattern for a bang up column.
>
> We are planning to have a number of big shots for our columnists— Harold Laski is one of them. They have all agreed to receive a small remuneration until we can see how profitable the whole undertaking is. We will pay you $15.00 (fifteen dollars) per week and my office will take care of all letters incidental to your column. You may choose your own title. Please let me know at once as I want to start announcing the names of our new contributors.

Hughes replied rapidly by wire that he would be "delighted to be Defender Columnist on terms of your letter." Lochard wired back that he expected Hughes's first column by the following Thursday and every Thursday thereafter. His length restriction was one thousand words. In addition to Hughes's title for his column, "Here to Yonder,"

21. LH, "The Negro Artist and the Racial Mountain," 163.
22. See "At Long Last," January 18, 1947; "Celebrities' Mail Bag," November 1, 1947; and "A Writer's Mail," May 24, 1947, in LH's *CD* column.

Lochard also solicited a "good" picture of him, further stating that if no existing photograph met that standard Hughes should have one taken and bill the *Defender.*

On November 21, 1942, the front page of the *Chicago Defender* proclaimed: "In This Issue—FIVE NEW COLUMNISTS!" In addition to Hughes, two of the other columnists should still be perceived by students of American life as "big shots," which Lochard had called them, since they have achieved enduring national fame, but all five continued their columns for many years, thereby proving their popularity at the time. Walter White, then secretary of the NAACP, began his "People, Politics, Places" column, and it was featured on the front page for its initial appearance. S. I. Hayakawa, a Canadian-born Japanese authority on language and later a United States senator from California, wrote "Second Thoughts." The two lesser-known columnists were U. G. Dailey and John Robert Adger. Dailey was a prominent Chicago surgeon who had taught at Northwestern University Medical School, and he offered medical information in "Until the Doctor Comes." Adger, a West Coast writer on foreign affairs, provided analyses on overseas events in "World Views." Although Hayakawa and some others of the many columnists for the *Defender* became nationally syndicated, none of the other columns gained the enduring fame Hughes achieved in "Here to Yonder."

This column in the *Chicago Defender* provided Hughes with his largest and most consistent audience ever. He gained a forum for sustained and contemporary communication with his favorite readers: the masses of African Americans, in all their diversity. Because the *Defender* thrived on racial news and commentary and because the audience was almost exclusively black, the *Defender* no doubt provided the perfect environment for the birth of Jesse B. Semple.

2

The "Here to Yonder" Column: Hughes in Two Voices

THE *CHICAGO DEFENDER* provided Langston Hughes with a regular weekly forum and an established audience already eager to read features centered upon African American interests. However, columnists come and columnists go. What would Langston Hughes do with this excellent opportunity? How would he distinguish his column from others? Would his column attract loyal readers? Would the deadline and the space restrictions inhibit him, or would he somehow fit his own style into the demands of weekly newspaper journalism?

Hughes launched his column in the November 21, 1942, issue of the *Chicago Defender*. Each week the column ran under the title "Here to Yonder," followed by a particular headline related to its contents.[1] The column varied from week to week in content, tone, and style. The Simple dialogue was one of the frequent formats for "Here to Yonder," but it did not appear until the column was three months old, on February 13, 1943. Even then, Simple did not appear every week. He was an occasional feature, sometimes running for two or three consecutive weeks, but sometimes absent for several weeks. "Here to Yonder" was Langston Hughes's forum, not merely the birthplace of Jesse B. Semple. As he appeared in the earliest columns, Simple was first merely a nameless voice from the masses, serving Hughes as a device to enhance the appeal of his editorial messages. Thus, to appreciate Simple's development, we must first distinguish Hughes's "Here to Yonder" column in general from the Simple conversations that gradually appeared more frequently in the column.

1. The title "Here to Yonder" was dropped with the October 16, 1948, issue, but I use it interchangeably with the column in general.

Hughes set up a contrast from the beginning of his column between the voice of Simple, a man of the black masses with provincial concerns, and the voice of the foil, an educated black man with a more global awareness. The two voices together provided commentary from "here" to "yonder" and connected the two spheres. Hughes used both voices in the nonfiction columns as well as in the Simple ones, because he truly loved African Americans in all their variety and because he could see the good points to be made by the two different types of Negro. By reading the early "Here to Yonder" columns, we can see why critics have often remarked about the similarities between Hughes and Simple as well as between Hughes and the foil. These columns explore sensitive issues, but in his own distinctive way, Hughes mixed humor into logic for a blues rendition of his views. An examination of the "Here to Yonder" columns provides three important insights into Hughes's political and artistic sensibilities: (1) Hughes spoke similarly in the Simple columns and in the nonfiction ones; (2) both the Hughes persona and Hughes the columnist emphasized that genuinely caring white people must be distinguished from reactionary whites; and (3) with or without Simple, Hughes valued humor.

In "Why and Wherefore," his first "Here to Yonder" column, Hughes establishes his overall intention as a columnist, thereby revealing both how he will fit into the established tones and topics prevalent in the Negro press and how he will distinguish his column from them. This first column also prefigures the Simple stories in several ways. Besides introducing a prototype for Simple, Hughes also introduces the basic Simple techniques of participant-observer reporting, inclusion of actual conversation, and expression of his own views through the voices of other people. Other early columns in the three months before Simple appeared indicate the breadth of subjects and the various techniques, such as direct quotation, humor, and historical survey, that Hughes would use to convey his weekly messages.

In "Why and Wherefore" Hughes mentions World War II as one of the "yonder" events that would affect people "here" in the United States, thereby introducing and establishing the significance of his column's title, "Here to Yonder." As did many of the news and feature articles in the black press, Hughes's first column illustrates the contradictions between the profession of American democracy and the practice of American racism. "An offensive against Hitler abroad demands for its success the intensification of the attack upon Hit-lerism at home," explains Hughes, conveying in a single sentence much of black America's exasperation with the hypocrisy of Jim Crow practices. Thus, in their approaching the same topics and in their fairly straightforward editorial style, Hughes's columns resemble those of other writers in the black press.

However, Hughes also established those topics and techniques that would clearly distinguish his column from the others. One Hughesian format was the autobiographical travelogue. He asserted that he had authority to write about things "from here to yonder" because, "for the last twenty years, half writer and half vagabond, I have travelled from here to yonder around the world and back again." He shared observations about American and international places and people in these travelogue columns.

Hughes also distinguished his column from the rest of the *Defender* discussions by stating and demonstrating in his first column his commitment to represent the viewpoints of average black people: "I know lots of folks, whose names have never been in the newspaper—as interesting as those whose names have been in the papers. I shall write about them, also. Your folks and mine—as colored as me—scattered all over the world from here to yonder. From week to week, they—and you—shall be the subjects of this column." Beginning in this introductory column, Hughes kept his promise to discuss common folk as well as celebrities.

His use of other voices to represent the viewpoints and behavior of the common folk prefigures this technique in the Simple stories. Hughes observes that the war overseas will cause the deaths of sol-diers from Harlem. He then amplifies his own observation by introduc-ing an anonymous spokesman who complains about the treatment of black soldiers. The conversation recorded in the column is presented as a true story in which Hughes participates, rather than as a fictional dialogue which Hughes creates. Nevertheless, this conversation with an ordinary man reveals that even in his first column Hughes set precedents for his future tales of Simple.

In the scene that Hughes records, the nameless man, a truck driver, has been drafted, and Hughes narrates, using slang, that "the cat was taking his first physical." At about that time, Hughes had just completed his own first physical for the military, so he certainly might have encountered such a person. Hughes had written to Arna Bontemps on November 2, 1942, "Man, I had no sooner written you last time than I got a wire from New York that the draft board had sent me a card to report for my first physical, which I did, and which resulted in the expected 1-A. So I am now 1-A!"[2] The conversation in the column, then, possibly was authentic. As he renders it, Hughes both listens and participates:

> He was talking and he didn't care who heard him. (Chalk up one point for the democracies—at least a man can talk, even a colored man.) He said, "I know they gonna send all us cats to a labor battalion. I'm a truck driver, and I know they gonna make me a truck driver in the army."
>
> "How do you know," I asked.
>
> "All the guys I know from Harlem," he said, "have gone right straight to labor battalions. Look at the pictures you see of colored soldiers in the papers, always working, building roads, unloading ships, that's all. Labor battalions! I want to be a fighter!"
>
> "I know a fellow who's gone to Officers School," I said. "And another one learning to fight paratroopers."
>
> "I don't know none," he said. "And besides, if they don't hurry and take this blood test, I'm liable to lose my job. This Italian I work for don't care whether the draft board calls you or not, you better be to work on time. He ain't been in this country but six or seven years and owns a whole fleet of trucks, and best I can do is drive one of 'em for him. Foreigners can get ahead in this country. I can't."
>
> "Some colored folks get ahead some," I said.
>
> "You have to be a genius to do it," he argued.
>
> Another man in the line spoke up, older, dark brown-skin, quiet. "Between Hitler and the Japanese," the other man said, "these white folks are liable to change their minds. They're beginning to find out they need us colored people."
>
> It was that third fellow who took the conversation all the way from the here of Manhattan Island to the yonder of Hitler, the Japanese, . . .
>
> . . . But I hope, since he wants to be a fighter, Uncle Sam will give him a gun, not a shovel or a truck. A gun would probably help his morale a little—now badly bent by the color line.

This very first "Here to Yonder" column includes several precursors to the mature Simple style. Notice first that Hughes reports a

2. Nichols, ed., *Letters,* 118.

scene in which he participates, just as he will initially participate in the Simple conversations. He never actually claimed that he was a sociologist, and he never claimed social study as the premise or purpose for his belletristic writings. Nevertheless, critics have often observed the value of his works—including his poetry—for a sociological appreciation of African Americans.[3] Even without extensive training or intentional effort, Hughes operated as an existential ethnographer, seeking emotional understandings of his Harlem brothers and sisters. But unlike a sociologist, who might aim for scientific objectivity, Hughes never set out to be objective in his column.

By writing as a participant-observer, Hughes shattered any false objectivity and removed any distance between himself and the issues of importance to his readers. Hughes's disposition was well suited to his role as observer. As Danny L. Jorgensen points out, "Some people, partly because of their ability to interact and develop relationships with people quite easily, take more readily to participant observation than people without these abilities."[4] Even in a situation that made him uncomfortable, Hughes gave others the impression that he felt right at home:

> Although he would admit privately that about two years passed
> before he was fully comfortable among the young black men [at
> Lincoln University, Pennsylvania], few saw his effort. "Langston was a
> remarkable person," Therman O'Daniel remembered. "He fitted in very
> easily—he could fit in anywhere. He had the personality to get along
> with other people, without the slightest pretentiousness. No doubt he
> had his private opinions and his private thoughts as a poet needing to
> create, but he was certainly one of us."[5]

3. See, for example, summaries included in Miller's *Langston Hughes and Gwendolyn Brooks,* where Rebecca Chalmer Barton calls Hughes a "poet-sociologist" (22) and Hugh Smythe indicates that *Simple Speaks His Mind* combines humor and sociology (25). For a definition and discussion of "existential ethnographer," see Norman K. Denzin, *The Research Act: A Theoretical Introduction to Sociological Methods,* 3d ed. (Englewood Cliffs, N.J.: Prentice Hall, 1989), 160.

4. Jorgensen, *Participant Observation: A Methodology for Human Studies,* Applied Social Research Methods Series, vol. 15 (Newbury Park, Calif.: Sage, 1989), 8–9.

5. Rampersad, *Life of Langston Hughes,* vol. 1, 127–28.

This comment about his behavior at Lincoln highlights the role Hughes played in his nonfiction columns or in the persona of the foil in the Simple dialogues. Whether or not he actually felt "fully comfortable," he could project "without the slightest pretentiousness" to the people he was observing that he fit in completely and was "one of them."

In this first "Here to Yonder" column and in the Simple stories, Hughes goes beyond third-person reporting to allow the other participants to speak for themselves. He includes three voices—his own, the truck driver's, and that of the quiet, dark brownskin, older fellow. The dialogue between Hughes and the other men shows distinct similarities to the Simple stories when we notice that Hughes calls himself "I" and never names the other men.

Because he sometimes shifted his own opinions to the mouths of his characters, Hughes distinguished his columns from the many other weekly columns in the *Defender* and in other black newspapers. Performing as a literary ventriloquist, he cleverly mixed his own opinions with those of blacks who had had other experiences. Hughes assumed the role he would take in the mature Simple stories by challenging the ordinary man's assumptions and by raising a different point of view—that of the more educationally and socially advantaged black Americans, "the talented tenth," as W. E. B. Du Bois called them.

Hughes, for example, tells the truck driver that he knows one person who has gone to Officers' Training School and another person who is learning to fight paratroopers. Because he was a writer, Hughes corresponded with "leaders" throughout the United States. He also took great pride in the achievements of blacks. With his unusual communications network and his proclivity for discovering the accomplishments of the race, he would quite likely have known about the exceptional men who had escaped the labor details in the armed services.

Since he was 1-A himself in November 1942, however, Hughes was busily engaged in trying to earn a deferment or to get some privileged duty for himself by enlisting rather than waiting to be drafted. He wondered if enlistees were more likely "to get in the Morale Division, or special services, maybe get sent to Latin America as a translator, etc????" Arna Bontemps suggested that Hughes "telephone Walter White immediately. He has a very fine contact with General Hershey and told me last week that he stood ready to help in a situation such as yours."[6] Bontemps also suggested that Hughes have White "ask General Osborn of the morale branch about that job with *Yank,* the overseas paper." As Bontemps viewed things, "the need for a Negro on the paper's staff remains." Thus, we can appreciate Hughes's awareness of mechanisms and personal contacts that could help a talented Negro in the right network escape the labor detail in the army.

Hughes never had to decide how to serve, however. He avoided military service, along with thousands of other men, thanks to Executive Order No. 9279, signed by President Roosevelt on December 5, 1942, which deferred the draft for men over age thirty-eight. Hughes was forty. Frank Marshall Davis, feature editor for the Associated Negro Press, wrote to Hughes: "Something tells me you are a very relieved individual."[7]

Hughes may have known of the Negroes who were exceptions to the rule, but the ordinary man could reply as does the truck driver: "I don't know none." The other men who speak represent viewpoints that Hughes can no longer express convincingly from a firsthand perspective, yet he wants those attitudes to be conveyed realistically and from the mouths of people who feel those needs and suffer those anxieties. Interesting to note is that it was "that third fellow who took the conversation all the way from the here of Manhattan Island to the yonder of Hitler." Hughes allows another speaker to offer a valuable analysis. Although Hughes may have shared the view, he did not mind relinquishing intellectual prominence in the column to someone else. Later, in the Simple stories, Simple very often gains the upper hand in his arguments with the college-educated foil.

The inclusion of other voices—ordinary people's voices—and the use of such other voices to carry important messages to readers significantly reflect Hughesian craft, both in the "Here to Yonder" column and throughout his published works. To render other voices authentically, Hughes had to listen carefully to both the diction and the content of the remarks of ordinary people he encountered. Simple

6. LH to Arna Bontemps, November 2, 1942, and Bontemps to LH, November 4, 1942, in Nichols, ed., *Letters,* 119.
7. Frank Davis to LH, December 8, 1942, Associated Negro Press correspondence, JWJ.

often urges his bar buddy to "listen fluently," and Hughes did exactly that to gather firsthand conversations. His diligent listening allowed him to faithfully record the idiosyncracies of speech and of anecdotal detail. To those journalistic skills of listening and recording he added creative talent for inventing voices as needed to represent specific attitudes and experiences. Quite often he used these invented personae to express his own opinions.

Hughes recorded and invented the voices of other people in the Walt Whitman tradition of hearing America sing. Comparing Hughes to Whitman, Donald Gibson wrote, "Both adopt personae, preferring to speak in voices other than their own." Hughes did not adopt a persona merely as a literary device, however. He was, as Gibson described him, truly "a man of large sympathies, at ease in the world, broad in outlook, and fantastically regardful of other people." Adopting many voices and arranging them artistically can be evaluated from a more technical literary perspective. M. M. Bakhtin identifies a variety of social speech types—"heteroglossia"—within any single national language: "social dialects, characteristic group behaviour, professional jargons, generic languages, languages of generations and age groups, tendentious languages, languages of the authorities, of various circles and of passing fashions." Bakhtin goes on to praise "a diversity of individual voices, artistically organized." The dialogic technique of the Simple stories immediately places into an artistic order the voices of Simple and the foil. However, through the oral narration rendered by Simple, the reader also encounters ministers, relatives, landladies, Irish police officers, Puerto Rican subway riders, bosses, significant female others, and random strangers whom Simple encounters on the streets and subways of New York. The foil steps in occasionally to narrate the setting, but the voice of Simple becomes both speaker and narrator in that Simple narrates many of the tales. We as readers do not witness these events from the standpoint of an objective third-person narrator; we witness Simple's recounting of them.[8]

8. Donald B. Gibson, "The Good Black Poet and the Good Gray Poet: The Poetry of Hughes and Whitman," in O'Daniel, ed., *Langston Hughes: Black Genius,* 66, 67; M. M. Bakhtin, *The Dialogic Imagination: Four Essays by M. M. Bakhtin,* ed. Michael Holquist, trans. Caryl Emerson and Michael Holquist (Austin: University of Texas Press, 1981), 262–63.

Richard Long and Eugenia Collier acknowledge both the regard of other people and the creative talent that Hughes brought to his portrayal of the numerous voices: "The astonishing feature of Langston Hughes' art is his unerring re-creation of the imagery, idiom, and syntax of black speech. This was not the result of chance, for Hughes' own spontaneous speech was quite different from that of the folk. His achievement was that of a connoisseur in love with the speech of black folk and with the folk themselves."[9] Thus, Hughes both heard and respected the language of his people.

Because he carefully observed other people, and because he genuinely valued their feelings, Hughes very often expressed in his writings the feelings of those other people whom he had observed. The Simple Minded Friend was the longest lived and most successful of those representatives of the feelings of other people, and these ordinary men in the first "Here to Yonder" column prefigure that aspect of having a character who speaks the truths of other people. Hughes's technique of having a designated spokesperson dialogue comfortably with an interpreter falls quite securely within the realm of participant observation:

> Obviously, no one can ever know a culture as well as someone who was born into it and who lives with it on a day-to-day basis. Yet most "natives" are unable to discuss and interpret their own behavior because they take so much of it for granted. Insofar as anthropology can make a special contribution to the study of human behavior, it does so because the fieldworker applies the perceptive faculties of a trained objective observer with the personal insight of someone who has lived as a member of the group over a long period. Neither of these aspects of his professional stance should be allowed to dominate the other.[10]

Thus, Hughes balanced the perspectives of ordinary Harlem residents with his own more privileged perspective. His unofficial ethnography was purposeful: to secure equal rights and opportunities for African

9. Richard A. Long and Eugenia W. Collier, eds., *Afro-American Writing: An Anthology of Prose and Poetry*, 368.
10. Julia G. Crane and Michael V. Angrosino, *Field Projects in Anthropology: A Student Handbook* (Morristown, N.J.: General Learning Press, 1974), 70.

Americans, or at least to raise the consciousness of his people to empower them to act on their own behalf.

In addition to the similarities in style, Hughes's first "Here to Yonder" column also resembles the Simple stories in content. Three of the topics covered in the brief conversation predict Simple's range: complaints about injustices in the treatment of black soldiers, use of news to verify injustices against black people, and contempt for the advantages white immigrants have over native blacks. Hughes certainly did not invent these topics, nor did he exaggerate their importance to ordinary black people. The Harlem Riot of 1943 revealed the frustration blacks felt regarding those same three areas, and the *Defender* carried many stories and editorials upon which black readers relied to verify the injustices they saw being perpetrated upon black Americans. Indeed, some of these same issues remain in the 1990s as continuing sources of irritation for African Americans.

In "The Birth of Jesse B. Semple," James Presley quotes from "Why and Wherefore" Hughes's promise to write about "your folks and mine—as colored as me." However, after suggesting that "Hughes had been looking for someone like Simple when he first started writing his weekly column," Presley could have gone on to show that Hughes had already found people like Simple in the quiet older man and especially in the truck driver.[11] This ordinary working man who reads and reacts to the newspapers and who contentiously raises the issue of racial discrimination is the very model of Simple, yet he has never been cited as the forerunner of the fictional creation.

In style as well as content, then, the first "Here to Yonder" column prefigures the Simple columns. On the other hand, an important distinction is that it reports a purportedly true encounter, whereas in the Simple stories the fictional aspect of the writing is emphasized and highly crafted. By involving himself as author in the Simple tales—rather than merely as reporter, as he did in this first column—Hughes was able to make significant improvements, such as the addition of humor and better-developed depth of character. These gradual embellishments have enabled Simple to survive as a fictional character.

After that first column, none of the other "Here to Yonder" efforts so directly prefigures the Simple techniques. His next two discussions

11. James Presley, "The Birth of Jesse B. Semple," 220.

offer the least interesting of his range—fairly historical, biographical commentary with no particular zing. His second column is a tribute to W. C. Handy, "Maker of the Blues," while his third eulogizes Josephine Baker, an entertainer erroneously reported dead. Hughes calls her a "Child of Charm." Throughout his years of writing the weekly commentary in the *Defender,* Hughes resorted to rather unremarkable biographical, bibliographical, and travel-centered topics fairly often.

The following two weeks, Hughes wrote his column in his most effective nonfiction voice. He focused upon the ludicrous practice of segregation and African American responses to it. "Jokes on Our White Folks," December 12, 1942, cites instances in which light-skinned blacks had thwarted the whole purpose of segregation by enlisting as "white" soldiers and by donating blood to the Red Cross as "white" donors. These instances, reported as anecdotes, retain the involvement of ordinary folks as well as the focus on absurd Jim Crow policies. Even as he mentions the jokes, however, Hughes carefully refrains from generalizing about whites. He specifies that the white folks he is discussing as the butts of the jokes are "our reactionary white folks, not the decent ones."

"He'd Leave Him Dying," the second in his memorable nonfiction commentary, appears December 19, 1942. It continues to address the policies of segregation mentioned in "Jokes on Our White Folks," but the tone changes from tongue-in-cheek to completely serious and affective. This time Hughes tells of a black soldier who is instructed to refrain from touching a white soldier who is dying. Because of segregation, this black soldier must keep his hands off any white soldier—even if the black soldier is a doctor. Hughes valued humor, but when human lives were wantonly sacrificed to the rules of segregation, he dropped the mask and mouthed no subtleties. His column rarely reached this level of urgency, but when the need arose, Hughes spoke completely without guise and without humor.

His January 9, 1943, column, "Music at Year's End," clearly written just before New Year's Day, presents a bleak view of reality, but it does not maintain the level of sincerity and seriousness that "He'd Leave Him Dying" presented. The Old Year's reflection uses a colloquial diction:

It was last year, 1941, that the war broke out, wasn't it? Before that there wasn't no defense work much. And the President hadn't told the

factory bosses that they had to hire colored. Before that it was W.P.A.
and the Relief. It was 1939 and 1935 and 1932 and 1928 and years
that you don't want to remember when your clothes got shabby and
the insurance relapsed. Now it's 1942—and different. Folks have jobs.
Money's circulating again. Relatives are in the Army with big insurances
if they die.

With this portrayal, Hughes reminds his readers that the buoyancy
they are experiencing has been achieved only after years of financial
hardship. Those earlier years were so bad that "you don't want to
remember." Hughes never feared to paint realistic pictures, but he
never allowed his writings to dwell on the negative side of reality.
Precisely this kind of fearless honesty won the praise of W. E. B. Du
Bois, who once defended Hughes's poetry this way: "The poet depicts
life as it is and he can be justly condemned only if he makes evil seem
more beautiful and good. This Mr. Hughes in his strikingly beautiful
poems has never done." In his columns, also, Hughes depicted "life
as it is," but he never painted troubles to make them "seem more
beautiful and good."[12]

In his January 16, 1943, column, "No Half-Freedoms," Hughes
insists that his readers continue to strive for full freedom. Citing
defenders of just causes ranging from Jesus and the money changers
in the temple to Frederick Douglass to volunteers in the Spanish Civil
War, Hughes warns African Americans not to heed the urgings of
southerners who seek "to soften and quiet down the Negro press
in its demands for freedom and equality for the Negro people in
America." This column establishes the precedent for his instructive
and straightforward interpretations of history and current events.
While he does not encourage thoughtless reactions to oppression,
Hughes does caution against complacency. Blacks were receiving
helpful advice as well as counterproductive suggestions, and Hughes
assumed the responsibility of helping to guide his readers into actions
that would benefit future generations.

Hughes discussed the broad issues of segregation and Jim Crow
laws, but he also covered specific problems, such as "colored" hotels,

12. Herbert Aptheker, ed., *The Correspondence of W. E. B. Du Bois,*
vol. 1, *Selections, 1877–1934* (Amherst: University of Massachusetts Press,
1973), 276.

which he complains about in "Hotels Non-Deluxe" (January 23, 1942). A world traveler and frequent lecturer, Hughes had ample comparative basis for his complaints that hotels for black people generally offered poor service, many inconveniences, and even some dirty shelves and drawers. He adds as an afterthought, "Most colored hotels are not owned by colored people." Again, Hughes shows his good sense of balance: he criticizes the problems with colored hotels, but he acknowledges that colored people are not fully responsible. Having identified himself in his first column as "half writer and half vagabond," he solidly asserts his intention to report the conditions he observes in his ongoing travels "from here to yonder around the world and back again."

Hughes's nonfiction columns occasionally reveal the kind of humorous exaggeration and wordplay for which Simple has become known. These nonfiction columns capitalize upon the same kinds of verbal humor that the bar buddy woodenly corrects in some of the Simple stories. Hughes's three-week series on Jim Crow shock expresses disappointment with the army and includes humorous reports and recommendations, and the column titles show that Hughes's penchant for rhyme is similar to Simple's: "Hey, Doc! I Got Jim Crow Shock!" (February 26, 1944); "Doc, Wait! I Can't Sublimate" (March 4, 1944); and "Hold Tight! They're Crazy White" (March 11, 1944). The link between these columns and the voice of Simple is strengthened by the fact that in the listing of Simple columns Hughes maintained he listed "Hey, Doc! I Got Jim Crow Shock!" as a Simple story, even though the column never mentions Simple.[13]

The title of the first column immediately establishes through punning the idea that "Jim Crow shock" exists and is a medical problem. Hughes names this "disease" by extrapolating upon the term *shell shock,* which 1944 readers recognized as what has subsequently been labeled "combat fatigue" or "post–traumatic stress disorder" (PTSD): mental fatigue or even a type of mental breakdown characterized by anxiety, depression, flashbacks, and so forth, often occurring after prolonged combat. "Jim Crow shock" humorously equates this condition with the mental fatigue or breakdown resulting from prolonged racism or senseless segregation—especially in the military setting.

13. *Mind,* drafts MSS, Folder 8 list, JWJ.

This concept shows how Hughes cleverly analyzed situations and aptly named them, as did Simple. Although Hughes makes this series on "Jim Crow shock" humorous, the news of that time adds a chilling seriousness to his comments. About a month after the series ran, the front page of the April 22, 1944, *Defender* reported: "Soldier, Oppressed By Jim Crow In Our Dual Democracy, Tries Suicide."

In the first column of the trilogy, "Hey, Doc! I Got Jim Crow Shock!" Hughes speaks of an actual incident involving a black soldier returning from a year in South Pacific action. This black soldier hit a white officer in a southern training camp and was then imprisoned. After relating the details of the case, Hughes takes tongue in cheek:

> It seems to me that his case might have been merely a case of Jim Crow shock, too much discrimination—segregation-fatigue which, to a sensitive Negro, can be just as damaging as days of heavy air bombardment or a continuous barrage of artillery fire. To fight for one's country for months on some dangerous and vital front, then come home and be subjected to the irritations and humiliations of Southern Jim Crowisms, Dixie scorn, the back seats if any in buses, is enough—I should think—to easily drive a sensitive patriotic colored American soldier NUTS.

Hughes suggests that a soldier suffering Jim Crow shock should be sent to see a psychiatrist rather than to the stockade. Certainly, psychiatric treatment would have been more humane than imprisonment. However, the irony that resides within Hughes's fictitious solution is that to treat the individual casualty either as a criminal or as a mental case does not speak to the real source of the problem: the institutional perpetuation of white racism. Hughes's expansion upon the analogy between shell shock and Jim Crow shock reveals that the common denominator between warfare and racism is their tragic human cost. As Simple will point out in a later column, "To be shot down is bad for the body, but to be Jim Crowed is worse for the spirit" ("Simple on Military Integration," *Best,* 81).

The humor that ordinary black readers appreciated was that the black soldier reacting to racism was not the person who needed mental adjustment. Other nonfiction columns and many remarks expressed through Simple clearly show that Hughes wanted white people to correct their own mental problem: racism. In his trilogy he suggests that white army men suffering color-domination madness should likewise see the psychiatrist. In the third column of the series, "Hold Tight! They're Crazy White," Hughes concentrates on the white problem. First he reveals the folly of blaming the victims of racism for their condition.

> It does not make sense to deny Negroes the vote and then call Negroes bad citizens when they have no chance to be good ones. It does not make sense to deny Negroes equal educational facilities and then berate the Negroes as being ignorant. It does not make sense to intimidate, brutalize, and hinder the progress of a people, and then blame that people for not progressing more rapidly. It does not make sense to want to call all Negroes by their first names, but expect to be called Mr. yourself. It does not make sense to eat the food that Negroes cook, yet refuse to eat with Negroes.

With emphatic repetition, Hughes points out many examples of irrational racism. He then goes on to speculate about possible solutions:

> This domination-complex which many southern whites have toward Negroes seems definitely pathological. I wish some big foundation like the Carnegie fund or the Julius Rosenwald foundation would put up some money to psychoanalyze their heads, and help to straighten them out a bit because, as we know, they will not listen to reason on the subject of the Negro. I figure the reason they will not reason is because they have no reason to reason with. Their color-neuroses have got them down. They need help to get back to their right minds. Our various boards of public health ought to do something about them, because they are dangerous.

In his trilogy Hughes coats a kernel of truth with a layer of humor, hoping to elicit both laughter and serious consideration of the effects of racism in the military—and of the possible solutions. His nonfiction proposals amuse us, but the notions make some sense. The ideas are far-fetched but plausible, much like Simple's often-quoted vision of the game preserve for Negroes in "There Ought to Be a Law":

> "Look here at these headlines, man, where Congress is busy passing laws. While they're making all these laws, it looks like to me they ought to make one setting up a few Game Preserves for Negroes."
> "Whatever gave you that fantastic idea?" I asked.
> "A movie short I saw the other night," said Simple, "about how the government is protecting wild life, preserving fish and game, and setting

aside big tracts of land where nobody can fish, shoot, hunt, nor harm a
single living creature with furs, fins, or feathers. But it did not show a
thing about Negroes."

"I thought you said the picture was about 'wild life.' Negroes are
not wild."

"No," said Simple, "but we need protection. This film showed how
they put aside a thousand acres out West where the buffaloes roam
and nobody can shoot a single one of them. If they do, they get in
jail. It also showed some big National Park with government airplanes
dropping food down to the deers when they got snowed under and
had nothing to eat. The government protects and takes care of buffaloes
and deers—which is more than the government does for me or my
kinfolks down South. Last month they lynched a man in Georgia and
just today I see where the Klan has whipped a Negro within a inch
of his life in Alabama. And right up North here in New York a actor
is suing a apartment house that won't even let a Negro go up on the
elevator to see his producer. That is what I mean by Game Preserves for
Negroes—Congress ought to set aside some place where we can go and
nobody can jump on us and beat us, neither lynch us nor Jim Crow us
every day. Colored folk rate as much protection as a buffalo, or a deer."

"You have a point there," I said. (*Best,* 62)

The foil approves Simple's logic by refusing to argue with him, and
Hughes in his nonfiction editorial had approved the fantasy technique
of psychoanalyzing whites as a way of protesting the injustices of
racism in the United States. This type of fantasy fits into a category
described by Melvin G. Williams as " 'get-even' dreams." "The get-even
dreams are almost always racial and are ego-building for Simple only
in the general sense that Blacks enjoy fantastic victories over whites."
Williams goes on to quote from James Thurber, creator of the well-
known daydreamer Walter Mitty, regarding the value of triumphant
daydreams: " 'In a triumphant daydream, it seems to me, there is
felicity and not defeat. You can't just take a humiliation and dismiss it
from your mind. . . . The thing to do is to visualize a triumph over the
humiliator, so vividly and so insistently that it becomes, in effect, an
actuality.' "[14] Hughes daydreamed victoriously as editorial writer and
as creator of Simple. Both voices offer a simultaneously humorous yet
serious perspective on contemporary events.

14. Williams, "Langston Hughes's Jesse B. Semple: A Black Walter Mitty,"
67.

Psychologist and sociologist Aaron D. Gresson also discusses day-dreaming. Quoting Freud, he notes:

"Unsatisfied wishes are the driving power behind phantasies; every separate phantasy contains the fulfillment of a wish, and improves on unsatisfactory reality." But John Dollard, in his classic study of caste, class, and race relations in the South, went even further, referring specifically to the oppressed: "sociologists who do not take this possibility into account are bound to misunderstand the personalities of Negroes and other oppressed collectivities; dreams and fantasies are as much social acts as blows and manifestoes."[15]

Gresson goes on to suggest that Simple demonstrates this truth: "Even after the super- and subordination structures of a given social order have been defined and institutionalized, they can be challenged—both in fact and fantasy." Moving on to "the psychology of the colonized" and making reference to sources such as Frantz Fanon's *Black Skin, White Masks* and *The Wretched of the Earth,* Gresson argues that when oppressed people feel violated, such violations can actually energize and empower them, rather than leaving them socially wretched. By truly acting to avenge himself, or even simply by verbally lambasting his oppressor in the presence of others, the oppressed person achieves "a useful alternative to the marginality/self-hatred perspective" and demonstrates "cathartic activity among the socially oppressed."[16] The Negro press in general, and Hughes's column—especially the Simple stories—in particular, illustrate the value of such catharsis. The writing and subsequent public discussions of them *might* have tangible benefits, but they *certainly* afford psychological advantages. By envisioning a better, more just reality, and *by talking about it,* the speaker begins to really improve his situation. If nothing else, the speaker is healthier—not merely wallowing in self-pity or in helplessness.

In addition to the daydreaming techniques, the nonfiction assessment in "Hold Tight!" offers a sophistication that would be uncharacteristic of Simple, while at the same time including verbal play

15. Aaron D. Gresson, *The Dialectics of Betrayal: Sacrifice, Violation, and the Oppressed,* 8.
16. Gresson, *Dialectics of Betrayal,* 28, 53, 54. See also a further discussion, more specific to LH, in Gresson, "Beyond Selves Deferred: Langston Hughes' Style and the Psychology of Black Selfhood."

like that which typifies Simple's lines. In an article about the Simple stories, Julian Carey says of Simple, "He is not sophisticated enough to diagnose the racist psyche, but he does know that he is not the problem."[17] Hughes, of course, *is* sophisticated enough to diagnose the racist psyche. He combines serious assessment with humorous extension. To clarify the "domination-complex" of white southerners, Hughes alludes to a book on the subject: E. Franklin Frazier, *The Pathology of Race Prejudice.* Such bibliographic reference is a common tactic in his columns. Then, using both flights of imagination and rhetorical strategies like those found in the Simple columns, he humorously indicts racist whites without using the Simple persona. He satirically fantasizes about ways in which such agencies as the Rosenwald foundation or the Carnegie fund could better develop humanity and civility between the races by offering funds to psychoanalyze racist whites. Beyond showing that racism is a problem worthy of funded research, he implicitly reminds his readers that the professed values and ideas of white America, which are symbolically embodied in such philanthropic agencies, are wholly at odds with the pathology of white racism. Obviously Hughes does not offer his suggestion for serious consideration, but he does seriously wish someone could assist racist whites in thinking clearly, thereby ceasing their domination complex. One year later Hughes would still be psychoanalyzing racist whites, comparing the "white Southerners in Dixie, our local Nordics" to the Germans, whom one American sociologist considered to be "victims of a mass psychosis."[18]

In "Hold Tight! They're Crazy White," Hughes deliberately repeats the word *reason* to play humorously with semantics and to stimulate thought about the psychology of racist southern whites. They need help, he says, because "they will not listen to reason on the subject of the Negro. I figure the reason they will not reason is because they have no reason to reason with." Forcing the reader to consider contextual meanings, Hughes shifts from *reason,* meaning "sound thought or judgment; good sense," to *reason,* meaning "explanation or justification of an act, idea." Then he shifts to the verb form of *reason,* "to think, talk, or argue coherently and logically," and back

17. Julian C. Carey, "Jesse B. Semple Revisited and Revised," 159.
18. LH, "Nazi and Dixie Nordics," *CD,* March 10, 1945.

to the noun, this time meaning either intelligence, as in "the power of rationally comprehending, inferring, judging, or thinking," or sanity, as in "proper exercise of mental capacity," and finally back again to the verb form. Obviously Hughes could have stated the matter in clearer terms: "They will not listen to rational thought on the subject of the Negro. I figure the explanation for their refusal to think or talk logically is that they lack the intelligence to do so." Such a statement lacks humor, however, and Hughes consciously softens the effect of his criticism with the leaven of humor. Jesse B. Semple will use the very same kinds of equivoques to discuss similar material.[19]

As we compare the rhetoric and language of Hughes as editorial columnist, of Simple, and of the foil (later named Boyd and regularly called that by some critics), we realize how closely Hughes identified with both Simple and the foil. Both personae speak for Hughes at times, and at times Hughes writes nonfiction editorials in the speech patterns of both personae. And when we compare the attitudes of just the two characters, Simple and the foil, in more detail, we may be inclined to agree with Harry L. Jones's theory of the consubstantiality of the two: "Boyd serves in one respect as Simple's immediate audience, although in actuality he is consubstantial with Simple, that is, Simple and Boyd share the same value scheme, attitudes, hopes, and aspirations for justice, truth, honesty, and racial equity which Simple promulgates over and over again. Boyd is the more moderate, less militant, Simple."[20] Since Hughes could voice the same kinds of sentiments and even use the same stylistic and rhetorical devices through the Simple/Boyd personae and in the nonfiction columns, we sense a dual authorial identity in the two types of columns. Even though Hughes established two separate voices for the Simple Minded Friend and the persona who represents himself and others of the more privileged and better-educated class of Negroes, he as an editorial writer speaks through both voices. He speaks both for the ordinary working black man who dreads Jim Crow as much as he

19. *Webster's New World Dictionary of the American Language,* 2d College Edition, New York: The World Publishing Co., 1970. See LH, "Reason and Right," *Claim;* a passage from that story is analyzed by Watkins in "Simple: The Alter Ego," 20.

20. Harry L. Jones, "Rhetorical Embellishment in Hughes's Simple Stories," in O'Daniel, ed., *Langston Hughes: Black Genius,* 138–39.

dreads Hitler and for the sophisticated college graduate who hopes
to lead the masses of black people. For Hughes, the two perspectives
are complementary, not contradictory.

Two columns concerning the 1944 presidential election exemplify
the identity of Hughes and his character Simple and further remind us
of the validity of Jones's theory of consubstantiality of Simple and the
foil, the Hughes persona. In the column "Simple and the Elections,"
August 12, 1944, when Simple declares himself to be for *Mrs.* Roosevelt, the Hughes persona teases him for such political innocence.
Two months later, on October 14, 1944, in "Mr. Dewey and Me," with
no Simple Minded Friend speaking, Hughes admits that he, too, had
to consider the wives of the candidates as he decided. He announced
his intention to vote his approval of Mrs. Roosevelt rather than Mrs.
Dewey. This reversal of position by the Hughes persona supports
Jones's theory that Simple and the foil—the Hughes persona—share
the same value scheme. Arthur Davis finds such consubstantiality
quite typical of Hughes. Calling it "twofold vision," he finds it not
only in the Simple stories, but also in the companion poems "Low to
High" and "High to Low" from *Montage of a Dream Deferred:*

> Insofar as an author may be his own creations, Langston Hughes is the
> earthy, prejudiced, and race-conscious Simple as well as the urbane,
> tolerant, and sophisticated "straight man" in the sketches. The two
> characters are opposite sides of the coin, and from their observations
> and insights, interacting one upon the other we get the twofold vision
> found in much of Mr. Hughes's best work, whether prose or poetry.[21]

The critics could have quoted Langston Hughes himself on the subject, for in an article explaining his Simple character, Hughes states
plainly, "The character of My Simple Minded Friend . . . is just myself
talking to me. Or else me talking to myself."[22]

A different way of shedding light on the interaction between these
two identities is by examining the language and grammar used by
the Hughes persona and by his Simple Minded Friend. In "Simple
Wants to Be Genius" (April 14, 1945) Simple's buddy lectures to him

---

21. Arthur P. Davis, "Langston Hughes: Cool Poet," in O'Daniel, ed.,
Langston Hughes: Black Genius, 19, 29.
22. LH, "Simple and Me," 349.

about the need to develop genius and about the benefits of genius to increase one's popularity. " 'Joyce likes you, I admit. And maybe one or two more I hear you talking about. But your landlady sure don't like you—unless you pay your rent. Whereas, if you was a good-looking, distinguished, renowned genius, she might like you, too.' " The bar buddy uses some terrible grammar in this remark. The comments sound conversational and even seem authentic for Hughes himself in a relaxed mood, but they indicate that Hughes was not paying careful attention to the consistent development of a distinct character for the bar buddy—including language and viewpoints that would contrast to those of Simple.

In another example the foil is trying to broaden Simple's point of view. Perhaps here Hughes is reporting actual conversations he has overheard or engaged in, so the informal diction may be authentic. Or, if he completely imagined the dialogue, Hughes may have employed the informal tone to attract rather than alienate some of his less polished readers who would benefit most from the message:

"You're as bad as Bilbo, daddy-o," I said. "You just want to talk up a fight. You and Mr. Cracker could get along—and do get along—when you are both after the same thing, and there is no way of getting it except by getting along. Look at the New York subway! Southern white folks ride on it and jammed up beside colored folks. All of them want to get home at 5:30, so they get along."

"I am not talking about no subway," said Simple, "I am talking about things in general."

"Things in general is made up of little things," I said, "and little by little, things are getting better for us in this world."

"I hope you are right," said Simple. "But I want 'em to get better faster than that."

"I want them to get better fast, too," I said. "But you have to build on what you got."

"I ain't got nothing to start with," said Simple.

"Nuts! You've got more than millions of folks in China or in Poland or in Persia have got. . . . What you really want is a job, pal. . . . You want sixty million jobs."

"I want just one," said Simple.[23]

23. LH, "This Snaggle-Tooth World," *CD*, July 28, 1945.

The Hughes persona reproves Simple for perpetuating the argument, but by comparing him with Bilbo, he adds some good-natured, teasing insult to the criticism. By evoking the name of one of the quintessential racists of the decade, the bar buddy surely captures Simple's attention. Clearly these two fellows are friendly enough to permit such tongue-in-cheek jabs as a comparison to Bilbo.

The passage indicates far more equality between the college-educated bar buddy and the average simple Negro than would remain in the collected Simple stories. In this episode the bar buddy uses terribly ordinary diction, including the word *get,* rather than the more formal *cooperate* for "get along" and *improve* for "get better." In several phrases the foil echoes Simple's language. For example, the bar buddy calls the average white person "Mr. Cracker," but the more polished interlocutor would never use such a phrase. Here, too, the foil uses slang, including the familiar "daddy-o" and the informal expletive "nuts!" These elements show that in this episode the foil's diction is not especially elevated over that of Simple or of the average man.

On the other hand, Hughes reworked a couple of his own essays so that they were subsequently spoken through Simple. "A Veteran Falls" appears in the *Defender* as nonfiction narrated in the columnist's own voice (December 7, 1946); Simple is not present. Later, when Hughes modifies it and includes it in *Simple Speaks His Mind,*[24] Simple tells the entire story and the bar buddy does not utter a line. Similarly, "Simple Down Under" (February 28, 1948) is an episode in which the foil speaks no lines at all. However, "Down Under in Harlem" had been published as a nonfiction editorial in the March 27, 1946, *New Republic.* This nonfiction commentary in a "general" publication—not the black press—contains similar language, organization, and comments. Thus, the writer Hughes expressed similar issues in similar ways through his own voice and through the voice of his Simple character.

One Hughesian theme in his nonfictional and in his Simple columns during the 1940s—and in his other writings—was that all white people are not alike. In order to help his almost exclusively black audience respond effectively to racism, Hughes reminds his readers

24. "A Veteran Falls" appears in *Mind,* 98–101, and is reprinted in *Best,* 49–52.

that all white people are not the guilty perpetrators of the brutal racist policies. He distinguishes many times between "reactionary white folks" and "decent ones." Hughes began making this point in one of his first columns, "Jokes on Our White Folks," December 12, 1942.

The distinction between "reactionary" and "decent" white people reiterates a clarification Hughes had begun making as early as 1930. In his first novel, *Not without Laughter,* Hughes had permitted several characters to offer their divergent opinions about white people, and the protagonist, young Sandy, in his drowsy thoughts, distinguishes between particular white folks as does Hughes: "Some white folks were nice, though. Earl was nice at school, but not the little boys across the street, who called him 'nigger' every day."[25]

This careful refusal to generalize about *all* whites reappears many times in the Hughes columns and often enters the Simple conversations via the careful notations of the foil. However, even Simple occasionally distinguishes "decent" whites from "evil" ones, praising as "decent" Eleanor Roosevelt and the couple who stood up to witness his marriage to Joyce.

With his distinction between "our reactionary white folks" and "the decent ones" in "Here to Yonder," Hughes remained characteristically respectful of individual differences. In columns purportedly addressed to whites, he assumes the basic human goodness of most white people and encourages them to improve. In fact, he asserts that blacks should be sure to communicate with the "nice white people" they know, "because we need their decency to save America." In his nonfiction voice, Hughes warns that, like a snake, Hitlerian ideas (racism in general, presumed white superiority over Japanese American citizens in particular) lie coiled and dangerous in America. The message concludes with an optimistic but sober warning: "Americans of good-will, the nice, decent church people, the well-meaning liberals, the good-hearted souls who themselves wouldn't lynch anyone, must begin to realize that they have to be more than passively good-hearted, more than church-goingly Christian, and much more than word-of-mouth in their liberalism, if they want to save America from . . . Hitler-land." Thus, Hughes generally assumed that some white people would work with blacks to end dangerous racism.

25. LH, *Not without Laughter,* 183.

Even in "Freight," an uncharacteristically solemn response to the deaths of talented blacks who were unfortunate enough to be injured in the South, Hughes tries to mention some whites who cared. Such a mention fails to translate the tone of the essay into optimism, however. Listing those needless deaths due to Jim Crow policies at hospitals compelled Hughes to consider the question from the Clark College student: "Is it true in the Southland, 'White folks will let any Negro die'?"[26] Thus, although Hughes carefully worked to distinguish caring whites from racist ones, he nevertheless gave voice to those African Americans who lamented the hateful actions of "white folks" with no adjectives to distinguish them.

However, Hughes knew that besides being unhealthy, consistently solemn and heartrending consideration of the racial issue was also an atypical response for the masses of black people. Hughes valued humor both in its historical contexts and in contemporary usage. He noted often how humor had aided African Americans in surviving racial oppression, and he chastised contemporary journals for being too serious. Referring to *Crisis* and to *Phylon,* Hughes wrote: "These magazines evidently think the race problem is too deep for comic relief. Such earnestness is contrary to mass Negro thinking. Colored people are always laughing at some wry Jim Crow incident or absurd nuance of the color line. If Negroes took all the white world's daily boorishness to heart and wept over it as profoundly as our serious writers do, we would have been dead long ago."[27] Not only did Hughes establish his own critical and aesthetic pronouncements on the value of humor, but he also followed advice on humor offered by the previous generation of black literary figures.

In his review of *Simple Speaks His Mind,* Carl Van Vechten cites an example of such early comment: "On frequent occasions the late James Weldon Johnson . . . was heard to observe: 'There is no doubt in my mind that the solution of the "race problem" depends on a sense of humor.'" Hughes felt that even serious writing needed the leaven of humor, so in his column he allowed readers to laugh as he satirized the contemporary national and international scenes in his own voice and through the use of fictional creations such as Simple.

26. LH, "The Snake in the House," *CD,* October 16, 1943; LH, "Freight," *CD,* May 10, 1947.
27. LH, "Let's Laugh a Little," Foreword to *Claim,* 11-12.

Saunders Redding, in his review of *Simple Speaks His Mind,* found its humor to be in the tradition of the "horse sense humorists" of 1875–1900, such as Josh Billings, Artimus Ward, Charles Heber Clark and his "Cooley," and Finley Peter Dunne, who created "Mr. Dooley." Redding elaborated by explaining that "the tradition demands a rich awareness, an unclouded eye, an unstopped ear. It demands the salt of sincerity. It demands a sense of humor delicately balanced between gross, playful burlesque and acute satire." Another reviewer believed the writing had a particularly Hughesian quality when it showed "a predilection for common life and everyday situations treated with a paradoxical mixture of genial humor and uncomfortable satire."[28]

Other critics place the humor in the Simple stories firmly into a context of black folk tradition, including both oral and written precedents. Roger Whitlow, for example, notices the oral heritage of "exaggerated tales of humor, the blues, spirituals, work songs, and legendary-men stories and the slave and animal tales" from which emerged black written folklore.[29] Some critics see Hughes as fitting right into this tradition by "transplanting" black folk narrative style into Harlem. On the other hand, some analysts refuse to credit Hughes with such a transplantation; they claim that black people brought the style to Harlem when they migrated from the South and that what Hughes accomplished was to record these authentic black narrative styles faithfully in his own works. As Richard Barksdale points out, this authentic black narrative style appears in Hughes's folk poems as well as in the Simple stories: "They contain many instances of naming and enumerating, considerable hyperbole and understatement, and a strong infusion of street talk rhyming." Specifically, he notes "that particular mixture of Hughesian irony and humor—a very distinctive mark of his folk poetry."[30] Hughes marked the Simple stories with many of the same characteristics.

The use of humor prevailed in Hughes's writings throughout his career, but it was especially noteworthy during the 1940s when he initiated Simple. Arthur Dudden's examination of political humor in the United States found that American society in the 1940s and 1950s

28. G. Lewis Chandler, "For Your Recreation and Reflection," 95.
29. Roger Whitlow, *Black American Literature: A Critical History,* 11.
30. Richard K. Barksdale, "Langston Hughes: His Times and His Humanistic Techniques," 14.

discouraged jokes about the government or its leaders: "The herd-like patriotic unities demanded by the Second World War and the Cold War aftermath effectively suppressed the traditional toleration for jesting at the nation's leaders." Dudden found four exceptions to the dearth of political humor during the late 1940s and early 1950s: the writings of Ring Lardner, James Thurber, Robert Benchley, and Langston Hughes. Although none of the four was *primarily* a political humorist, Dudden felt that all extended H. L. Mencken's example of "antidemocratic derision," ridiculing "the bloated pride in the nation's achievements and the blind faith in the progress of democracy," yet professing "to be entertained rather than revolted by the nation's follies." To support his reference to Hughes as political humorist, Dudden cited the Simple stories.[31]

Despite the similarity Dudden notes, however, Hughes and Mencken took essentially opposite positions in their stances toward democracy, although ridicule mattered in both views. Mencken's humor was grounded in his skepticism about democracy—its adulation of the average man (whom he called the "boob") and the collective will of the majority (the "booboisie"). Hughes's sympathies, on the other hand, were profoundly democratic. He both identified with and boosted the pride of the average man; Simple, after all, became his mouthpiece. His humor pointed out the failure of American society to live up to its democratic ideals. As his poem "Let America Be America Again" hauntingly comments, "America never was America to me." For Hughes, especially in his Simple voice, the average black man overcomes racism by maintaining his morality and his sense of humor. Whereas Mencken laughed at people, Hughes laughed with them. Whether one evaluates the humor as an example of the folk tradition or as political humor, Hughes uses and advocates the use of humor to balance one's mental outlook.

These topics and tones represent the wide range printed by the time Hughes introduced his Simple Minded Friend and in Simple's early years. He had already used some direct quotations, some humor, some historical survey. He had directly or indirectly offered advice to both blacks and whites, and he had acknowledged both the famous

31. Arthur Power Dudden, "The Record of Political Humor," 61, 60, 61-62 n. 40.

and the unknown. By any standards, the column should be judged a success. It ran for nearly twenty years in the *Chicago Defender,* and Hughes was later syndicated into several other papers, ultimately moving into the "general" press. The significant trademarks of his column, however, were cast in the early years. Most important of all the trademarks, without a doubt, was his Simple Minded Friend, whom we later came to know as "Simple."

3

Simple Comes to Life

IN HIS "HERE TO YONDER" column, Langston Hughes experimented with the Simple Minded Friend and with nonfiction editorial writing. The earliest fans read Simple's first conversation with columnist Hughes in the February 13, 1943, *Chicago Defender,* three months after Hughes began writing "Here to Yonder" on November 21, 1942. This character attracted significant attention from the readers, and because of his popularity he was developed into a particular individual with a nickname, a personal history, and a predictable range of topics to discuss. As he developed into a more rounded fictional character, he acquired the full name Jesse B. Semple and began to dominate the "Here to Yonder" column.

Hughes introduced Simple in three consecutive columns on February 13, 20, and 27, 1943. All three columns focused on the war and involved some disagreement between the writer and his Simple Minded Friend. Entitled "Conversation at Midnight," the original dialogue with Simple presents a fellow who hates curfews. Only his love of "the right to stay up late" persuades him that he would best serve his own interests by joining the (segregated) army to battle the Nazis, who would impose worse limitations than Jim Crow. The same topic recurs two weeks later in "My Friend Wants to Argue." The Simple Minded Friend raises a reasonable point when he is challenged to join with white Americans in the fight against global racism; he asks, "Now, how am I going to fight with them in a Jim Crow army?" Although the *with* is not italicized, Simple's question actually points out two flaws in his buddy's point of view. First, as long as the United States supported Jim Crow policies, how could blacks feel that they were really allies with their white counterparts? How could blacks fight against global racism when their own government enacted racist policies against them—even in the armed forces? Second, the segregated troops prevented blacks from fighting literally "with" whites. They might have fought against the same enemy, but they did not battle shoulder-to-shoulder.

These dialogues authentically represented vital issues for blacks in the 1940s, because many blacks questioned the validity of a Jim Crow army. Other blacks, who better understood the horrors of Nazism, interpreted the contrasts and encouraged their brothers to defer the struggle to conquer racism in the United States so that the Allies could defeat the greater evil—Nazism.

In a recorded interview, Hughes stated that he had invented the Simple Minded Friend in order to present a view opposite of the pessimism blacks expressed regarding the war. He wanted to convey that Hitlerism was worse than Jim Crow.[1] He could have used his own editorial voice, eliminating the Simple Minded Friend. After all, he already had commented in his columns on reactionary white folks, cold-hearted segregationists, and deceptive southern advisors without inventing a "friend." Nevertheless, he wanted to offer a balance in thought, and he wished to involve his readers in some representative fashion. Rather than merely preaching against pessimism, he wanted to acknowledge the skepticism many blacks shared regarding the rhetoric about democracy that contradicted the unpleasant realities of racism. While allowing the doubts, Hughes intended to dominate the logic. He wanted to persuade his readers that their best interests were served by supporting the Allies in the war effort.

Sandwiched between these two columns contrasting Jim Crow to Nazi oppression, "Wives, War, and Money" offers the first glimmers of Simple's eventual personality. After suggesting that the economics of depression lead to crime—especially mugging—the Simple Minded Friend complains about low pay during the war:

> "You want to make money out of war?" I asked. "You want to make money out of people killing and being killed?"
>
> "I want to make money out of something," said my Simple Minded Friend.
>
> "You are mighty cynical," I said.
>
> "It is no sin to want to make money, is it?"

1. St. Clair Bourne, director, "Langston Hughes: The Dream Keeper," *Voices and Visions.*

Simple reveals both his never-ending need for more money and his penchant for misinterpreting words—hearing "sin" in "cynical."

These first three conversations with the Simple Minded Friend were the first of many sequential columns. The writer had clearly formulated his Simple Minded Friend as an assistant for his weekly editorials, so he tried him three times to ensure that the public had ample time to respond to him. In these three columns the Hughes persona dutifully imparts to his Simple Minded Friend the broader view of certain facts and popular opinions. For example, Simple seems unaware that Jim Crow is not as bad as Hitler's regime. Hughes tactfully addresses the ignorance with which his views are greeted. This teaching role is one many of the better-educated African Americans celebrated, because the great migration brought thousands of rural, unsophisticated blacks to settle in the urban North, Midwest, and West. They seldom viewed world politics as being significant to them. After reading previews of these first three columns, Arna Bontemps commented on their value for bringing sophisticated concepts "down to earth" for ordinary people:

> Your "Simple Minded Friend" seems to me a very happy creation, especially as a device for treating topics which would otherwise seem high-flown or academic. You can use him to show the application of theoretical questions to his life. International events might thus be related to his affairs. The *Good-Morning Stalingrad* techniques. I would not advise a) using the "Friends" *every* week or b) wasting him on the kind of material which needs no pointing up. It would be ideal, I'd think, to do an occasional "Friend" piece about the perplexity that comes to the common colored citizen when he tries to apply certain current statements of American ideals and war aims to life as he knows it. It might, in other words, be a way of commenting on current events and pronouncements.[2]

Hughes evidently believed in such a mission, because in a subsequent "Here to Yonder" column he wrote that "old residents" have responsibilities toward "cotton patch Negroes."[3] The history of migration

2. Bontemps to LH, in Nichols, ed., *Letters,* 121–22 (this letter is out of place; dated Monday, February 22, 1943, the letter should follow LH's letter of February 17, 1943, on pp. 124–25).

3. LH, "Dixie to Golden Gate," *CD,* May 6, 1944.

reveals that many rural African Americans arrived in urban centers bereft of knowledge about indoor plumbing, regular garbage pickup, and other city habits. For example, Booker T. Washington found himself teaching his unsophisticated rural brothers and sisters about table settings and tooth brushing when he began his own career in education. Perhaps the voice of a Simple Minded Friend allowed Hughes to meet his responsibilities as an old resident through his column.

As the sobriquet "Simple Minded Friend" implies, in the earliest "Here to Yonder" columns, the Simple character, like the truck driver and the older man in the first column, was not named. More important, in his first appearances he revealed little information about himself as an individual, and his personality was not clearly developed. He merely represented the general, working-class readership of Hughes's column. Hughes deliberately avoided biographical details in the beginning, because he knew that in real situations black folks neither volunteered nor inquired about strictly personal details, such as name, place of employment, or salary. This valuable anonymity permitted average readers to imagine that someone they knew was entering the "Here to Yonder" column, voicing the opinions of other average readers.

Hughes defends his purposeful exclusion of biographical details in one of his earliest letters to Maria Leiper, the editor at Simon and Schuster who worked most closely with him to polish his Simple manuscript:

> Regarding the suggestion that Simple's and Joyce's jobs be made clear: I deliberately do not do so because, since many Harlemites have rather lowly jobs which they often consider beneath their qualifications and education (and which they very often are), one may know people in Harlem for years without really knowing exactly what kind of work they do—sometimes because of shame to admit that their jobs are not up to what friends might expect of them. Negro readers, I think, get this nuance in reading these stories. But I could find no natural way of inserting it into the script. It just wouldn't be mentioned much between Simple and a casual friend, perhaps never brought up as a direct question. The same is true about Simple's educational background. People who have not gone to school very much are seldom clear about just where, when, or how far they have gone. What I wish to give the reader is the same knowledge of Simple as he would get if he were

to see him often for a year or so—which would be only what Simple himself would impart by conscious and unconscious words.[4]

Hughes asserted not only his authorial control, but also his authenticity as an observer of black culture. He knew what he wanted to reveal about his characters and what he did not want to reveal in order to preserve the true nature of interactions between casual acquaintances. In this regard, he offered empathetic observations acquired from his unofficial ethnography.

Hughes's concern for authenticity suggests the interaction between fact and fiction in his crafting of Jesse B. Semple. When called upon to explain how Simple began, he always admitted that his character had not merely popped into his mind:

> I cannot truthfully state, as some novelists do at the beginnings of their books, that these stories are about "nobody living or dead." The facts are that these tales are about a great many people—although they are stories about no specific persons as such. But it is impossible to live in Harlem and not know at least a hundred Simples, fifty Joyces, twenty-five Zaritas, a number of Boyds, and several Cousin Minnies—or reasonable facsimiles thereof. (Foreword to *Best,* vii)

Hughes was even more direct in an explanation preceding his reading of several Simple stories on an album:

> A great many people ask me if the leading character in my book *Simple Speaks His Mind* is a real character. Of course, he's not a real character in the sense that he's based on a real person. He's a composite. But he did grow out of a conversation that I had with a young man during the war. This fellow lived near me, just down the street, in fact, but I didn't know him very well. I knew him just well enough to say hello when I ran into him in the street. But one Saturday night I happened to run into him in Patsy's bar on Eighth Avenue. He asked me to come back to the booth and meet his girl friend.[5]

4. LH to Maria Leiper, August 29, 1949, LH correspondence, Simon and Schuster file, JWJ.

5. *Langston Hughes Reads from "Simple Speaks His Mind,"* record album.

Hughes comments that this conversation had occurred with a fellow whom he did not know very well. Thus, Hughes understood—or at least this important conversation taught him—the etiquette of familiarity. As he narrates the tale on his album, he agreed to go with this young fellow to meet his girlfriend, and the fellow treated Hughes to a beer.

> Not knowing much about the young man, I asked where he worked. He said, "In a war plant."
> I said, "What do you make?"
> He said, "Cranks."
> I said, "What kind of cranks?"
> He said, "Oh, man, I don't know what kind of cranks."
> I said, "Well, do they crank cars, tanks, buses, planes or what?"
> He said, "I don't know what them cranks crank."
> Whereupon, his girl friend, a little put out at this ignorance of his job, said, "You've been working there long enough. Looks like by now you ought to know what them cranks crank."
> He wasn't quite as polite with her as he had been with me. "Aw, woman," he said, "you know white folks don't tell colored folks what cranks crank."
> Well, now, I can't quite explain the processes of the creative imagination, and I don't know why it was that some months later out of this conversation there came into being in my newspaper column in the *Chicago Defender* a character whom I nicknamed "Simple." His real name, it turned out, was Jesse B. Semple. He began to talk about the war, about the problems of Negroes and democracy. Gradually he began to talk about himself more personally, about his love affairs, about his former wife that he was trying to get divorced from, and eventually he became what I feel to be a fairly well-rounded character.

Hughes confirms that the nature of Simple's conversations only gradually turned to personal details. Although he certainly denies that he copied the actual conversations with his young neighbor to produce the fictional creation of Simple, Hughes frankly reveals the strong connection between reality and his own fiction.

People familiar with the Simple episodes always refer to the "cranks" story as the beginning of the interaction. However, evidence that even that "authentic" beginning was crafted lies in the manuscript drafts accumulated for *Simple Speaks His Mind.* In an episode called

"Contender," the crank story operates independently of the girlfriend. In fact, the girlfriend is more like Zarita, caring more about a steady flow of alcoholic treats than about her escort's familiarity with his job.

Contender

It was during the war that I first met Simple. It was in a bar down the street around the corner from where I live. He was sitting in a booth with a girl who was not Joyce. After the introductions the conversation drifted to work conditions and war plants. Simple said he worked in a plant that made cranks.

I said, "What kind of cranks?"

He said, "Cranks! Cranks! Just cranks!"

I asked, "But what do they crank?"

He said, "I do not know! I don't crank with those cranks. I just make 'em. I reckon white folks do the cranking—in facts, I'm sure they do—because it took a special order from the President to even get colored folks a job making them. So I do not know what they crank."

"Well, it would seem to me you'd be curious about what those cranks crank," I said. "The colored race will never get ahead until we learn about things."

"I'll never learn about things until I get ahead then," said Simple. "There is no way for me to find out what those cranks crank where I am now. Mine is the only department where they allow colored folks to work anyhow, because that is the hardest work. But I'll bet you if I ever get a chance to crank with those cranks, I can really crank—because I believe a colored man can do anything anybody else can. I am a Race Man, and I really stand up for my people."

"Well, sit down now and buy me a zombie!" said the girl in the booth. "This is Saturday night. We out for some fun. We're not out for no arguments about race. I been colored all the week on my job down in Sutton Place. Yes, Miss, this! And Yes, M'am, that. I want to forget it tonight. Put a nickel on Louis Jordan and 'Let the Good Times Roll.'"

The juke box blared, the drinks came, and that was the end of our discussion for the evening. But the next time I ran into Simple at the bar, he took up the conversation right where we left off and it has been going on ever since, usually in the form of an argument. It does not always concern race. Sometimes it concerns his landlady who is his *bête noire*. Sometimes it concerns Joyce who is his girl friend. And sometimes it is about what you wish for in your soul but don't know how to express except in terms of the things you contend with every day. Simple is always contending with something.[6]

This episode, in which Simple is clearly less lovable than in the version eventually published in the foreword to *The Best of Simple,* left the questioning about the cranks to the foil, rather than to an embarrassed girlfriend. Thus, while Hughes has reinforced the impression that the "meeting" with Simple happened in a certain way, the written record suggests that Hughes crafted even the beginning.

However Simple first occurred to Hughes, the character continued to appear in his column. Simple's fourth appearance in "Here to Yonder" responded to a trilogy of columns about Hollywood and proved without a doubt that Hughes, the columnist, was the "I" with whom the Simple Minded Friend conversed at the beginning of the Simple episodes. Voicing an average person's opinion about the stereotypes of blacks in movies, Simple reveals his changing function in the column. Instead of griping about an issue that he selects, Simple gripes about an issue that Hughes's previous columns have presented to the public. He directly engages Hughes in discussion about his earlier suggestions regarding Hollywood. The column begins, "My Simple Minded Friend said to me, 'Hey, listen! I have been reading your columns about Hollywood and I do not think it is fair for you to jump on the Negro actors, and not mention the Jews.' " Thus, even without calling him by name, the Simple Minded Friend is clearly addressing Hughes.

Simple challenges the basic premise from Hughes's three-week series on racial bias in Hollywood: "Time Now to Stop, Actors," "Further Comment on Hollywood," and "What You Can Do about Hollywood," March 13, 20, and 27, 1943. In the columns Hughes boldly condemned black actors who accepted roles that perpetuated shallow stereotypes. Going further, he encouraged the public to write protest letters to Hollywood studios whenever they saw "an offensive portrayal of a Negro" and to write constructive letters, as well, informing the studios that "Negroes are just as much a part of American life as anybody else . . . in crowd scenes, in factory scenes, in trains . . . —clean, decent, non-caricatured Negroes." He also encouraged active

6. LH, "Contender," LH MSS #3534, Folder 1, JWJ. This draft is amended in Hughes's handwriting.

support of the NAACP—which was campaigning against Hollywood stereotypes—and called for direct verbal complaints to movie-theater managers who showed movies with insulting portrayals of blacks.

Simple, brimming with race loyalty, hates to hear black actors being criticized when the people with power are never held responsible. He claims that the Jewish moguls "own Hollywood." Hughes disagrees about ownership, but Simple persists. "My point is, the Jewish people are oppressed in Europe, just like we are here, so we ought to get more cooperation out of them than we do." Simple has connected "here" to "yonder."[7]

The use of Simple in "Jews, Negroes and Hollywood" foreshadows the mature Simple columns and collected episodes, where Hughes would trust Simple to deliver the essential message. In them, Simple would no longer directly confront Hughes the columnist, poet, and race man; instead he would argue with a Hughes persona—more stereotypically intellectual than the author himself, and when the average black working-class man would meet the college-educated black man, the author most often would let Simple express the more logical point of view. The more sophisticated speaker would recite platitudes and spout the proclamations of the American dream, while the more down-to-earth person would shatter the illusions of what *should* be or what *could* be. In this fourth appearance of Simple, Hughes provides a glimmer of that disillusioned common sense with which the average man offers clear-eyed and logical analysis.

After Simple has reasonably suggested that Jewish producers should sympathize with black victims of oppression rather than contribute to the perpetuation of that oppression, Hughes, as writers often will, defends his previously published position. He reiterates the essential point from his March 13, 1943, column, that black actors could refuse stereotyped roles. They could get jobs elsewhere—even if they abandoned acting. This focus on the black actors' responsibility fails to influence Simple. He closes his commentary by suggesting changes for Jewish producers *and* for writers such as Hughes. "Well, if I was a Jewish producer I would not give a Negro a bad part. And you guys who write columns ought to put the pressure on them to give us something better." Since Hughes has placed Simple's suggestion

7. LH, "Jews, Negroes and Hollywood," *CD,* April 17, 1943.

in the emphatic final paragraph, the columnist has replaced himself with Simple and has let Simple become the one who puts pressure on the movie producers to provide better roles for black actors. Clearly Simple's outspoken stance indicates the growing courage of black Americans and a determination to improve conditions for blacks in America.

Two weeks after Simple's comments on Hollywood, Hughes reverses the process of having Simple respond to previous non-Simple columns. In "Mugging" (May 1, 1943), he responds to a Simple column but only mentions Simple indirectly. Hughes reminds readers that a few weeks earlier ("Wives, War and Money," February 20, 1943), Simple had wished all young boys were in the army because so many of them were muggers. The narrator had argued with Simple in February, but having recently outrun a potential mugger, Hughes has switched his allegiance and now agrees with Simple. If confronted by another mugger, Hughes plans to say, "Writers don't make money, nohow, especially cullud writers, and if they do they can't keep it. Them's just my door keys you hear jangling in my pocket. Put away that knife, cat, and let me see your draft card!" This reference to one of Simple's previous conversations reveals Hughes's intention to integrate Simple's ideas with his own, thereby installing the Simple Minded Friend as a regular feature in the column. Moreover, while adopting Simple's attitude toward muggers, Hughes also seems to have adopted his grammar and lingo, thereby further legitimizing Simple and the ordinary people he represents.

Hughes again recognizes Simple when he devotes his May 15 column, "Ode to My Simple Minded Friend," to him. Even the title reveals that literary convention is being inverted. Who could offer an ode, traditionally a lofty and serious tribute, to a "Simple Minded Friend"? As the title predicts, the poem is humorous and undignified. One quatrain reads:

> Simple said, I like to argue
> Just for the sake of sound,
> That's why I'm glad
> When you come around.

The poem affirms Hughes's growing commitment to the dynamic between the two perspectives. It shows the pleasure in argument and amplifies the sense that the Simple Minded Friend is a real person.

Not until June 26, 1943, does Simple appear again in conversation with his bar buddy. This fifth conversation is the first one in which Simple dominates both the number of lines spoken and the logic. "Let the South Secede" is the title of the column and the premise of Simple's argument. He wants the South to form a separate nation; "then we can fight it—just like we fight Hitler!" Hughes tries several arguments, but Simple counters each one.

> "But," I said, "you forget that there are certain progressive elements in the South like the CIO unions. If we work with them, we might wipe out some of the abuses down there peacefully, both against labor and against Negroes."
>
> "We MIGHT is right," said my Simple Minded Friend, "but it is a mighty big MIGHT. And you are one of the biggest but-and-if men I know—always maybe- and might-ing about things. By the time you get through if-ing, the way crackers are beating and killing up Negroes—even mobbing soldiers—half of us will be dead, and the other half crippled and lame—or else done gone crazy like Bigger Thomas in NATIVE SON."

Simple admits the possibility that "certain progressive elements" might work with blacks to ameliorate conditions in the South, but he stresses the idea that such cooperation is improbable. The attack on the bar buddy for being "one of the biggest but-and-if men I know" helps readers appreciate that Hughes and other blacks promoting interracial cooperation realize that less optimistic blacks view their efforts with great skepticism. Moreover, by naming Bigger Thomas, Simple reveals his own appreciation of the power of literature. The reference to *Native Son* reveals the extensive popularity of that novel, since Simple rarely alludes to books, preferring newspapers and magazines, music, or sports events. Of course, the negative association with that novel reflects Hughes's disappointment with the excessive violence and madness evident in African American literature.[8]

To advance his argument, Simple repeats his idea: "What I say is, let the South secede *right now* so we can fight it—like it ought to be fought—as an enemy of the Four Freedoms." His buddy attempts

---

8. LH expounded on his disdain for excessive violence and madness in African American literature in "The Need for Heroes," which is discussed in the Introduction.

another attack on that argument: "I guess you want to start the Civil War all over again?" Simple immediately deflates that argument: "That's the trouble! The Civil War ain't never ended—at least not ended right. The South never accepted the Constitution." Realizing that he can not get the idea of fighting out of Simple's mind, the bar buddy tries a different approach:

> "Hitler'd just love to see Americans fighting among themselves," I said, "and anybody that starts such talk as that, IS giving aid and comfort to the enemy. Fighting among ourselves is wrong."
> "Am I fighting? No! I'm just talking. Is the South fighting me? Yes! So WHO is giving aid and comfort to the enemy? Me—or the South?"

Simple's logic on that point defies contradiction. Racist violence indeed sprang from southern whites, but blacks merely argued that such racism equaled the horrors of Hitler's policies. When the bar buddy suggests that progressives should try to change the South, Simple laughs and claims victory in the argument:

> "Now, I got you! How are we starting out to change Germany and Italy? Huh? By force of arms, that's how! By the biggest army ever raised in the history of America! By shooting them down! Now, how would you propose to change the South, Mr. Hughes?"

Simple actually calls the name of his companion here, leaving no doubt that Hughes himself at this point is the bar buddy, "one of the biggest but-and-if men I know," with whom Simple converses in this very early column. Hughes gradually developed and eventually named his two characters, Jesse B. Semple and his foil, Ananias Boyd, but in the early columns Hughes himself was engaging in dialogue with his Simple Minded Friend.

Simple's next appearance came two months later, on August 28, 1943, and this one, "Simple Looks for Justice," was the first column to be chosen for inclusion in *Simple Speaks His Mind.* This episode is the third consecutive "Here to Yonder" column discussing the Harlem Riot of 1943. "Letter to White Shopkeepers" (August 14) analyzes the riot, helping the merchants to understand why their stores were damaged. It points to several problems in the pattern of merchant-customer relations in Harlem. A week later, "Suggestions to White Shopkeepers" interprets the problems raised in "Letter" and offers specific actions to make white-owned businesses less vulnerable to future riot damage. Hughes places the problems into three general categories: employment practices, overcharging, and lack of community involvement.

First, Hughes cites a lack of black employees or retention of the bare minimum requisite number of black employees as being both common in Harlem and unfair. Moreover, he mentions that even those blacks hired as clerks are frequently required to perform custodial tasks as well, even when white coworkers are permitted to relax. Most offensive of all, though, is the fact that, besides underemploying or not employing black people, newly arrived Europeans—even those who have not learned English—are given immediate and respectable employment. These discriminatory practices in employment would have been unfortunate anywhere, but in Harlem such conditions created daily tension.

Second, Hughes observes that merchants in other parts of New York sell identical items at prices lower than those in Harlem, and he attacks the higher pricing, a practice both unfair and insensitive, considering the lower wages and higher rents that were the companion conditions of Harlem economics. Furthermore, Hughes points out that the profits made from overcharging Harlem patrons enabled white merchants to establish bigger and finer stores in downtown New York, "where we can NEVER work, sometimes cannot even trade." Profits gained in Harlem also enabled white shopkeepers to live in beautiful "neighborhoods with trees and lawns" and "where the garbage is collected regularly," but "where we cannot live." Thus, just as white people could find jobs and job conditions unavailable to blacks in Harlem, they could also overcharge and then apply the profits to stores and homes that were off limits to blacks.

Merchants may have been unaware of the intensity of resentment of these unfair advantages because they were guilty of a third injury to Harlem: lack of community involvement. Hughes points out to the merchants that they have no firsthand knowledge of neighborhood issues, such as the absence of regular garbage collection and playgrounds for the children, because they refuse to join neighborhood action groups. Furthermore, Hughes condemns these white shopkeepers for neglecting the black press, for failing to advertise in black papers. He points out that these merchants are also guilty of ignorance or apathy regarding the broader concerns of black Americans, such as the anti-lynching bill and the anti–poll tax bill in Congress.

Following two weeks of direct address to white shopkeepers, on August 28, "Simple Looks for Justice" appears, giving Simple the opportunity to explain to his non-participating friend why he broke windows. Hughes's column was one of the only printed sources to offer a first-person perspective from a participant in the riot. Since Simple voices the same desire for justice that motivated some of the rioters, he distinguishes Hughes's column from other editorials of the period. Newspaper columnists did not riot; ordinary people did. Now in his sixth appearance, Simple offers a perspective that readers expect to differ dramatically from that of the Hughes persona. The explanations from Simple carry none of the pedagogical burden so evident in comments from Negro leaders and in other newspaper columns.

Simple is not just a participant; he is one of the crowd. Unlike some of the other fictional participants (the protagonist from *Invisible Man*, by Ralph Ellison, or Pink Jones from "In Darkness and Confusion," by Ann Petry), Simple neither begins the riot nor views it with awe. Unlike many of the essayists who comment on the riot, the character Simple is never interviewed by the press. He merely becomes one of the masses. "I have never been nowhere near news except when I was in the Harlem Riots. Then the papers did not mention me by name. They just said 'mob'" ("Name in Print," *Sam*, 230). Thus, Hughes created in Simple a voice for any person from the masses who broke windows in the 1943 Harlem riot.

Most analysts of the riot during the 1940s conceded that Harlem had a right to be angry, but, like Hughes, they refused to condone violence as the appropriate vehicle for legitimate anger. "You had no business breaking up stores," Hughes tells Simple. "That is no way to get Justice."

Jesse Semple quickly answers that violence *is* a legitimate means by which to achieve justice, and in so doing, he offers one of the few defenses of the rioters' actions to be found in print. "That is the way the Allies are trying to get it, bombing the insides out of Hamburg and breaking up everything in sight Over There!" Simple had expressed the same justification for violence in "Let the South Secede." Indeed, the use of violence as a catalyst for social change seems to be quite American. As Arthur Schlesinger puts it in his scathing analysis of violence in American history, "Violence, for better or worse, *does* settle some questions, and for the better. Violence secured American independence, freed the slaves, and stopped Hitler."[9]

Whether deliberately or unwittingly, Hughes allows Simple to defend violence in the same way that Frantz Fanon would do in such works as *Black Skin, White Masks* (1952) and *The Wretched of the Earth* (1961). Subsequent sociological and psychological analysts have found that when oppressed people perceive violation of their rights, violence can have great psychopolitical value. While early social scientists launched and supported theories linking violence to psychopathology among the oppressed, these and other, more recent studies find exactly the opposite connection. "Violence is a cleansing force. It frees the native from his inferiority complex and from his despair and inaction, it makes him fearless and restores his self-respect. The Negro rioting in the USA is, from this point of view, both a political protest *and* a catharsis."[10] Thus, while many of the outsiders and nonparticipants condemn the violence, another perspective— Simple's view—celebrates the healthy consequences of such action.

A later column, "Simple's Rainy Day" (November 25, 1944), resembles "Simple Looks for Justice" in its first-person participant viewpoint on working-class people's inclination to spend their hard-earned wages on ostentatious fashions—zoot suits, stetson hats, and so forth —rather than saving money for a rainy day:

> "Them few dollars I could put away now would not do me much good nohow—if the next depression lasts as long as the last one did. I did not have any fun for a gang of years, that is why I am having my sport now. . . . I never had twelve dollars to pay for no sharp hat before, so I intends to have a sharp hat now. And I got it. I also intends to see that Joyce looks ready when she steps out with me, because from 1932 to 1942 I did not have no money to buy neither my wife nor nobody else no clothes, so I intends to see that some *one* of my womens looks ready now. . . . I intend to have three suits, too, before this war is over. I mean three Sunday suits."

9. Arthur Schlesinger Jr., *Violence: America in the Sixties,* excerpted in *Toward Social Change,* ed. Robert Buckhout (New York: Harper and Row, 1971), 137.

10. Leonard Bloom, *The Social Psychology of Race Relations* (Cambridge, Mass.: Schenkman, 1972), 57.

Simple explains that he is deliberately spending too much on fashion. Hughes, in a nonfiction editorial, had offered a similar explanation seventeen months earlier:

> Naturally, when the children of depression were able to buy a suit, having been penny-pinched so long, they got a coat that was much too lengthy, pants that had much too much cloth in them, and hats whose brims were like umbrellas—plenty of brim! . . . In the light of the poverty of their past, too much became JUST ENOUGH for them. A key chain six times too long is just long enough to hold NO keys.[11]

Not only did Simple intend to own flashy outfits, but he also refused to buy property. " 'A little piece of property?' yelled Simple. 'You know jumping well a man can't get on WPA if he owns property. And if you got no income, you can't pay taxes. And if you don't pay taxes, they take it away from you. That's what happened to Grandpa. I do not want no little piece of property! I will spend my money NOW.' " "Simple's Rainy Day" allows Simple to express for himself—and for other working poor—why he spends money as fast as he earns it. The Hughes persona—speaking for most of the strivers and bootstrap pullers—questions such action. The column offers a valuable exchange of views, respecting both.

Besides offering the valuable political and economic viewpoints of ordinary working black Americans, Simple was also emerging in a few columns as the dominant speaker in the dialogues with the Hughes persona. "Simple and the Landladies" (October 9, 1943) and "Equality and Dogs" (December 11, 1943) exemplified the pattern upon which Hughes settled for *Simple Speaks His Mind.* Simple dominates the number of lines spoken and determines the subject of discussion. He offers humorous comments about everyday life, never forgetting his keen racial pride. Nevertheless, Simple's function in the column had not yet become fixed by late 1943, nor was the "characteristic" subject matter fully settled.

For example, in "Simple and the Darak [*sic,* Dark] Nuance" (November 13, 1943), Simple offers detailed economic analysis: "If Jim Crow can keep us scared to death, out of factories, and out of unions, and poor, then we have to work cheap and look how much money the

11. LH, "Key Chains with No Keys," *CD,* June 19, 1943.

folks we work for make off of our labor." This Marxist, leftist argument in the early (and uncollected) Simple columns stands in stark contrast to the June 1945 episodes in which Simple joins the NAACP. By then, he has cast his lot with a bastion of anti-Communism. This early criticism of capitalism is a piece of economic analysis more likely to be expressed by the political left than by the average Negro in the 1940s. In fact, the more intellectual voice of the bar buddy could offer such analysis with more conviction—and in his nonfiction editorials Hughes did periodically give similar views. Simple's characteristic economic commentary focuses on the high cost of food, rent, and clothes. However, his typical criticisms of racial injustice often ignore strictly economic issues and focus upon the frustrations of biased treatment: day-to-day Jim Crow.

"Happy New Year" (January 1, 1944) shows that Hughes had not yet settled on how he would use Simple. In this episode we find the Hughes persona talking most, beginning with his questions about Senator Rankin, a segregationist: "Why do you suppose Rankin is yelling so loud these days? . . . Because Hitler is getting beat . . . and Rankin is scared it [racial superiority] will get shot to hell in Dixie, too!" Simple discounts his buddy's ideas, saying, "You sure can latch on to some far fetched connections, Jack." The educated character has begun a long discussion of national politics as they might be affected by international situations—the pattern of his "Here to Yonder" concept. Yet his conclusions are frantic and flawed; he does not offer the calm and intellectually sound commentary later associated with the foil. In direct contrast to the collected stories, Simple remarks on the unlikely nature of his bar buddy's analysis, calling the connections "far fetched." The column continues, with the Hughes persona talking unless otherwise indicated:

> " . . . Happy New Year, because we have got those cashiers, and we have got Negroes working in places this year where they never worked before, and the anti-fascist pressure of the Allied armies in Europe is being felt even way down in Dixie. . . .
>
> "British imperialism is on its last pair of legs. . . . the Four Freedoms, the Moscow Conference, the Teheran Conference! Maybe the declarations the Allies gave out there sound like a lot of words to you. But the Declaration of Independence and the Preamble to our Constitution and the Emancipation Proclamation probably sounded like just a lot of words too. . . ."

"But didn't Churchill take every one of them Four Freedoms back in reference to the colonies?" [Simple asks.]

"Some folks took the Emancipation Proclamation back, too, and swore they wouldn't abide by no parts of it. . . . Maybe Mr. Churchill doesn't *intend* to give up his grip on Africa and India. But . . . forces are at work in the world mightier than Mr. Churchill. You and me, for instance."

"You and me?" asked my Simple Minded Friend. "How do you figure you and me amount to so much?"

"Because you and me are the people—the common people—who don't like being kept down. And we are the majority in the world. And we are not going to be kept down, either."

"You talking about colored people, too?" [Simple asks.]

"Are you white?"

"No" [replies Simple.]

"Neither am I."

Hughes speaks at least four lines for every line Simple squeezes in. In addition, Hughes carries the conversation. He brings up the subjects of discussion and launches the overall pattern of analysis. Simple merely comments upon or questions the assertions he makes.

As noted earlier, Hughes instructs Simple. He provides a global interpretation of the political and economic scene in the United States. He tells Simple the new year promises to be truly happy because blacks have been hired as cashiers in places where they had only been allowed to sweep floors before. He goes on to contradict the assessment that important political documents such as the Emancipation Proclamation and the Constitution are merely "a lot of words," thereby encouraging Simple to have faith in the Four Freedoms. He urges Simple to view himself as an empowered member of the masses—"the common people—who don't like being kept down. And we are the majority in the world."

This kind of instructive lecture hardly represents the clever dialogues found in the collected Simple stories. Although "Landladies" and "Equality and Dogs" had already appeared, Hughes had not yet settled on a particular formula for his use of the Simple Minded Friend in his column. "Here to Yonder" was his vehicle, and he granted himself the privilege of instructive discourse. While "Landladies" had been amusing, humor is sparse in "Happy New Year," where Hughes was so concerned with delivering his message that he virtually ignored any dramatic possibilities involving Simple, whose questions are merely echoes or prompting cues that allow the Hughes persona to expound upon the great American potential for freedom. Because Hughes dominates the topic, the tone, and the quantity of lines spoken, we can see that in this column the Simple Minded Friend was, in fact, the nameless foil for the Hughes persona.

The scanty number of lines spoken by Simple and even the assignment of lines in the closing formula—allowing the bar buddy (Hughes) to speak the last word—represent almost the exact opposite of the patterns of division in the mature Simple tales. In this early effort Simple challenges an assertion Hughes has made about the masses not being kept down. "You talking about colored people, too?" Rather than replying directly, Hughes answers the question with a question of his own: "Are you white?" Simple never denies his race—not even in these earliest versions. He merely answers, "No," to which Hughes replies, "Neither am I." The response is a bit flippant, but it ends the dialogue with a matter worth considering. Democracy and the Four Freedoms were as much for people of color as they were for Europeans and their descendants. Since African Americans had heard these exciting promises along with everyone else, it should have been clear to the United States government that it needed to keep these promises at home as well as abroad.

In the pattern of conversation subsequently adopted as the standard ending formula for the collections, not only does Simple generally have the final word, but his final word most often adds humor. Take, for example, "Income Tax." In the *Defender* version, Simple concludes with, "No matter what kind of forms they are, *income* or *female*—they can sure give you trouble!"[12] In the collection, the episode ends with a similar play on words:

"Well, you certainly have opinions about everything under the sun," I said. "You ought to have a newspaper since you have so much to say."
"I can talk," said Simple, "but I can't write."
"Then you ought to be an orator."
"Uh-um, I'm scared of the public. My place is at the bar."
"Of Justice?"
"Justice don't run no bar." ("Income Tax," *Mind,* 123)

12. LH, "Simple's Income Tax," *CD,* March 15, 1947.

Another good example of Hughes's use of humor as his standard ending formula appears in "Possum, Race, and Face," which Hughes created from three separate columns. He closes the long episode with Simple once again hearing everything he wants to hear:

> "Nobody, white or colored, has any business getting on a bus or streetcar drunk," I said. "If you are drunk, you should take a taxi home. Drunks are nuisances, staggering around and talking out of turn—like you are when you are high. I do not agree with you this evening."
>
> "If you agreed, there would be no point in having an argument," said Simple, pushing back his glass.
>
> "There is not very much point in *your* argument," I said.
>
> "Except," said Simple solemnly, "that I think colored folks should have the same right to get drunk as white folks."
>
> "That is a very ordinary desire," I said. "You ought to want to have the right to be President, or something like that."
>
> "Very few men can become President," said Simple. "And only one at a time. But almost anybody can get drunk. Even I can get drunk."
>
> "Then you ought to take a taxi home, and not get on the bus smelling like a distillery," I said, "staggering and disgracing the race."
>
> "I keep trying to tell you, if I was white, wouldn't nobody say I was disgracing no race!"
>
> "You definitely are not white," I said.
>
> "You got something there," said Simple. "Lend me taxi fare and I will ride home." ("Possum, Race, and Face," *Mind*, 225–26)

Simple has raised a point that the foil neglects: "if I was white, wouldn't nobody say I was disgracing no race!" African Americans frequently measure each other's actions against the value or detriment they might have for "the race." Whites, meanwhile, direct movies, marry, commit crimes, or merely get drunk as individuals rather than as representatives of their race. Simple makes sense. However, the foil's point, rather than Simple's, gains acceptance.

The foil insists that Simple should not embarrass the race by going home on public transportation while he is drunk. As is typical for the collected stories, the ending formula leaves the reader laughing. The poor foil has won the argument, but he has been outsmarted, as in this taxi fare scheme. Simple allows the foil to persuade him of the advantages of riding the taxi home, but then he borrows the taxi fare from his buddy. In such a situation, it would be hard for the college-educated man to feel that he was smarter than Simple. The cleverness, the humor, and the allocation of the last word to Simple distinguish these collected stories from the early, uncollected columns.

Its deliberate political agenda clearly removed "Happy New Year" from the eventual pattern of the Simple stories, in which political nuances assume more subtle roles, yielding to humor and narration. This increase in artistic concerns over political ones also corresponds chronologically to the end of World War II and the reduced threat of Hitlerism. Thus, the difference between the early political columns and the more humorous collected versions owes much to the lessening urgency of political realities. Whereas Hughes admitted a political consideration in his creation of Simple, he was certainly motivated by artistic concerns—and financial considerations—when he sought to revise the Simple conversations for publication as a book.

Having established his Simple Minded Friend, Hughes used Simple more and more frequently as the years progressed to carry the message of the column. Furthermore, Hughes crafted his Simple Minded Friend into a more identifiable person. Considering Simple's longevity and the extent of his popular appeal, Hughes eventually had to give him a real name. So, on November 3, 1945, the name *Jess* first appears in the column—not *Jesse B. Semple,* but *Jess.*

> "So your grandpa was a drinking man," I said. "That must be who you take after."
>
> "I also am named after him," said Simple. "Grandpa's name was Jess. My name is Jess, too."
>
> "Jess," I said, "is certainly not an Indian name." ("Simple's Indian Blood," *CD*)

This first reference to Simple's name stands out because Simple must announce, "My name is Jess." As chronological analysis of the columns reveals, in 1945 the bar buddy is still called "Mr. Hughes," so the bar buddy has a name and an identity, serving as a persona for Hughes the columnist. Until this column, however, three years after the Simple Minded Friend first appeared in "Here to Yonder," he has not yet given his name, nor has his bar buddy ever asked his name. This reminds us that the relationship between these two men has developed in the rather impersonal environment of a bar, where people willingly tolerate individuals' preferences for privacy.

The first use of the name *Jess* appeared in isolation. Almost another year passed before the name reappeared in the newspaper. Hughes was not yet concentrating on enhancing the unique identity of a character called Jess; he was still experimenting with the function of the voice in his column. For example, in early 1947 he jumped from "Simple after the Holidays" (January 11, 1947), a funny episode revealing that Simple gave Joyce a chicken cooker instead of a fur she wanted for Christmas, to "Simple and the Year Gone By" (January 25, 1947), a totally topical column in which the Hughes persona seeks to edify the poor Simple Minded Friend. Hughes did appreciate Simple's growing popularity with his readers, and he sensed more dramatic potential with the enhanced development of these two characters. Whereas he had begun the conversations with Simple during the war to address specific political concerns, he was free as the war ended to deviate from his original intentions. He developed the personalities of the characters by distinguishing them more from each other. He defined Simple's name and enhanced his characterization. The extent and consistency of these improvements became more evident as Hughes began to circulate his manuscript for consideration by publishers; by 1949, he was carefully crafting his character Simple in his column and in his revision of old columns for book publication.

One of the first changes in characterization was that Simple increasingly criticized his bar buddy, pointing out how cautious he was. In "Simple Speaks of Shouting" (November 10, 1945) the bar buddy hesitates to tell Joyce that he shares Simple's appreciation of gospel music and shouting. "She's liable to get a low opinion of me," he says. Simple blasts the intellectual: "That is the trouble with you smart people. You are always afraid somebody will get a low opinion of you." Two months later, in "Simple Views the News" (January 5, 1946), he tells his buddy, "To be a race man, you are mighty lenient to these white folks." On the other hand, in "Simple's Psychosis" (May 18, 1946), when the Hughes persona attempts to pin psychological labels on Simple's attitudes, Simple argues his way clear of the attacks. The intellectual tells the average guy, "You have got a white-complex, also a dog-psychosis. You need to be psychoanalyzed."

"For why?" said Simple.
"To change your mind," I said.
"It is not my mind that needs to be changed," said Simple. "It is them white folks. . . . I tell you it is them that thinks about me!" said

Simple. "What I mainly thinks about is the good times I have had, not
the bad—white folks or no white folks."

"You do seem to enjoy yourself," I said. . . . "I guess you do not
need to be psychoanalyzed. That is only for people who are not having
a good time out of life."

The college-educated bar buddy cannot argue that Simple fails to have
a good time out of life. Simple then turns the tables on his buddy.
Simple figures that if psychoanalysis is "only for people who are not
having a good time out of life," then:

"It must be for white folks," said Simple, "because they always talk
like they are worried. Sometimes you talk like white folks yourself."

"Only when I am talking with you," I said. "Some of these
arguments you hand out worry me. I have got to stop taking you
seriously or else I will have complexes."

"Then let's us have a beer," said Simple. "That is very good for
a man's complexions. Lend me a quarter and I will set you up. I am
always kinder broke towards the end of the week."

"I am broke, too," I said.

"Then we will not have no beer," said Simple. "We will just keep on
having complexions."

Simple not only forces his more intellectual buddy to admit that he
sometimes seems unduly worried, but he also converts *complexes* to
complexions, which two race men would never deny having. This
humorous twist of both the logic and the language reveals one of the
techniques Hughes masters via the Simple conversations.

By 1946, Hughes was negotiating with Current Books to publish
a book of the Simple columns, and his column begins to reflect
his attention to the craft of the stories. For example, he began to
distinguish the foil's life history and behaviors from his own, thereby
increasing the fictional identity of his character. One episode, "Simple
and the GIs" (February 9, 1946), occurs chronologically within the
span when Hughes's name appears as the bar buddy to whom Simple
speaks, but the episode clearly differentiates between the Hughes
persona and Hughes himself. In this column the Hughes persona is not
sympathetic to draft evasion, whereas Hughes himself had strategized
to evade standard military duty. This type of fictionalization reveals
that Hughes clearly saw the dramatic value in contrasting Simple with

a bar buddy quite different from him. Nevertheless, he had not yet completely withdrawn himself as the model upon whom the bar buddy was based. As late as March 8, 1947, in "Simple, Soaring, and Sleeping," he wrote, "Now that I have my first job in twenty years—I am a Visiting Professor at Atlanta University—I asked my Simple Minded Friend what I should buy with my money since it is a brand new experience for me to have a regular income." With this statement, he both involves the Simple character and uses factual details about his own life. Thus, careful scrutiny reveals that for at least four years after he initiated the column, Hughes without a doubt portrayed the person who conversed with Simple as himself.

Experimentally, then, Hughes vacillated between the original model for the column, in which the worldly fellow instructs his more provincial companion, and a more dramatic and more highly crafted fiction. In mid–1946, he began to write more of the Simple columns in the style that would come to characterize the collected stories. The episodes that appeared on July 6, 13, and 27, August 17, September 28, and October 5, 1946, were all revised for publication in *Simple Speaks His Mind*. In these conversations Simple humorously observes that some of his human parts come in pairs, while others come solo, and he reflects on his appreciation for Harlem and the problems associated with vacations in the country. Simple's name reappears on October 26 in "Simple's Landlady's Dog," when his landlady uses it in expressing her profound gratitude to Simple for walking her dog. "Thank you! You certainly nice, Mr. Jesse, you certainly nice!" Again notice that only the first name is used.

By the end of 1947, Hughes occasionally omits the phrase *my Simple Minded Friend* and uses the nickname *Simple*. "Simple and Jackie," celebrating Jackie Robinson as the first African American in National League baseball (September 6, 1947), uses the long phrase, as does "Simple Begs to Differ" (October 11, 1947). "Simple Writes a Book" (September 27, 1947) and "Simple and Temptation" (October 25, 1947), on the other hand, use only the nickname.

The introduction of the name *Jess* and the sporadic removal of the long phrase *my Simple Minded Friend* signaled the more significant changes that ultimately gave Simple his enduring fictional form. We find when we analyze the columns chronologically that the voice of the foil increasingly withdraws, leaving the majority of the columns' messages in Simple's voice. For example, by the time Hughes wrote

"Simple Down Under" (February 28, 1948), the foil does not speak at all, and in "Simple Thinks He's Simple" (September 18, 1948) the foil speaks only one line. By the time he had settled on Simple as a character fully able to sustain the column and present his own ideas (which are, of course, Hughes's own reflections, too), he had also developed Simple sufficiently for a collected volume.

Evidence that Hughes was refining his characterization of Simple emerges in details that Simple provides in 1948 and 1949. We learn that Simple actually selects drinks according to the severity of his problem. In "Simple Goes on Record" (July 17, 1948), when Simple tells his buddy how Cousin Mabel sold all his collection of classic jazz albums, he is so deeply disturbed that he needs I. W. Harper's—not beer. On the other hand, in "Simple's If" (August 7, 1948), global troubles overwhelm Simple to the extent that he refuses to drink anything—even a beer.

Simple even reveals details about his failed marriage in "With Money, Love Is a Sweet Orange, Without, It's a Lemon" (May 28, 1949). In the same column, he spells out his proper name, thereby indicating how carefully Hughes was crafting the character by that time. Simple declares that lack of money contributed to the destruction of his marriage, recalling that his wife wanted him to be responsible for keeping food on the table. Simple rejects that charge:

> "She hollers, 'You ain't even responsible.'
> " 'That's right,' I said, 'my name's not Responsible. I am Jess Semple. You knowed my name all the time.'
> "She said, 'That *e* ought to be an *i*. Your friends nicknamed you right—Simple. You are simple, too, if you think you can keep a woman on nothing to eat.' "

By the time this column appeared, Hughes had received his first report from Simon and Schuster on the manuscript *Simple Speaks His Mind.* The publisher's readers did not ask him to spell out a name for Simple, but they did call attention to the expressions "Jack" and "Richard" used when Simple spoke to his buddy. Thus, the attention to names and Hughes's desire to give Simple maximum personality led to his including within the "Here to Yonder" columns a careful spelling of both Simple's correct name and his nickname.

Infused with humor and increasingly well-rounded in character development, the authentic Negro-to-Negro dialogues between Hughes and his Simple Minded Friend proved to be a vehicle that far exceeded the author's original intentions in "Here to Yonder" of educating average black people about the evils of Nazi Germany. Not only had he discovered for himself a clever and versatile medium in which to express his own sometimes contradictory views, but he had also established a realistic character whom black readers accepted as one of their own people. Fan mail preserved in the James Weldon Johnson Collection of Yale University's Beinecke Rare Book and Manuscript Library reveals how warmly the readers received Simple. As early as June 2, 1944, a reader informed Hughes that he and his office-mates were "happy to read another dialogue with your 'Simple Minded Friend.' We hope your conversations with him will not be so far between from now on."[13] Perhaps accepting his reader's suggestion, Hughes added eleven more Simple columns in 1944. These numerous Simple tales in that year spoiled the insatiable fans. By January 31, 1945, readers bitterly complained about Simple's absences from Hughes's column. "For two whole weeks, now, we have looked for word of Mr. Simple in your weekly column, but to no avail. . . . Mr. Simple has become a pleasant habit to us; a habit we wouldn't like to break." As Hughes's reply to this lament reveals, in 1945 he was committed to the continuation of Simple: "please don't worry— Simple is a fixture."[14]

Readers clearly enjoyed the Simple conversations, but more importantly, they identified with the Simple Minded Friend. One fan wrote, "Your character, Simple, talks for the majority of everyday colored folks, in like lingo. What he has to say is to-the-point, plain, bold—the way he says it so enjoyably amusing." Another reader concluded that Hughes performed a great service to the general African American population by allowing Simple to speak. "The majority of my friends are simple minded also and we just love to see our thoughts in print where some of our more *complicated* minded brothers and sisters, both *white* and *black,* might see them and *stop* and *think a moment* about what we are thinking about."[15] How ironic that while Hughes

13. Harvey C. Summers to LH, June 2, 1944, *CD* correspondence, Fans, leaf no. 14, JWJ.
14. Charlie May Singleton and Marie D. Boswell to LH; reply, LH to Singleton and Boswell, June 1, 1945.
15. Mrs. Rice to LH, March 3, 1945; Joseph Gardette to LH, March 7, 1945.

originally intended to instruct the less sophisticated brothers and sisters by using his Simple character, some of the fans rejoiced that Simple could educate the more "complicated minded" readers. Fans clearly appreciated the representation afforded by Simple.

One letter from a mother and daughter in Leland, Mississippi, could almost have been written by Simple. With spelling and punctuation of the original preserved, a line from the letter reads, "i takes a great deal of pleasure of reading your here to yonder colum." Another reader explicitly wrote, "I am referring myself as your simple minded friend," and added, "Mr. Langston Hughes see if you can make a column from this. I am not a writer. I was only thinking of some of the funny things that go on in this country."[16] This man offered several examples of strange racial behaviors he had observed. He sensed that Hughes could weave them into his column, perhaps through the language of the Simple Minded Friend.

Some readers sincerely believed in the authenticity of the Simple Minded Friend, even going so far as to offer via Hughes messages and even gifts for Simple. One reader sent Simple "one of Holford's famous inhalers," strictly warning Hughes "that this inhaler is not for you but for your simple-minded friend. If you need one for yourself you may buy it." This generous fan expressed his concern because "Simple likes a gang of lush [alcoholic beverage]. I am afraid that he will not be able to work some Monday morning." He then went on to provide explicit directions for using the inhaler: "When you meet him on the street early some morning full of that gage, simply stick the bottle under his nose. Remember bottle not cork. Believe me my friend he will become as sober as a judge should be."[17] Although this response was not typical, it did demonstrate the degree of realism Hughes achieved with his character, despite the initial namelessness and lack of personal history.

Let the record show that not all readers liked Simple. Nevertheless, even the most hostile letters verify that the Simple Minded Friend was portrayed realistically. For example, one woman wrote Hughes in May 1943 to urge him to help blacks cease criticizing each other "to the extent of refusing to associate or even live in the same neighborhood

16. Emma Sullivan and Mrs. L. B. to LH; Mr. T. H. Hill to LH, June 9, 1944.
17. Theo. R. Pardue to LH, January 14, 1946.

with the loud mouth, vulgar speaking, zoot suited, knife-toting moron." She felt confident that Hughes could write about this issue "without creating class hatred." She urges Hughes to address within his column the idea that Simple and his ilk—those who embarrass the race—cannot be tolerated by the blacks seeking upward mobility. She remarks, "We do not hate the simple minded friend in your column—but he must learn through severe and extended criticism that he is not wanted and that there is no place for him where this race is going." She discusses Simple as if he is a real person for whom she feels pity, but whom she feels compelled to train.[18]

Another reader absolutely disdains the way Simple discredits the race, but fully recognizes that Simple is a fictional creation: "I read your articles in the Chicago Defender every week and find most of them very interesting. Although sometimes I'm very annoyed at your fictitious friend 'Simple.' Truly some of the things you say about him are so absurd and such a discredit to 'The Race,' it makes me shudder to think that those incredulous words came from the brains of such an intelligent person as yourself."[19] While that reader uses a level of diction that suggests an education, other readers wrote letters which quite "simply" stated their displeasure, such as this one:

> Having just finished reading your column ["Simple's Cousin Slick Gets the Cure from Sister Clarina-Ray"] I'm very mad at you. You hadn't oughta wrote that. You hadn't oughta go picking on religion and that nice lady that tried so hard to reform that characterless creature. With due respect to the manner in which you master the art. I for one can see what's wrong with the situation. You simply cant get blood out of a turnit. But how many other bone heads that read this paper know that the lady was giving that which is Holy to the Dogs. Casting pearls before swine. Really, Mr. Hughes, having met you once at Friendship house, And having been so thrilled at having met you. And having seen how young and handsome you are. (I fancied you were an old man with a beard) And Having obtained your autograph, and all that kind of stuff. And like I said, having read this work of Art you created. I am very much mad at you.[20]

18. Mrs. William Condol to LH, May 20, 1943.
19. Ann Edwards to LH, April 11, 1946.
20. Estelle White to LH, November 27, 1948.

This fan was devoted to reading and meeting Hughes, but none of that devotion stemmed her displeasure.

Hughes's fan mail conclusively verifies widespread interest in the topics he discussed and popular affirmation of Simple's realism. Hughes must have been pleased to stimulate so much response from his readers. Therefore, Simple—who spoke for the readers—provided Hughes an opportunity to express his appreciation to his readers by giving them a voice in the column.

Inspired by enthusiastic fans and interested publishers, Hughes began in 1945 to envision the dialogues between Simple and himself as material for a book. He sent to his literary agent, Maxim Lieber, a group of Simple columns to query about their potential for publication. As part of his motivation for launching this project, Hughes mentioned the black interest in the columns by reporting to Lieber, "I get dozens of fan letters every month from Negroes about these columns."[21] The support of fans and his interest in publishing a book of the Simple columns led Hughes gradually to include more Simple conversations in his "Here to Yonder" column. He increased them from ten in 1943 to fourteen in 1944 and eighteen in 1945—plus one column which was not a Simple conversation in the newspaper, but which he converted to a Simple episode for book publication. He maintained about the same number of Simple columns, seventeen, in 1946 and 1947, but he increased the quantity to twenty-two in 1948 and twenty-three in 1949. By that time, he had a contract for publication in hand and was actually printing in the *Defender* columns that he had written with the book in mind.

The authenticity of Simple's portrayal and the universal humor in the episodes may have ultimately convinced Simon and Schuster to risk publishing them, but Langston Hughes needed to persevere for several years in order to realize his goal of seeing Simple preserved in book form. A look at the process of seeking a publisher and revising the columns for publication will add further insight to our appreciation of Hughes's craft.

21. LH to Maxim Lieber, March 26, 1945, LH correspondence, Lieber file, JWJ.

4 _____

Negotiations: Finding a Publisher for Simple

HUGHES HAD BEEN both lucky and unlucky with publishers, but his Simple manuscript compiled "the worst record of any major manuscript in his career."[1] A reason for this dismal record was that Hughes sought more than just *any* publisher. He insisted upon a publisher who would keep Simple as a character of the people—one of the common folk—by making the book accessible at a low cost and by preserving all the qualities that had endeared Simple to his *Chicago Defender* audience. Both the negotiations for a publisher and the revisions required by the eventual publisher indicate the attachment Hughes felt to his creation, Simple. At the same time, these processes show that Hughes was mature and confident as a professional writer.

The idea of a collected edition of Simple stories begins with the correspondence between Hughes and the publisher and editor of the *Chicago Defender,* John Sengstacke. It may have been Sengstacke who first interested Hughes in making Simple an entity apart from the newspaper in which he frequently appeared. Thanking him for his letter of October 12 and for his check sent upon returning the manuscript of Simple stories Hughes had submitted for possible publication in book form by the *Defender* company, Hughes wrote to Sengstacke on November 2, 1946, "I also appreciate your interest in the possibilities of the 'Simple' material for a book, and, since you are not entering the book publishing field yourself, I shall submit it elsewhere."[2] The *Defender* of October 12, 1946, carried a letter to

1. Rampersad, *Life of Langston Hughes,* vol. 2, 155.
2. LH to John Sengstacke, November 2, 1946, LH correspondence, *CD* file, JWJ.

the editor that ended with a postscript: "What became of that idea of mine, suggesting that all the choice items in some five years of 'The Grapevine' by Charles Cherokee be assembled for a book published by the Chicago Defender Publishing Company?"[3] Obviously, Hughes was not the only columnist writing memorable weekly columns, and the notion of collecting "choice items" for a book was not reserved for him alone. Because he was editor of the *Defender,* Sengstacke was aware of the Charlie Cherokee proposal even when he suggested the publication of a book to Hughes.

Years later, when an offer of publication was in hand, Hughes again thanked Sengstacke for having provided the inspiration for the project:

> Due to your interest, way back in 1945 you will recall, I gathered together my Simple columns from *The Chicago Defender* into the semblance of a book which you very kindly considered for publication. And returned to me with a most generous token payment.
>
> A year or so later another publisher took the book, offering a good advance pending revisions, but we could not see eye to eye on how the final draft should be put together, so I returned the contract.
>
> It might interest you to know that Simple has finally gone to press this week. Simon & Schuster are bringing it out in the Spring under the title of *Simple Speaks His Mind,* and seem quite excited about its promotion as a rare book of Negro humor and comment.
>
> I owe the initial interest in Simple as a book to you, so I thought I would tell you about it. Thanks![4]

As Hughes has described the process, it was a fairly simple matter of following the suggestion to make the collection into a book, then rejecting one publisher's offer, and finally accepting the offer from Simon and Schuster. The process, however, involved considerably more complications than that.

Hughes had sent to his literary agent, Maxim Lieber, a group of Simple columns to see if Lieber felt "their humor would appeal to a standard publisher."[5] Hughes specified "standard" publisher because he had another option already: the *Negro Digest* wanted to publish a

3. Dutton Ferguson to Editor, *CD,* October 12, 1946, 14.
4. LH to Sengstacke, December 8, 1949, LH correspondence, *CD* file, JWJ.
5. LH to Maxim Lieber, March 26, 1945, JWJ.

booklet of the Simple columns. Hughes's letter to Lieber suggests that the *Negro Digest* would have published the columns without much revision, because Hughes told Lieber he would revise the columns if his agent thought they might be worthy of consideration by a "standard" publisher.

Lieber replied to Hughes by noting that the columns as they had originally appeared were not the material for a book.

> Minna [his wife] and I both read all of *My Simple Minded Friend*'s columns and enjoyed them thoroughly. In order to make a successful book, it would be necessary to integrate them into a cohesive whole. Whereas no continuity is needed for a newspaper column, it is needed in a book. The columns as they now stand are excellent pamphleteering material and were they given integration and continuity would make a very powerful book, with wonderful humor and irony—a book such as *The Good Soldier Schweik*.[6]

Offering to hold the columns and expecting that Hughes would want to "weave them into a book pattern," Lieber provided the first indication that Hughes had before him a major editing and revising task if he would convert popular columns into an excellent book. At that point, however, Hughes may not have been centrally concerned with the quality of the collection.

The record of correspondence with publishers and with his literary agents reveals that Hughes sought to maximize his financial gain from each creative effort, and with his many projects running simultaneously, he probably felt that he could not always devote full creative attention to a project he considered to be already "completed." The second volume of Arnold Rampersad's biography of Hughes reveals the hectic pace and variety of Hughes's publishing career. However, Malcolm Cowley, who has researched the biographical and professional similarities of writers in various decades, reports that most professional writers—not just Hughes—attempted to make each separate project yield a double or triple income.[7]

Still pursuing an easy transformation from columns into a published book, Hughes again wrote to his agent informing him that

6. Lieber to LH, April 17, 1945, JWJ.
7. Malcolm Cowley, *The Literary Situation* (New York: Viking, 1954), 178.

the Negro Digest Publishing Company of Chicago had written that
they wished to publish the "Simple Minded Friend" columns in a
pocketbook-sized, paper-bound book to sell for fifty cents. Ever mindful of the economic constraints of his audience, Hughes liked the idea
of selling Simple books at fifty cents per copy, thereby making Simple
available to the audience that had supported him in the *Defender.* Further evidence of Hughes's economic considerations for his audience
appear in Milton Meltzer's description of the inexpensive printings of
poetry that Hughes sold for twenty-five cents on his lecture tours. In
fact, he even had individual poems available as ten-cent broadsides,
suitable for framing or pinning on the wall.[8] When readers were
paying ten cents per copy for the *Chicago Defender,* the fifty-cent
edition of a collection of Simple columns would certainly have been
a bargain.

Hughes also noted that the *Negro Digest* wished to have the
book illustrated by Ollie Harrington, another very popular feature
contributor to the black press. Hughes genuinely admired Harrington's cartoon subject "Bootsie," which appeared in the *Pittsburgh
Courier.* Hughes was eager to have Simple assume visual form in the
sketches of such a compatible artist as Harrington; his excitement
shows in his correspondence. When he finally received the offer of
publication from Simon and Schuster, he attempted to add illustrations
by Harrington.

> I don't much like the idea of illustrations as such—not actual scenes so
> much as decorations or suggestions of settings and persons. If we have
> these, Ollie Harrington would probably be the man to do them. His
> "Bootsie" in the *Pittsburgh Courier* is a famous cartoon character not
> unlike Simple. Although I don't think our drawings should be cartoons.
> But Harrington is a fine artist, and not all of his work is of a cartoon
> nature. Then, too, (and this is VERY important) he knows Negro tastes
> and how NOT to offend them, even when drawing humorously—which
> we would not want to do.[9]

Hughes never convinced Simon and Schuster to use Harrington as the
illustrator for *Simple Speaks His Mind,* but he did interest Dodd Mead

8. Milton Meltzer, *Langston Hughes: A Biography,* 153–54.
9. LH to Maria Leiper, August 29, 1949, LH correspondence, Simon and
Schuster file, JWJ.

in publishing a collection of the "Bootsie" cartoons. Obtaining expatriate Harrington's Paris address from Jean Blackwell Hutson, Hughes asked the artist if he wanted to pursue such an opportunity with Dodd Mead.[10] Harrington rejoiced in this opportunity and gratefully granted to Hughes the requested privilege of writing the introduction for the book of collected Bootsie cartoons. His remarks in that introduction to Bootsie speak as well to the character of Simple and the nature of Hughes's art:

> The trials and tribulations of Bootsie and his friends are typical of the trials and tribulations of the average Negro from Lenox Avenue in Harlem or Hastings Street in Detroit to Central Avenue in Los Angeles or Rampart in New Orleans—woman problems, pocketbook problems, landlady problems, and race problems are the same. . . .
>
> As a social satirist in the field of race relations, Ollie Harrington is unsurpassed. Visually funny almost always, situation-wise, his pictures frequently have the quality of the blues. Behind their humor often lurks the sadness of "When you see me laughin', I'm laughin' to keep from cryin'."[11]

Hughes obviously delighted in Harrington's work and was therefore pleased that the Negro Digest Publishing Company planned to illustrate Simple with art by Harrington. Combined with the low price per copy and the anticipation of minimal revision, the appropriate illustrations made the offer quite attractive to Hughes.

Hughes asked his agent to send off to the *Negro Digest* the necessary permission forms and to request an advance of $100 from them. Maxim Lieber, however, still had his mind on the editing and revising he envisioned as necessary for a high-quality book of Simple stories. In his reply to Hughes, he addressed this matter: "I'm very glad that it is this company that is doing the book as it is a good one and you will not be pressed to do any rewriting which I said would be necessary if we were to submit the material elsewhere. I still hold to my original contention, however, that if you *did* rewrite you would have a much more exciting book."[12] Although Lieber deprecates the *Negro Digest* approach, he would not interfere with

---

10. LH to Ollie Harrington, March 14, 1957, LH correspondence, JWJ.
11. LH, Introduction to *Bootsie and Others,* iii.
12. LH to Lieber, November 24, 1945; Lieber to LH, November 28, 1945.

a publishing offer. Nevertheless, he clearly reiterates his conviction that if Hughes revised the columns for "integration and continuity," he would produce a much more stimulating book.

The lethargy of the Negro Digest Publishing Company eventually forced Hughes to seek another publisher and led to the extensive revisions for which Lieber had hoped. Hughes sent a copy of the Simple Minded Friend columns to the company late in December 1945, but they never replied with an advance or with steps toward publication. Hughes inquired of Lieber in January and in March regarding the status of the book, but each time his agent told him there had been no reply. Finally, in June 1946, Hughes abandoned the project with the *Negro Digest* and sought another publisher for Simple.[13]

Hughes's next effort at publication was directed to Bernard B. Perry, an editor at Current Books. Negotiations with Current Books ended up being lengthy and awkward. Hughes apparently initiated the contact in late May or early June 1946. Lieber wrote to Hughes on June 5, 1946, that, without having read the columns, Perry wanted to issue a $2.00 or $2.50 edition of Simple, rather than the $1.00 edition for which Hughes was asking; then, six months later, the company would consider issuing a reprint at $1.00 or less. This letter confirms that Hughes had especially liked the Negro Digest Publishing Company's offer to issue the book at a cost of fifty cents. It also gives early indication that Perry was not sensitive to either Simple or Hughes, because the editor had not read the columns and he had disregarded Hughes's suggestions regarding price and marketability.

The months passed, and Perry held on to the manuscript. He requested additional material, which Hughes sent. Finally, in late February 1947, Current Books offered a contract for Simple, but Perry's earlier insensitivity had forewarned Hughes of significant incompatibility. Perry suggested several changes that superseded the efforts Lieber had recommended. By this time Hughes had accepted a one-semester position as a lecturer at Atlanta University. In addition to a full schedule of academic requirements, he was also lecturing throughout the country on weekends during that semester. Thus, he had neither time nor inclination for what he considered wasteful revisions of the Simple text.

13. Lieber to LH, January 22, 1946; LH to Lieber, March 4, 1946; and LH to Lieber, June 1, 1946.

The Current Books contract offended the author. Hughes exercised his authorial prerogative and refused Perry's offer in a lengthy and poised letter. He first wrote to Maxim Lieber:

> The Current Books contracts came but, after reading them and Bernard Perry's letter of February 14 outlining what they would like to have me do with the book, just about the LAST thing I would like to do is sign the contracts. There isn't any really good reason why I should sign them, is there?
>
> In the first place, I don't believe Current Books has the least idea what the material or the character is about, judging from the list of sketches which they suggest eliminating.
>
> In the second place, this impression is further confirmed by the suggestions for new sketches which they offer, such as "Simple at a Black and Tan Radical Party"—which Simple has never been at and would hardly likely ever be at, but if he were I would not want to make fun of it; "Simple and the Civil Liberties Union," also "Simple and the Turkish Bath"—which there are just about two Turkish Baths in the whole of the U.S.A. that colored people can go into, and only folks with money go to those. Such ideas are way off the beam.
>
> In the third place, there is no way for me to completely revise the book by April first (or May first either) with my teaching four days a week here, and the week-ends mostly taken up with out-of-Atlanta lecture trips to Birmingham, Mobile, New Orleans, etc. I have a busy enough spring as it is without adding a dead-line like that to my schedule. Since they've had the manuscript for the last six months, why such a rush all of a sudden?
>
> Certainly the manuscript as it now stands needs a lot of work, condensation, arrangement, and revision—but along the lines of its own character and subject matter. It does not seem to be the kind of book for Current Books, and I would find it difficult, I am afraid, to make it to their liking. I greatly appreciate their interest in it, but I would be delighted to *not* have them publish it, if it's O.K. by all concerned. Is it O.K. by you?[14]

After four years, Hughes had developed quite an attachment to Simple, and he considered him almost as a separate person rather than as a fictional creation. In telling Lieber that Simple has never attended nor would he ever likely attend a Black and Tan Radical Party, Hughes

14. LH to Lieber, March 2, 1947.

has thereby personalized Simple, reporting his activities as if they were a matter of historical record.

A most significant point in this letter to Lieber is that, even though Hughes resists the suggestions made by Perry, he has clearly accepted the need to revise his columns for eventual publication as a book. He is only willing, however, to change the material "along the lines of its own character and subject matter."

A few days later, but before he had received any affirmations from Lieber, Hughes wrote more briefly and humorously to Arna Bontemps. He repeated his objections to the Current Books offer:

> I have just turned down the contract for the "Simple-Minded Friend"
> book, because "Current Books" did not seem to me to understand
> what the character was all about and wanted many more changes
> and extensions than I am prepared to make. They offered a splendid
> advance, in fact, more than I have ever gotten on any book before, but
> even at that I do not see why a firm that does not understand Simple
> should be publishing him. He does not understand it either and he told
> me not to bother with them, and I do not blame him.[15]

Even more plainly than in the letter to Lieber, Hughes reveals that Simple is to him a very real character, strong-willed and opinionated. Neither the author nor the character could tolerate compromises that would endanger the qualities that had made Simple so authentic—so much like someone the readers knew. Not even the largest advance Hughes had ever been offered on a book could persuade him to change the characteristics and experiences that readers of the *Defender* had come to love. His brief remarks to Bontemps highlight his resolution to reject Bernard Perry's insensitive suggestions.[16]

Lieber supported his client's feelings about the Current Books offer. His reply enhances the picture of the professional relationship between an author and his agent:

15. LH to Bontemps, March 8, 1947, in Nichols, ed., *Letters,* 217.
16. One should note, however, that Perry became an editor at Indiana University Press and eventually published Hughes. He published Hughes's translations of Gabriela Mistral in 1957; Hughes's anthology *Poems from Black Africa, Ethiopia and Other Countries* in 1963; the collection *Five Plays of Langston Hughes,* edited by Webster Smalley, in 1963; and Hughes's anthology *New Negro Poets USA* in 1964.

As a fully responsible agent, exercising my trust seriously, I was obliged to forward to you the Current Books contract. However, I must assure you I'm relieved to have your unequivocal reaction. Your letter to Perry is in the best diplomatic tradition. As our Mr. Vandenberg would say, 'it's fair and firm.' Seriously, Perry's letter to you displayed the naivete of his class—the middle class. We are surely far from the millennium, at least in these United States. Our so called best friends, here, the liberals, have no idea how late it is, and how fascism, which they are helping to usher in by their stupid and ill-advised red baiting, will soon strangle them.

By all means, send Perry the letter you've prepared, and maybe some day, in your own good time, you'll have a finished script of *Simple* that will satisfy us all; and rest assured I'll not be cajoled into tying you up into other assignments.[17]

Lieber clearly agrees with Hughes that Perry understands neither the character Simple nor the author Hughes. Yet Lieber never wavered in his belief that Hughes would need to edit and revise the manuscript in order to create the important and powerful book that should emerge from the raw material of the Simple columns.

Correspondence records prove Lieber correct in calling Hughes's letter to Bernard Perry diplomatic, because Hughes did not offend the editor of Current Books. Within six months, Lieber informed Hughes that Perry "and his associates feel deeply distressed that they made suggestions without knowing what they were talking about and they are now ready to accept the kind of book you think should be written. How about it?" Hughes, already disenchanted with Perry, responded coolly to another opportunity to publish Simple with Current Books. He replied to his agent that he would consider the offer when he returned from the West Indies in about three weeks.[18]

His cool reply did not signal refusal. By mid-January, 1948, he had "devised" about a dozen more chapters of *Simple Speaks His Mind* and wished Lieber to forward them to Bernard Perry. In Hughes's assessment, the new chapters improved the manuscript. However, Perry rejected the collected columns. He wrote to Lieber that the pieces were "repetitious" and "too thin to make a book." In light of the earlier exchange, Perry felt he would be unwise to offer any

17. Lieber to LH, March 10, 1947.
18. Lieber to LH, September 25, 1947; LH to Lieber, September 27, 1947.

editorial suggestions directly to Hughes. However, he wondered if "Mr. Hughes would consider writing a novel around the character of Simple." Lieber communicated the rejection to Hughes and urged him to submit the manuscript to other publishers, even to Knopf, which had by this time published his first novel, *Not without Laughter,* and four collections of his poems.[19]

Hughes had already inquired of his first publisher, receiving a negative response from Blanche Knopf. However, he followed Lieber's suggestion (and his own inclination) to continue to submit the manuscript to other publishers. He was also attempting to establish a solid critical base for Simple by soliciting scholarly comments that might be used to promote the character.

Ira De A. Reid, professor of sociology at Haverford College, Haverford, Pennsylvania, had already boosted Simple's academic value by soliciting the first academic article on the subject. Noting that *Phylon* would be willing to pay the only honorarium it could offer, "and this only once a quarter," he asked Hughes, "Will you do an article on the character Mr. Simple? I think it is an amazing character and one worthy of essay treatment."[20] The resulting article, "Simple and Me," appeared in *Phylon* in 1945. It offered the first reflective examination of Simple published outside of the *Chicago Defender,* and it elevated the character by discussing him in a refereed academic journal.

Comfortable with Reid's awareness of and respect for his Simple tales, Hughes solicited from the sociologist some brief comments (six to ten lines, one-quarter to one-half page) that might help to publicize and promote his book-length collection. Hughes wrote that he had assembled and arranged the Simple columns written for the *Defender,* "combining some, and putting them into book form to be submitted shortly to a publisher." He assured Reid that commentary on the character should be easy for him, "as you remember the character from the *Defender,* since there is no change in the book, except the addition of a few new columns which will appear in the paper shortly." Hughes greatly underestimated the time-consuming process of editing and revision that his Simple collection would require, but

19. LH to Lieber, January 12 and 20, 1948; Bernard Perry to Lieber, January 23, 1948; Lieber to LH, January 27, 1948.
20. Ira De A. Reid to LH, October 18, 1945, LH correspondence, JWJ.

he rightly gauged Reid's willingness to comment on Simple. Reid responded promptly with a few lines that Hughes no doubt savored:

> "Mr. Simple" is the wisdom of the people. He talks the easy language of folk who know none of the tricks of cocktail hour prattle, or the dilemmas of dialectic debates. He talks to the point because he doesn't have to be a two-tone, double-talking liberal. And he makes so much sense. The highly quotable "Mr. Simple" belongs in "Bartlett's" for he and "Mr. Dooley" are ideological twins, even if the former does have a bit more color in his arguments.[21]

Hughes successfully solicited additional critical comments from Arna Bontemps and Charles S. Johnson. Along with these comments, he submitted to his agent in March 1948 another draft of the Simple tales, hoping Lieber would offer the manuscript to Rinehart and perhaps to Random House. This time, however, Hughes indicated a genuine willingness to edit the collection: "I am, of course, open to editorial suggestion for further cutting if it should seem too long, or some of the material seem repetitious. Also, perhaps the chapters might be arranged to better advantage, if such a suggestion is brought up. I have inserted several short stories as told through Simple's mouth—such as, 'Rock, Church, Rock,' 'Get Over John,' and 'Tain't So.'"[22] Besides being willing to cut or rearrange the episodes, Hughes mentioned his insertion of several short stories. He added "Banquet in Honor" and several more stories to the manuscript Perry had rejected in January.

With these insertions during the first three months of 1948, Hughes revealed a completely new strategy in his crafting of the Simple stories. Fishing for a commitment from a publisher and eager for an advance, Hughes stretched his manuscript by including non-Simple fiction that he had adapted to make Simple its narrator. Before the first Simple manuscript was published, Hughes printed a few of the short stories in the "Here to Yonder" column. However, the technique did not always succeed. A brief analysis of "Tain't So" and "Banquet in Honor" suggests why some of these short stories ultimately had to be deleted from the Simple manuscript—as happened with "Tain't So"—while a few survived as Simple stories and were even among those most highly acclaimed by critics—as with "Banquet in Honor."

21. LH to Reid, February 2, 1948; Reid to LH, February 23, 1948.
22. LH to Lieber, March 8, 1948.

"Tain't So," which appears in *The Langston Hughes Reader,* describes an elderly white woman, Miss Lucy Cannon, who follows her friends' recommendation to see a gifted healer in order to cure her many aches and pains.[23] The healer is a black woman who tricks Miss Lucy into feeling better. Miss Lucy becomes outraged when she learns the healer is black, and she basically overlooks her healing because of her anger.

To force "Tain't So" into a Simple format, Hughes added an introduction and a conclusion that place the story into one of Simple's conversations with his buddy in the bar:

> "That Negro with the turban talking to Tony down yonder at the end of the bar is what you call a Mental Healer," said Simple. "He coins money."
>
> "I am always doubtful of Harlemites who wear turbans," I said, "and the Negroes who patronize such fakers are certainly gullible."
>
> "Negroes are not the only ones who go to Mental Healers," said Simple. "There was a rich white lady who used to come up from Birmingham every season to White Sulphur Springs. . . ."
>
> "And what happened?" I asked.
>
> "You might not believe it," said Simple, "but my Uncle Joe were a Christian man and would not lie. He told this tale."
>
> "Get on with the story," I said.
>
> "Refill the glasses while I tell you about it," said Simple. "This old Miss Lucy Cannon . . ."

From this point, the story reads exactly as it appears in *The Langston Hughes Reader.* To close the story within a Simple framework, Hughes tacked on an appropriate ending:

> As Simple drained his glass, I said, "You certainly remember some extraordinary stories."
>
> "Order a couple more beers," said Simple, "and I will remember you another one."
>
> "Thanks," I said, "that's enough for one evening. Goodnight."

23. "Tain't So" was first published in *Fight against War and Fascism,* May 1937, and has been reprinted in three Hughes collections: *Laughing to Keep from Crying, The Langston Hughes Reader,* and *Something in Common.* (See Donald C. Dickinson, *A Bio-bibliography of Langston Hughes: 1902–1967,* 175.)

"So you're running out on me," called Simple as I reached the door. "Tis so," I said.[24]

Hughes lets the bar buddy invert the refrain of the story, "Tain't so," thereby adding one of the traditional Simple techniques: wordplay. "Tain't So" is mildly amusing, but the situation of the glib healer in Hollywood seems too far-fetched to remind ordinary black folks of their own existence. Simple, after all, did not witness or participate in this event; he merely recounts the story as told to him by his Uncle Joe. Although readers may rejoice that racist old Miss Lucy Cannon must pay the black healer who tricked her into feeling better, the entire situation is so exaggerated that despite Simple's contention that his Uncle Joe "were a Christian man and would not lie," it can only be considered a tall tale.

"Banquet in Honor," on the other hand, seems plausible. As James Emanuel indicates, "Banquet in Honor" was originally a short story that Hughes wrote in 1941 in California—two years before Simple was created.[25] It tells of an elderly black writer/artist, versatile and accomplished, who is being honored by Joyce's society friends. This Dr. So-and-So-and-So surprises the entire audience by rejecting the alleged honor and using the opportunity to admonish these Negroes for failing to support young black artists who struggle to survive. Nearly all readers have attended some formal dinner—a tribute to the pastor, a fraternity banquet, or a special event such as this one held by society ladies. Simple's involvement throughout the action adds to readers' enjoyment of the occasion. Readers do not merely hear the narrative of Dr. So-and-So-and-So surprising his sponsors with indignation at their failure to appreciate young black artists. We also hear Simple's comment about Mrs. Sadie Maxwell-Reeves's bosom and Joyce's outrage about Simple's laughter. Simple goes beyond telling the story; he participates in it. Since we "know" Simple, we can envision him at this banquet, laughing at the embarrassed society ladies who planned the event. Thus, whereas "Banquet in Honor" successfully converted a short story into a Simple story, "Tain't So"

24. Hughes MSS, JWJ, Catalogue #3532-2, Folder 9.
25. James A. Emanuel, "The Short Stories of Langston Hughes," 261. "Banquet in Honor" was first published in *Negro Quarterly,* Summer 1942. (See Dickinson, *A Bio-bibliography,* 161.)

and other short stories failed to match the style and caliber of the Simple tales.

Lieber gladly received the revised manuscript in March 1948 and sent it to Rinehart, where it was declined.[26] Sloane Associates also evaluated the *Simple* manuscript and declined to publish it. By October 1948 the manuscript was with Little, Brown. Hughes was giving considerable attention to the effort by this time, and he had evaluated the draft with future readability in mind: "The columns which are purely topical and would date very quickly, I am not including in the manuscript. But the Negro Problem is always with us and probably will be for the next 50-11 years, so most of these columns will hardly be dated for several literary seasons."[27] His assessment of the purely topical columns reveals his sensitivity to the tastes of future generations of readers. As printed in the *Defender,* the Simple columns contained references to particular news stories that were completely familiar to the weekly readers. After all, his original intention had been to help his less worldly readers better understand their relationship to global news—particularly Nazism. His revisions exchanged the focus on news for improved characterization and greater continuity of plot. The revisions took two forms: deleting whole columns and substituting more generic terms for names of politicians, brand names, and other words specific to the 1940s.

Many of the columns proved too topical for inclusion in the book. "Simple and the Elections" (August 12, 1944), for example, discusses presidential candidates in the 1944 election. Clearly such a column would have offered mainly historical interest as years pass. Similarly, "Simple Starts at Rock Bottom" (July 21, 1945), which discusses Bilbo, Rankin, and Eastland—outspoken racists of that time—proved too closely linked to the news to have universal appeal for future generations of readers.

Even when humor and race consciousness fit the traditional Simple pattern, when the subject matter revolved around names and events that might have lost their impact with passing years, Hughes omitted

---

26. Lieber to LH, March 18 and May 3, 1948. Rinehart did, however, publish *Simple Stakes a Claim* in 1957. The details of this occurrence appear in chapter 7.

27. LH to Lieber, October 7, 1948, JWJ.

the columns from the manuscript being circulated to publishers. For example, "Simple and the Secret" (March 23, 1946) involves Simple's willingness to reveal American knowledge of the atomic bomb to Haile Selassie, Ethiopian emperor from 1930 to 1936 and from 1941 to 1974. Although Selassie remained sovereign for many years, Hughes rightly predicted that future generations might not understand Simple's vigorous opposition to the Dutch in Indonesia and the British in India. Appendix A is a chronological list of the first seven years of Hughes's "Here to Yonder" columns; it reveals that many of the early Simple columns were excluded from the book-length collections.

Even within columns that were not "purely topical," Hughes substituted for names and other references that would have dated quickly. For example, in "Simple and Harlem" (October 5, 1946) Simple had spoken of Adam Powell. As revised for the book, "Toast to Harlem" mentions only "a colored congressman" (*Best,* 21). "Simple Lets Off Steam" (March 1, 1947) included a plea from the foil for Simple to take a global view when he feels tempted to complain about being cold in winter: "Think of the DP's in Germany and Italy. And the poor English with their coal and food shortages. Even the London bakeries have been given orders to bake *only* bread—no pies or cookies or cakes. Things are critical over there. Maybe if you started feeling sorry for some of those poor people in Europe, you wouldn't have so much time to feel sorry for yourself." Even though that passage survived at least one typescript sent to the editors at Simon and Schuster, "Letting Off Steam" as it was published in *Simple Speaks His Mind* contains no such references. Likewise, in "High Bed" Hughes substituted Fords for Kaiser-Frazers, cars well known in the 1940s.

In at least one instance, Hughes's attempt to revise required more than one change of historical reference. For example, "Simple's Selfish Peace" (September 15, 1945) became a portion of "Simple Prays a Prayer." As published in the *Defender,* the episode began, " 'I reckon there are all kinds of Victory Prayers to pray,' said my Simple Minded Friend, 'but the one I would pray is . . .' " When Hughes was circulating the manuscript, though, the war had ended, so he changed the line to read, " 'I reckon since the war is over and we don't want to have no more, there are all kinds of Victory Prayers we could pray. . . .' " For the book, Hughes revised the line again. This version reads more like a short story:

> It was a hot night. Simple was sitting on his landlady's stoop reading a newspaper by streetlight. When he saw me coming, he threw the paper down.
>
> "Good evening," I said.
>
> "Good evening nothing," he answered. "It's too hot to be any good evening. Besides, this paper's full of nothing but atom bombs and bad news, wars and rumors of wars, airplane crashes, murders, fightings, wife-whippings, and killings from the Balkans to Brooklyn. Do you know one thing? If I was a praying man, I would pray a prayer for this world right now."
>
> "What kind of prayer would you pray, friend?"
>
> "I would pray a don't-want-to-have-no-more-wars prayer, and it would go like this . . ." (*Best*, 6–7)

Hughes effectively changed from the wartime/postwar focus. He retained the necessary desire to be rid of war, but he placed this desire within a general framework, evaluating the standard types of bad news predicted from scripture ("wars and rumors of wars") and still evident in today's newspapers.

Hughes showed uncanny perception about concepts that would prove anachronistic, and unfortunately his predictions about the longevity of the race problem have been proved true. Consequently, generations of readers continue to enjoy the ups and downs of Simple, unhampered by distractions of identification: Who is Adam Clayton Powell? What is a Kaiser-Frazer? What are DPs? Obviously, footnotes could explain such items, but footnotes would distract from the entertainment value of the Simple stories. Thus, the stripping of "news" from the Simple columns proved essential to the creation of the successful book of Simple stories. By his successful pruning of the "dated" terms and episodes, Hughes overcame a typical liability with the kind of political humor his Simple stories express. In the preface to his *Treasury of American Political Humor,* which includes a Simple episode, Leonard C. Lewin explains: "Most political humor is topical, and therefore perishable; not much of the older material can come through to us as humor without long and destructive explanation."[28]

Critics have remarked about the longevity of Simple's popularity, which is exceptional for a comic figure. Roger Rosenblatt, for

28. Lewin, ed., preface to *A Treasury of American Political Humor,* 16.

example, comments that, "unlike tragedy, which endures from age to age, humor generally thrives only within the lifetime of a particular taste. If Simple turns out to be the exception to this rule it will not be because the jokes he made held their flavor, but because the image of man he represented was important to hold on to."[29] This praise for the universal qualities in the Simple stories certainly holds validity. However, for many observers of American race relations, "the image of man" is an incomplete credit for such a "race man" as Jesse B. Semple. Instead, they might argue that Simple is the exception to the rule of humor's characteristic brevity because the ironies of racism and the failures of democracy in the United States have continued. Or, as Hughes himself phrased his prophetic vision, "the Negro Problem is always with us and probably will be for the next 50-11 years, so most of these columns will hardly be dated for several literary seasons."

In her analysis of the rhetoric of human rights as expressed in the Simple columns, Lucia Shelia Hawthorne supports this conclusion: "The fact that the columns still have natural pertinence is an indication that little has changed for black people in this country. It is both rhetorical and social comment to say that the Simple columns are, unfortunately, only slightly 'dated.' . . . We understand the Simple columns today because today's reality is only a little different from the realities of Simple's days."[30] Much has changed since 1971, when Hawthorne arrived at her conclusions, but even in current discussions of Simple, his contemporaneity continues to be praised. Actor Anthony Thompson, who performed in a one-man theatrical adaptation of Simple during the mid–1980s, says that individuals from his audiences seek him out after his performances to marvel over the appropriateness of Simple's remarks for their own situations and to relate their own tales about being black in America. In the mid–1990s, average African American working people continue to complain about aching feet or other injuries and to bemoan the fate of blacks in America. Thus, Hughes effectively preserved Simple's timeless complaints.

29. Rosenblatt, *Black Fiction,* 118.

30. Hawthorne, "A Rhetoric of Human Rights as Expressed in the 'Simple Columns' by Langston Hughes," 128, 155–56.

After his efforts to remove ideas that would become dated, Hughes told his agent how he felt about further revisions of the manuscript:

> Personally, I think there is too much material for a single book and we could weed some of it out. And if a publisher takes the book and gives an advance, I am perfectly willing to attempt a new editorial job on it—but my temperament at this moment will not permit me to make it into a novel. I am more inclined to making it into a radio program which I think it will become—that is, if radio can grow up enough to take a little controversial comedy.[31]

Despite Hughes's work to delete topical columns and to substitute for overly specific historical references throughout the stories, he failed to convince Little, Brown to publish the Simple manuscript. Such unsuccessful efforts to publish a collection of stories could have discouraged a less determined writer, but Hughes continued to urge his agent to submit the manuscript to other publishers. Finally, on February 21, 1949—more than three years after the search for a publisher began—Maxim Lieber wrote to Hughes, sending him an advance of $900 from Simon and Schuster for *Simple Speaks His Mind.* Hughes delighted in the generous advance and in the fact that the large, well-respected publishing firm of Simon and Schuster had agreed to the project. He could not have known that Simon and Schuster would work very cooperatively with him and that he would have a sensitive editor in Maria Leiper. That Hughes finally shaped *Simple* under the advisement of Leiper and the Simon and Schuster office proved supremely auspicious.

Hughes very quickly began to appreciate his good fortune. On February 25, 1949, Hughes and his agent met with Leiper to discuss the book. On May 5, she sent them eleven pages of single-spaced typed editorial comments from the people who had read the Simple text. Indicative of her sensitivity and conscientiousness, she added three pages of her own comments to introduce and to interpret the extensive—and sometimes cruel—remarks. Leiper's report pleased Hughes. He informed Bontemps that she had sent him "a very good and complete chapter by chapter editorial comment to

31. LH to Lieber, October 7, 1948.

aid me in revisions."[32] He carefully examined Leiper's remarks about each episode, which he refers to here as chapters.

By the end of June, Hughes had written a new beginning and a new ending for *Simple*. As was often the case for this prolific writer, he just wished for more time. He told his friend Bontemps, "If I could take ten straight days out on the book alone, I could have it done shortly, in fact, in ten days. Just needs cutting, rearrangement, and a slight plot thread binding it together."[33] Apparently Hughes had no opportunity to focus upon the book alone, because he did not return the manuscript until late in August. By that time he had made several changes. A data sheet saved with the draft shows that he had originally submitted fifty-five columns to Simon and Schuster. The August revisions reflected omission of sixteen columns, as the publishers had suggested. In addition, three or four were divided into two episodes, and eight to ten new columns were added. The number of episodes submitted in August totaled fifty, with a total length of 222 pages.[34] In his August 29 cover letter to Maria Leiper, Hughes indicated that this draft was "very carefully revised following the editorial notes which you gave me (and which were, by the way, excellent)." Leiper quickly sent a two-page summary of the first reader's report of the revised version of *Simple*. Based on this report, Hughes volunteered to drop "Tain't So" and "Get Over John" before any other readers examined the new draft of the book.[35]

By mid-October, Leiper was prepared with a full report from all readers on the revised version. She sent Hughes a fourteen-page missive, again meticulously detailing the suggestions of the editorial board. A month of revision, documented by a flurry of brief letters exchanged between Leiper and Hughes, led to a third report from the panel of readers at Simon and Schuster. The necessary revisions decreased, so the document from Leiper was merely five pages long.

32. Maria Leiper to Maxim Lieber, May 5, 1949, LH correspondence, Simon and Schuster file, JWJ; LH to Bontemps, June 22, 1949, in Nichols, ed., *Letters,* 263.

33. LH to Bontemps, June 30, 1949, in Nichols, ed., *Letters,* 263.

34. *Just Simple* Data, August 22–27, 1949, Folder 8, Hughes MSS #3532-1, JWJ.

35. LH to Leiper, September 8, 1949, JWJ.

Indicating the quality of improvements, she began her letter with praise: "Every time you touch your book, you make it better." Leiper humorously considered, then disallowed, the interminable process that such consistently advantageous revisions could involve: "Dear me, this could go on forever, I suppose. But no, the production department wouldn't permit it. They're already eager to get their hands on the manuscript." Following that humorous and congratulatory introduction, she moved into editorial suggestions with the confident prediction that this memo would "go over things for—probably—the last time."[36] Indeed, within a month, the final draft of *Simple Speaks His Mind* was ready to go to press.

Thus, from a strictly chronological perspective, Hughes had written Simple columns for two years before he considered book-length collection. His search for a publisher had taken over three more years and had included disappointing rejections from publishers who kept the manuscript for many months. Once Simon and Schuster agreed to publish the book, Hughes revised the text repeatedly for seven months. Converting Simple from a newspaper celebrity to the protagonist of his own book was *not* a simple process.

36. Leiper to LH, November 14, 1949, JWJ.

5

Readings and Revisions

WONDERFUL CHANGES—often subtle, but important—occurred in the language, characterization, and continuity of the Simple stories after Hughes began receiving and responding to editorial suggestions from Simon and Schuster. An examination of these changes shows how the transformation of the Simple tales from columns to book was completed and enhances an appreciation of Hughes's skill as a writer.

Beginning with the first draft of the manuscript, the panel of readers at Simon and Schuster noticed the exceptional features of the Simple stories and offered sensitive suggestions. The orientation toward the mass African American audience required for publication in the *Defender* proved vital to the eventual publication of the Simple stories in book form. Segregation bred ignorance, among other things. Fear of the unknown had aided the separation of the races. Because they did not contribute to the polite alienation so common to desegregation, Hughes's Simple stories attracted the editors at Simon and Schuster. Initial readers of the Simple manuscript predicted that the stories would allow white readers to gain an honest appreciation for the frustrations and survival strategies of more than one socioeconomic class of blacks.

Correspondence from Simon and Schuster indicates that the initial readers for the Simple manuscript were fascinated by both the language and the subject matter of the dialogues. Like most whites, they had not been reading the *Defender,* so the Simple dialogues— particularly the attitudes expressed in them—were new to them. Furthermore, they had never before engaged in genuine dialogue with an average Negro about day-to-day life. Therefore, they found Simple's viewpoints very interesting. In particular, the authenticity of

the conversations intended for a black audience gave white readers
a remarkable vantage point.

> There is a prickling sense of being an eavesdropper, when one reads
> this material; at least, that's how it struck me. So clearly, the pieces
> weren't set down for me to read, they were addressed by one Negro
> to other Negroes. As things are in this country, unfortunately, there
> is almost always a barrier set between even the friendliest white and
> Negro. Here it is absent, as I've never found it is, for example, in novels
> by Negroes—which, of course, are addressed to whites as much as (or
> more than) to Negroes.[1]

Another reader agreed with that view, and a third reader embellished
the opinion, saying that the book has "a key-hole type of fascination
for a white man, and it opens a door freshly, revealingly, invitingly,
unostentatiously."[2] This appeal remained intact at the end of the revision process, since reviewers of the final product, *Simple Speaks His
Mind*, praised the same authentic Negro voice that had attracted the
editors at Simon and Schuster. William Gardner Smith, a reporter for
the *Pittsburgh Courier*, noted in his review: "Because most of these
columns were written for a Negro audience, they are uninhibited,
intimate, to the point." Carl Van Vechten, a close friend of Hughes
and a great admirer of his craft, made a similar observation. "Since
these papers were originally written for a Negro newspaper and,
consequently, an exclusively Negro audience, there is no attempt
at obfuscation."[3] This attractive authenticity remained in the book
form of the stories largely because Hughes did not edit the fiction to
accommodate the significant change in audience from almost exclusively black to largely white. He left the characters, the scenes, the
topics, and the language as they had originated in the *Defender*.

Although the authentic Negro tone, topics, and dialect could have
inhibited sales potential for the book, the editors were willing to
risk publication. One reader expressed his confidence that the book

---

1. "*Simple Speaks His Mind:* Readers' Reports," First Report, reader no.
3, Hughes MSS, JWJ.
    2. Ibid., readers no. 7 and no. 6.
    3. Smith, review of *Mind;* Van Vechten, "Dialogues—But Barbed," review
of *Mind,* in Mullen, ed., *Critical Essays,* 75.

would succeed because "it should arouse interest among a satisfactory number of literate white people who have never before seen such a candid portrait of a Negro written by a Negro for other Negroes." Another reader, although recognizing the need for richer character development, hoped for the book to "retain its original quality, as a book written by a Negro for Negroes. It must never have an eye on the white folks."[4] Clearly, then, the *Chicago Defender* origins of Simple proved vital to his authenticity and to the appeal his character had for the publishers of *Simple Speaks His Mind.*

Whereas the racial message was viewed by some of the first Simon and Schuster readers as a sales liability, the more common opinion was that "the sales problem may be overcome by a thorough revision job, which will make the material seem more of a book and less a collection of newspaper columns."[5] This suggestion should have come as no surprise to Hughes, since Lieber had said exactly the same thing three years earlier. The surprise may have been the extent of the revisions required, and the unquestionable improvements rendered because of those changes. Whether or not he fully realized the amount of work that lay ahead of him, Hughes honestly appreciated the remarks and suggestions from Simon and Schuster. Following the editors' suggestions, he concentrated on three basic areas in his revisions: improving characterization through use of consistently distinctive diction for the two principal speakers, clarifying characters' identities through consistent use of names or references, and adding a story line to connect the episodes and to give a sense of time.

Although Hughes recognized on his own the need to remove topical and easily dated references from the stories, he apparently needed help appreciating the similarities between the foil's diction and Simple's diction. As discussed in the review of the development of Simple in the "Here to Yonder" columns in chapters 2 and 3, Hughes based the bar buddy upon his own life, views, and expressions. We have seen that Hughes sometimes named himself as the bar buddy in the first four years of the Simple columns. So Boyd, the bar buddy, and Hughes, the writer, employed the same rhetorical patterns, and therefore Simple did to some extent, too, in the early years.

4. *Mind,* First Report, readers no. 8 and no. 6.
5. Maria Leiper to Maxim Lieber, May 5, 1949.

Hughes's friendly correspondence, examples of which are conveniently published in *Arna Bontemps-Langston Hughes Letters, 1925-1967,* edited by Charles H. Nichols, shows that he sometimes used improper grammar and slang deliberately, sounding like the colorful "blue collar" workers he enjoyed so much. As a result, the early foil occasionally calls Simple "man," a common street expression, rather than "my good fellow," or "friend," the more polished appellatives. "Man, I do not know what to reckon," says the bar buddy in "Simple's Selfish Peace" (September 15, 1945). The foil also lapses into a double negative from time to time, and he uses the mundane "Huh?" rather than a more sophisticated "I presume?" to elicit affirmation from Simple. Hughes himself found no shame in using the colorful colloquialisms of the average Harlem resident. In fact, he strongly advised young people to beware of the stereotypes created by the media. "Listen, boys and girls, . . . Don't let the radio sketches that give you only dialect comedians make you believe that lack of proper English is always attended by servility, grotesqueness, and stupidity."[6] For Hughes, lack of proper English was merely another dialect, another vernacular, another respectable means of expression. Not surprisingly, then, since his voice originated as Hughes's own, the bar buddy in the *Defender* columns also uses some poor grammar and slang—often similar to the errors in Simple's language. Such remnants of the early Simple columns prompted readers of his manuscript to suggest the need for better developed and more consistent characterization. Maria Leiper elaborated upon that suggestion when she collected the readers' reports for Hughes and Lieber. In parentheses she especially emphasized the inconsistency in the dialogue and characterization of the foil: "The greatest inconsistency in characterization, it seemed to me, was in your interlocutor. Most of the time he was formal, stilted, prissy, stuffy—as, I feel, he should be, to make a good foil for Simple. But every so often he became idiomatic to the point of slanginess. I'd keep him pedantic throughout."[7] Hughes had already begun to elevate the diction of the foil in his column. As he gradually withdrew his own personality and replaced his former role with a more stereotypically

6. LH, "Need for Heroes," 185.
7. *Mind,* First Report, reader no. 7, and Maria Leiper's parenthetical comments regarding reader no. 7's comments.

"upper class" persona, he also deliberately rendered the foil's diction more formally. The lapses in diction occurred mainly because he had compiled his columns for the book manuscript without editing them for consistent characterization. Thus, the later columns, written in 1948 and beyond, tended to portray the more sophisticated foil; the earlier columns often projected a foil very much like Hughes himself—down-to-earth and likely to throw slang into his conversation. Only after Hughes had received extensive editorial guidance from readers who seemed to fully appreciate Simple's nature, and after he had begun to consciously heighten the intellectual aspect of the bar buddy, did he revise the diction of the foil to distinguish clearly between what Eugenia Collier notes as perfect contrasts: "the writer's extremely proper (and pallid) diction" and "Simple's warm accents and colorful idioms."[8]

Some of Hughes's changes to accomplish this more distinctive contrast between Simple and the foil are quite minimal, as in "Last Whipping," where "mad" in the newspaper column becomes "angry" in the book. In "Nickel for the Phone," Hughes revises the foil's question, "did you make up with Joyce?" to "did you effect a reconciliation with Joyce?" The best examples of the more polished diction appear in episodes written after Hughes became sensitive to the need to maintain consistently elevated diction for the foil. "A Letter from Baltimore," for instance, appeared in the *Defender* on September 10, 1949. In this episode the foil is greeted by a grinning and financially solvent Simple. The foil responds to Simple's joy and his offer to buy the beers: "What, may I ask, is the occasion for this sudden conviviality?" After he explains that his wife, Isabel, is seeking an uncontested divorce and tells the foil that he once knew a woman who framed her divorce decree, Simple threatens to throw his out instead of signing it. The foil reminds him, "That would render it invalid, also null and void." Both of these sentences demonstrate how debonair the foil eventually sounded.

Besides distinguishing his characters' diction, Hughes also enhanced characterization by emphasizing the proper name of his Simple Minded Friend and by withdrawing his own name from the bar

8. Eugenia Collier, "A Pain in His Soul," in O'Daniel, ed., *Langston Hughes: Black Genius,* 125.

buddy. As noted in Chapter 3, he did not name his Simple Minded Friend "Jess" until the character had been appearing in the column for three years. Since the editors at Simon and Schuster wanted a clear demarcation between these two main figures, they urged Hughes to distinctly name the Simple Minded Friend and to clear up confusion about names that they thought might be referring to the foil by eliminating them. Hughes responded to the thoughtful comments of his editors, appreciating that their confusion probably represented a similar confusion the larger white audience would experience. He carefully revised his earlier episodes to include Simple's proper name, and he began to include it in his *Defender* columns, as well. He and his editor agreed that the foil should remain nameless, but they also had to agree on whether to use nicknames for him.

In her May 5, 1949, letter, Maria Leiper advises Hughes to leave the foil nameless, even to drop the term *Jack* when Simple addresses him: "I would keep the narrator nameless. Every so often he is referred to as Jack or Richard; seems to me he should be anonymous Mr. Interlocutor to be the best possible foil for the very human, lively Simple." The funny aspect of that advice is that the editors lacked familiarity with the colloquial use of "Jack" or "Jim" or any other name snatched at random to underscore a point. When Simple says, "Yeah, Jack, it's payday!" he is not calling his companion by the name *Jack.* That word simply punctuates his comment and emphasizes it. Although Hughes knew the colloquial practice, he followed the advice of the editors at Simon and Schuster to leave his foil anonymous. He wrote to Leiper, "I cut out the word 'Jack' as you suggested, although it is not the narrator's name, but merely a Harlem equivalent of 'fellow' or 'boy.' "[9] Once she understood its use, Leiper offered to let Hughes return "Jack" to the text, but she suggested a typographical change. "Your word 'Jack.' By all means put it back if you wish. No one will be confused by it, as I was, if you follow the simple procedure of spelling it with a small 'j,' as bud, or fellow, or man appears when used as a salutation in your text." We see the lowercase "jack" in "Confused," but for the most part, Hughes preferred to omit "Jack" rather than present it in lowercase. In this way he could faithfully represent Harlem and still be understood correctly by white

9. LH to Maria Leiper, August 29, 1949.

readers who might buy the book. Not until the third volume, *Simple Stakes a Claim*, did "Jack" reappear, capitalized and in its normal vernacular use.[10]

Inserting and improving the explanation of Simple's full name did not create any problem for Hughes. He simply revised his first, rather mild use of Simple's name: " 'I also am named after him,' said Simple. 'Grandpa's name was Jess. My name is Jess, too.' "[11] Whereas this 1945 column announced Simple's name for the first time, by 1949, when Hughes edited this passage for inclusion in the book, both the bar buddy and the readers already knew Simple's name. The first change was to add the middle initial *B* and some explanation of its addition to the name. However, when Hughes added the initial, he still had not fully settled on the distinction between Semple and Simple. He had written *Semple*, but over the *e* was typed the letter *i*. Finally Hughes settled on two revisions for the passage: he improved the foil's grammar a bit, and he extended Simple's commentary on his name:

> "So your grandpa was a drinking man, too. That must be whom you take after."
> "I also am named after him," said Simple. "Grandpa's name was Jess, too. So I am Jesse B. Semple."
> "What does the *B* stand for?"
> "Nothing. I just put it there myself since they didn't give me no initial when I was born. I am really Jess Semple—which the kids changed around into a nickname when I were in school. In fact, they used to tease me when I were small, calling me 'Simple Simon.' But I was right handy with my fists, and after I beat the 'Simon' out of a few of them, they let me alone. But my friends still call me 'Simple.' "
> "In reality, you are Jesse Semple," I said, "colored."
> "Part Indian," insisted Simple, reaching for his beer.
> "Jess is certainly not an Indian name." (*Best*, 18)

In the column the foil said of Simple's grandfather, "That must be *who* you take after." For the book, the foil uses the preferred objective case, *whom*. Another change is that the number of stage directions,

10. Maria Leiper to LH, October 18, 1949. The lowercase *jack* appears in "Confused" (*Mind*, 174), and the vernacular use of capitalized *Jack* appears in *Claim*, 63, 83.

11. "Simple's Indian Blood," *CD*, November 3, 1945.

such as "I said" and "said Simple," was reduced for the book. Whereas the column interrupted the foil's line about the grandfather, the book leaves the line unbroken. Similarly, the column broke the foil's line, " 'Jess,' I said, 'is certainly not an Indian name,' " and the book leaves it whole. The most important improvement in this episode, however, pertains to substance rather than punctuation. It is Simple's offer of information about his self-placed middle initial and about his correct last name. Most readers chuckle to learn that Simple gave himself a middle initial, but not a middle name. He wanted his name to be complete, and he showed enough self-determination to give himself the initial he needed. This same assertiveness allowed him to defend his nickname. He could live with being called "Simple," but he fought with schoolmates to eliminate "Simon," which referred to "Simple Simon" from Mother Goose. By showing that "Simple Simon" was an insult that he would not tolerate, Simple also reveals that the nickname "Simple" pleases him. By standing up for himself, he transformed a taunt into a positive appellation.

The second time the name appeared in the column, the landlady used it to express her profound gratitude to Simple, who had walked her dog. "Thank you! You certainly nice, Mr. Jesse, you certainly nice!"[12] When the story was edited for inclusion in the book, Hughes used Simple's last name and allowed Simple to amplify the significance of her using it: "All I got was, 'Thank you, you certainly nice, Mr. Semple.' She used my real last name, all formal and everything. 'You certainly nice, yes, indeed' " (*Best,* 70).

Readers well acquainted with the collected stories may remember how Simple mentions his name in "Final Fear":

" 'Suffered!' cried Simple. 'My mama should have named me Job instead of Jess Semple. I have been underfed, underpaid, undernourished, and everything but *undertaken.* I been bit by dogs, cats, mice, rats, poll parrots, fleas, chiggers, bedbugs, granddaddies, mosquitoes, and a gold-toothed woman' " (*Best,* 60). The episode as it appeared in the newspaper, however, made no mention of the name.

These insertions of the full name and Simple's explanations about the significance of using a person's proper, formal name resulted partially from astute editorial guidance. Leiper pointed out the problem

12. "Simple's Landlady's Dog," *CD,* October 26, 1946.

with the spelling of Simple's real name and of his nickname: " 'Jess Semple'—we've forgotten that's his real name. After all, I think it was as long ago as on page 19 that you mentioned it; so the first feeling is that this is a misprint. Perhaps you could insert a phrase to the effect that she was so high and mighty she used his whole name, and his formal right name, too. Otherwise it worries us not merely here, but several times later when it comes."[13] Hughes apparently understood her remarks to pertain to *Jess* and *Jesse,* which was not her intention. She elaborated and clarified her suggestions about a month later, responding to some revisions she had not anticipated:

> I'm afraid my letter wasn't very clear when I wrote about Simple's real name. I wasn't referring to his first name, Jess, but to Semple. He was Simple for so long, that when suddenly the word Semple appeared, I thought it was a misprint. Then, when I came upon Semple several times, I thought for a while this was repeated carelessness. I don't think it matters at all how often you use Jess, we remember that right from the start, and there's no confusion attached to it, anyway. But Semple, hmm, let's see. Page 117, the landlady says "Mr. Semple"—maybe a few words here about her using his formal, right, real name? For it is so long since we were told it.[14]

With such specific and reasonable suggestions, Hughes added the full name several times, making it clear that Jesse B. Semple was the true name for our "Simple" friend. For example, in "A Ball of String" Simple complained: "I do not like Zarita nor no other dame calling me up at a bar, having the bartender strewing my right and full name all over the place, 'Hey, there, Jesse B. Semple! One of your womens wants you on the phone. . . .' That bartender ain't got no business letting everybody know my business and I don't care to have my name known to everybody, neither." Not only does Simple clarify his "right and full name," but he also reminds the audience of the privacy that people in a bar often hope to preserve. Not even Joyce resorts to his real name, unless she is angry.[15] With his editor's suggestions,

13. Leiper to LH, October 19, 1949.
14. Leiper to LH, November 14, 1949.
15. "A Ball of String," *Mind,* 196. Joyce's angry use of "Mr. Semple" appears in "Banquet in Honor," *Best,* 48.

Hughes established Jess as a very easygoing fellow whose friends usually address him by his nickname rather than by his right name.

This addition of the name represents one of the last changes Hughes made in the Simple manuscript, according to the drafts retained in the James Weldon Johnson Collection at Yale. Other changes were needed besides the distinction in diction between Simple and the foil and the clear and consistent use of Simple's name, however. The editors also noted the lack of continuity in Simple's life story. Writing separate columns for a weekly newspaper, Hughes did not have in mind the chronology and character development needed in a book of collected fiction. Some of the earliest readers at Simon and Schuster commented specifically on the characterization and the plot. "Simple, and his friends, and the man he talks to, aren't sufficiently real. If they could be developed, turned into flesh-and-blood people, it would be a fine book," commented one reader. Another said, "The basic improvement I should like to see made is to give it some movement, and as other readers have suggested, more developed, consistent, characterization." The most specific suggestion detailed possible additions. "Indicate what kind of job Simple has and how he gets along in it; develop the triangle situation with wife and mistress so that something happens; have him, perhaps, finally leave the landlady he hates; show a little more precisely what Simple's relationship is to the narrator."[16] These suggestions are thoughtful responses to the Simple stories, and Hughes accepted the wisdom in them.

An examination of the "Here to Yonder" columns shows that the Hughes persona encounters Simple by chance as two men might meet from time to time in a bar or on a street corner. As Hughes has told the saga of the origins of these stories, such random encounters were exactly the way Hughes met the Simple prototype. The "Simple" character just begins talking, revealing details about his life and his loves only at random, never in a purposeful, chronological order. Readers of the columns did not readily know about Simple's migration from Virginia, his separation from Isabel, or his affection for Joyce. Simple's desultory conversations revealed segments—sometimes about his past, sometimes about his present. Thus, what appears in *Simple*

16. *Mind,* First Report, readers no. 6 and no. 7.

Speaks His Mind as facile and well-developed characterization was actually the result of thoughtful editorial guidance, arduous revision, and careful craft. Hughes agreeably shaped the stories so that they appeared more like a book than like the random newspaper columns they had been. He wrote to Leiper:

> Today I sent you the Simple book (completed manuscript except for such further revisions as your editorial department may suggest) under the title, "LISTEN FLUENTLY." It has been carefully revised following the editorial notes which you gave me (and which were, by the way, excellent). More than a dozen chapters have been dropped, and a number of others shortened. The plot line of Simple's first wife, the divorce, and Joyce has been strengthened and the narrator's character built up a bit. A completely new sequence of chapters has been devised and links inserted so that a number of them seem to flow, story-wise, one into another; also the round-the-year flow of seasons help to hold them together. Some completely new chapters have been inserted, including new opening and closing chapters.[17]

Thus, Hughes made several changes including deletion and insertion to strengthen the fictional value of the book-length collection.

The new opening chapter Hughes mentioned, "Feet Live Their Own Life," resulted from the editorial request that he provide more background for the characters. In his first draft of the manuscript, he had begun the book with "Conversation on the Corner." "Feet" offers a far broader introduction to Simple's life. It mentions his birthplace, his childhood in crowded conditions with an extended family, his reason for drinking, his reasons for liking Joyce, and his attraction to Zarita. It also enumerates (and exaggerates) some of his many jobs and frustrations, including his participation in the Harlem Riot of 1943. "Conversation," which was shifted to the fourth story in the book, also explains Simple's relationship with Joyce. It focuses primarily upon the former marriage and the expensive divorce still pending, however. The more general "Feet" better prepares the inexperienced reader to understand Simple's attitudes and activities. In addition, throughout the collection Hughes enhanced the story line involving Simple's first wife. He combined chronologically distant columns to

17. LH to Maria Leiper, August 9, 1949.

explain more clearly how the marriage to Isabel had felt to Simple—as in "Conversation on the Corner." He gave the collection a sense of passing time by indicating Simple's progress or frustration in accumulating the $133.34 needed for his share of the $400.00 divorce. Finally, he added "A Letter from Baltimore," which ends the finished collection with Simple securing his divorce from Isabel. That episode did not appear in the *Defender* until Hughes was busily engaged in revising for the editors at Simon and Schuster.

Besides creating entire new episodes to advance the story line regarding Simple and his marital status, Hughes also added more description and more frequent appearances by particular characters to existing columns, thereby clarifying the characterization. For example, he added to "Conversation on the Corner" a few descriptions of Joyce. Simple appreciates not only that she is a working woman, but also that she is "decent. She won't come to see me." Simple also calls her the "one girl friend I respect." Zarita, on the other hand, "talks too loud—come near getting me put out of my room."[18] Hughes also reviewed his use of characters. For example, in "High Bed," he substitutes Aunt Lucy for a character he had called "Grandma." He never mentions Grandma in the other episodes, but he uses Aunt Lucy in "Last Whipping." The substitution contributes to greater continuity.

Other revisions increase clarity and keep Simple in the domain of the ordinary Negro. For example, Hughes changed "from Atlanta to Athens" to "from Athens, Georgia, to Athens, Greece," while describing the rocket trip Simple planned while he was in his "High Bed." Otherwise, the drive from Atlanta, Georgia, to Athens, Georgia—a distance of only sixty miles—might have been envisioned when Simple spoke of traveling from Atlanta to Athens. Thus, the revision clearly indicates an international journey.

From his hospital bed, Simple requested that his friends bring food and spirits to compensate for the regular hospital fare. In the earlier draft of "High Bed," Simple was in a private room at the hospital. The editors suggested that a ward would be more appropriate than a

---

18. Handwritten additions to typescripts in Hughes MSS #3532-1, Folder 8, JWJ. Hughes notes, also by hand, that these revisions are from August 22 to 27, 1949.

private room, so Hughes added a sentence about the sausage which Zarita had brought, but which Simple was not permitted to eat. "She [the nurse] said it would be a bad example for the rest of the patients in this ward."[19]

Simple needed other conveniences in the hospital, including a stocking cap. In the column, he did not explain to his audience the cosmetic aid they all recognized. "Even if I was dying I would comb my own head and better not nobody else touch it! But say, boy, if you want to do me a favor, bring me a stocking cap when you come back. That is one thing these white folks do not have in this hospital. I wonder if it is against the rules to wear a stocking cap in this here high bed?" The wider audience—white readers in particular—would not understand why a man would want a stocking cap. As Hughes had discussed in a nonfiction editorial, "Those Little Things," something like a stocking cap revealed just how little whites really knew about blacks. Consequently, for the book Hughes permits Simple to explain exactly why he wants to wear a stocking cap on his head: "But say, boy, if you want to do me a favor, when you come back bring me a stocking-cap to make my hair lay down."[20] These changes helped to create the kind of character who could remain authentically black, but who could be understood universally.

As Appendix B shows, several episodes were drawn from two or more columns or from bits of columns. In "Ways and Means," for example, Hughes combined attitudes and lines from four different columns. He borrowed some ideas from "Letter to White Shopkeepers" (August 14, 1943) and "Suggestions to White Shopkeepers" (August 21, 1943), but basically he merged "Simple Looks for Justice" (August 28, 1943), which had told Simple's version of the story of the Harlem Riot of 1943, with "Simple and the NAACP" (June 16, 1945), in which the bar buddy praised Simple for joining the NAACP. The foil seemed confident that Simple could vent future frustrations through the more intellectual methods of the civil rights organization. By combining Simple's firsthand account of the riot with his enthusiastic

19. Hughes MSS #3532–2, Folder 9, JWJ.
20. "High Bed" column, December 9, 1944; "Those Little Things," July 24, 1948; "High Bed" as published, *Best,* 55.

response to joining the NAACP, Hughes allows Simple to persuade his brethren. The foil only needs to endorse the decision Simple has already made.

Tracing all the additions and revisions that gave Simple his personal history would be tedious. We can, however, examine one of the stories Hughes wrote specifically for the book. "Blue Evening" offers a convenient summary of Hughes's responses to the editorial suggestions offered by Simon and Schuster.

After carefully reviewing his earlier columns, and after thoughtfully considering the editorial suggestions, Hughes wrote a few Simple tales specifically for publication in the book-length volume. "Blue Evening," originally named "Where the Blues Come From," was written for the July–August 1949 draft. It contributed to the flow of stories before and after it by enhancing the plotline regarding Joyce and by clarifying the narrator's role.

Hughes had already inserted descriptive lines in previous episodes to indicate that Joyce was a hardworking, moral woman. Simple says he loves and respects Joyce, yet we see him continue to drink with Zarita in the bar and associate with her in other situations. Consequently, readers could easily doubt the sincerity of Simple's professions of love for Joyce. "Blue Evening" removes all doubt. In this episode we learn of Joyce's admirable gentility in the face of what she sees as devastating evidence of Simple's infidelity:

> "She did not say a word. She just turned her head away and looked like tears was aching to come to her eyes.
> "I says, 'Joyce, baby, listen,' I says, 'I want a word with you.'
> "She said, 'I come around here to bring you your yellow rayon-silk shirt I ironed special for you for Sunday. Since your landlady said you was at home, she told me to bring it on upstairs myself. Here it is. I did not know you had company.' "

Joyce even apologizes for standing in the way of the fellow returning with the beer Zarita had ordered. Simple follows her as she leaves, thereby seeing clearly that the landlady has instigated this trouble.

> "When I got to the bottom of the steps, my landlady was standing like a marble statue.
> "Landlady says, 'No decent woman approves of this.' Which is when Joyce started crying.

"Boy! My heart was broke because I hates to be misunderstood. I said, 'Joyce, I did not invite them parties here.'

"Joyce says, 'You don't need to explain to me, Jess Semple,' getting all formal and everything. She says, 'Now I have seen that woman with my own eyes in *your* bedroom with her stuff spread out every which-a-where just like she was home. And people I know from their looks could not be *your* friends because I never met any of them before—so they must be hers. Maybe Zarita lives with you. No wonder you giving a birthday party to which I am not invited. Good night, I am gone out of your life from now on. Enjoy yourself. Good night!'

"If she had fussed and raised her voice, I would not have felt so bad. But the sweet way she said, 'Enjoy yourself,' all ladylike and sad and quiet, as if she was left out of things, cut me to my soul. Joyce ought to know I would not leave her out of nothing."

Hughes has offered a detailed exchange which clearly reveals the very deep emotional attachment Joyce and Simple feel for each other. We have seen that she has ironed a shirt especially for Simple to wear on Sunday. Otherwise, she would not have visited his room. She was hurt by seeing Zarita making herself at home in Simple's room, even to the extent of hosting a birthday party—to which Joyce had clearly not been invited.

The reader can completely sympathize with Simple. Unlike other episodes when he seems to exaggerate his many woes, "Blue Evening" describes a plausible coincidence—with the landlady helping to create a part of the trouble. We clearly see how pushy Zarita is. We also see how conniving the landlady can be. Most importantly, we see how poised Joyce is, even under pressure.

While he finds this situation painful to recall, Simple needs a friend. He trusts his bar buddy to support him at a crucial time like this. The draft of "Blue Evening" sent to Leiper on August 9, 1949, had already been revised several times, especially the beginning and ending. A brief examination of those stages of revision will shed some light on the kind of relationship Hughes wanted to establish between Simple and the foil, since this interaction prompted so much revision.

The opening lines of "Blue Evening" were written at least three ways before Hughes arrived at the language and setting he sought.[21]

21. Hughes MSS #3532-2, Folder 9.

The first draft was straightforward. It began, as did many other Simple stories, with a statement from Simple:

> "I never thought it would happen to me," said my bar buddy.
> "What?" I asked.
> "That a woman would put me down."

But Hughes wanted something more for this crucial story. The second draft preceded Simple's initial remark with a description from the foil:

> I could tell something was wrong the minute I walked in and saw him on the corner stool alone.
> "I never thought . . ."

This revision offers a visual image of Simple, along with the foil's subjective interpretation of the image. Just by seeing Simple *alone* on the corner stool, the foil knows that Simple is troubled in body or spirit.

This change enhances character development because it reminds readers that these two men have met and have talked many times in the bar. They have established a normal pattern, and they have shared both happy and sad times. Another revision extends this level of interaction between them. The assumptions to which the foil jumps are spoken to Simple:

> The minute I walked in and saw him on the corner stool alone, I could tell something was wrong.
> "Another hang-over?" I asked.
> "Nothing so simple," said my bar buddy soberly. "This is something I thought would never happen to me."
> "What?" I asked.
> "That a woman . . ."

The opening line is arranged to give the reader a glimpse of Simple before the foil interprets the vision as meaning something is wrong. The nature of the relationship between Simple and the foil was such that it tolerated some kidding, even some outright criticism of shortcomings. This aspect of the relationship is illustrated with the question about the hangover. The foil has already announced that he knows something is wrong with Simple, but his question briefly sidetracks the reader into believing the problem is a mere hangover.

One may conclude that the foil has seen Simple quietly sitting alone in the bar on some other occasion when the problem was just the consequence of overindulgence in beer (or something stronger). In addition, the effect of the description is enhanced by the question, because the reader can now add to a mental image of Simple alone on the corner stool the image of a man with a hangover.

In the final version published in *Simple Speaks His Mind* little is rewritten. Instead, several words are omitted:

> When I walked into the bar and saw him on the corner stool alone, I could tell something was wrong.
> "Another hang-over?"
> "Nothing that simple. This is something I thought never would happen to me."
> "What?" I asked.
> "That a woman could put *me* down. . . . "

The changes are in the interest of economy of language this time. The end product is clear, concise, and effective. The reference to sobriety is omitted in Simple's reply, but is later stated more clearly when Simple refuses the foil's offer of a drink, saying, "I feel too bad." The foil's reply is to Simple, but it also alerts the reader to the significance of the narration Simple is about to deliver: "Then it *is* serious."

The introductory lines now convey a vivid image of these two men, about to share what is obviously an unpleasant and deeply disturbing story, one ultimately revealing the break-up of Simple and a woman. The beginning of the story does not directly state that the woman is Joyce. After several trials, then, Hughes had arrived at an opening that satisfactorily portrayed the situation.

Whereas the incidents constituting the main action of the story did not trouble Hughes, the ending, like the beginning, required several drafts to satisfy him. A few of the changes related to the overall coherence of the lines spoken by Simple, but the more noteworthy adjustments affected the relationship between Simple and the foil. The first version of the ending contains the ingredients of the final draft, but it is not crafted as smoothly:

> "Since she lives on the third floor, you can hardly play Romeo and climb up. And I don't believe Joyce would like her name called aloud in the street," I said.

"I will have to call it," said Simple, "if she don't let me speak through the door. I can always explain that by saying that I have lost my mind, that she has driv me crazy. And I will stand in front of her house all night."

"The law would probably remove you," I said.

"They would have to use force to do it," said Simple. "I would not care if the polices broke my head. Joyce has done broke my heart."

"You've got it bad," I said.

"Worse than bad," said Simple. "Here, take this quarter and buy yourself a beer whilst you waits till I come back."

"Remember, I can't wait all night," I said.

"Then go home," said Simple.

This first draft of the ending lacks intensity and contains a few rough edges in sentence structure. "And I will stand in front of her house all night" fails to convey Simple's meaning adequately. His goal is to see Joyce, not merely to appear on her doorstep all night. A little later when Simple says, "I would not care if the polices broke my head. Joyce has done broke my heart," the phrasing communicates, but it lacks a smooth transition from head to heart. Both these problems are somewhat ameliorated in the next draft, but the final exchange between Simple and the foil required several drafts. The second draft of these closing lines improves very little:

"I will have to call her," said Simple, "if she don't let me through the door. I can always explain it by saying that I have lost my mind, that she has driv me crazy. And I will stand in front of her house all night if she don't answer."

"The law would probably remove you," I said.

"They would have to use force to do it," said Simple. "I wouldn't care if the polices broke my head tonight, anyhow, since Joyce has done broke my heart."

"You've got it bad," I said.

"Worse than bad," moaned Simple. "Here, take this quarter and buy yourself a beer whilst you wait till I come back."

"I can't wait all night," I said.

"Then go to hell," said Simple.

Simple's urgent desire to see Joyce is more clearly communicated, and the connection between his head and his heart is coherent. Despite these improvements, however, the final exchange has been made worse. The foil's line has not been improved, and Simple's closing line is profane and desperate—a bit abrupt and completely heedless of the friendship that these two men have valued. Let us examine subsequent revisions of these final lines.

The third draft preserves the quality of the relationship between the two men, and it simultaneously clarifies the intensity of the moment for Simple:

> "I have my own affairs to attend to," I said, "so I can't wait all night."
> "Then don't," said Simple. "Don't. If you can't even watch with me one hour, then don't."

The foil's diction has been elevated, more in keeping with the characterization Hughes was enhancing for the book. Simple's response has been lengthened and tamed. His words are childlike in their piercing accusation. "If you can't even watch with me one hour" apparently alludes to Jesus Christ's disappointment with his disciples in Gethsemane when they could not "watch with me one hour" (Matthew 26:40). Such an allusion would amplify the profound sorrow and heaviness Simple felt. But Hughes remained dissatisfied. Childlike words were not quite the finishing touch for this moment when Simple has been deeply wounded—first by Joyce and then by his bar buddy. Hughes made changes. The fourth draft combines the accusation from the third version with the anger from the second draft:

> "I have my own affairs to attend to," I said, "so I can't wait all night."
> "I thought you was my ace-boy," said Simple, "But everybody lets you down when troubles come. If you can't even watch with me one hour, then don't. To hell with you! Don't!"

Here we have a reply from Simple that conveys both the anger and the profound disappointment he experiences when his friend fails to appreciate his need for unrestricted moral support. Nevertheless, the allusion to Christ may have been too powerful, too sacred for a scene in a bar.

Subsequent drafts came in other sittings. The fifth and sixth drafts are dated November 2 and 4, 1949. Draft number five contains one typewritten revision and two handwritten ones:

> "I thought you was my ace-boy. But everybody lets you down when trouble comes. If you can't wait, then don't. To hell with you! Don't!"
>
> [By hand] He left a whole glass of beer on the bar when he walked. [crossed out]
>
> [By hand] I started to say I would wait. But Simple had gone.

Hughes has changed *troubles* to the singular form and has dropped the specific reference to one hour as the time the foil needs to wait, as well as the biblical wording "watch with me." His first handwritten addition would have contradicted his earlier—and significant—revelation that Simple felt too bad to drink. Simple had declined a drink, so he should not have had a whole beer to leave behind. The second addition adds the warmth and the human frailty of a true friendship. The foil wants to retract his earlier remark about having affairs to which to attend, but Simple is not present to hear these kinder words.

The final draft, as it appears in the book, shows how thoroughly Hughes examined even the subtle nuances of the words in this exchange:

> "I have some affairs of my own to attend to," I protested, "so I can't wait all night."
>
> "I thought you was my ace-boy," he said and he turned away. "But everybody lets you down when trouble comes. If you can't wait, then don't. To hell with you! Don't!"
>
> I started to say I would wait. But Simple was gone.

Although few and subtle, the changes in the final draft enhance the dramatic quality of the scene. The foil *protested* that he could not wait all night. This verb conveys more of the foil's inability to replace his own responsibilities with his friend's needs. It also carries with it the connotations appropriate for the type of Negro the foil characterizes: one who protests. Some readers may even think of a line from Shakespeare: "Methinks the lady doth protest too much," bringing to mind the indecision and betrayal in *Hamlet*. Whether Hughes intended to pack so much into the verb or not, he certainly improved the scene by replacing the mundane *said* with the more specific *protested*.

A second change, also small but powerful, is the descriptive phrase inserted into Simple's last line: " 'I thought you was my ace-boy,' *he said as he turned away."* Thus, the last few lines are spoken by Simple as he walks away from the foil. They may have been muttered under his breath, or they may have been shouted, but they were not spoken to the friend's face. Hughes has significantly intensified the drama and the emotion in this scene by having the abrasive "To hell with you!" spoken *away* from the friend, rather than toward him. Simple is hurt. He has lost his girlfriend, and he does not even have the faithful support of his alleged friend.

More logically now, the reader can understand why Simple was not available to hear his buddy's change of heart—that he would wait. After all, Simple had turned away and presumably had begun to walk off immediately after hearing the bar buddy protest that he could not wait for Simple all night. Yet, Hughes adds one last change: "I started to say I would wait. But Simple *was* gone." The verb no longer assists action ("Simple *had* gone"); it conveys state of being, or in this case, state of absence. Simple was not just leaving, nor is the foil responding to the act of his leaving. Simple was gone. The bar stool was empty. The ears to hear "I can wait" were gone. The scene in its final version ends very poignantly and powerfully.

The net result of these many insertions, changes, and revisions is that by late 1949, when Hughes put the finishing touches on his manuscript, he was crafting fiction. He was no longer merely meeting weekly deadlines or amusing the readers of the *Chicago Defender.* He was no longer assembling previously typed episodes. Now he was presenting to the general American audience—and to posterity—an average black man in Harlem. He wanted to write honestly so that the activities and emotions of this average man would become universal. The critical and popular responses to the Simple stories suggest that Hughes accomplished his goal.

6

Simple Takes a Wife— and Broadway

SALES FOR *Simple Speaks His Mind* delighted both Langston Hughes and his publisher, Simon and Schuster. Early reports on the publication date, April 14, 1950, showed sales of more than 8,000 paper copies (at one dollar each) and 4,000 cloth (at three dollars each). His editor, Maria Leiper, wrote to Hughes monthly, offering the newest figures along with the required cautionary note about possible returns later on. By October 18, Leiper reported sales totals of 14,875 paper copies and 4,515 cloth copies. As the publication anniversary approached, she informed Hughes, "Stock on the paper *Simple* is dwindling, so we're going to press with a new edition of 5000."[1]

Ever cognizant of the need for an affordable edition for his loyal but financially strapped readers, Hughes asked Simon and Schuster about the possibility of a twenty-five-cent reprint. His editor replied that the company always held off for more than a year before making serious attempts at such sales. More important than the calendar year, however, were current sales. Leiper noted that "with *Simple* we'd wait until sales of the dollar edition had pretty well stopped. I am happy to say that is not yet the case."[2]

The second edition of *Simple Speaks His Mind* was off the press by early May 1951. In November of that year, Leiper commented on the financial figures for Hughes: "I see that all those books you have ordered lately have outbalanced your royalty account—but then, on the $554.04 worth you've bought you have, I hope, realized a tidy profit. *And,* this is almost the only royalty statement I've seen, this season,

---

1. Maria Leiper to LH, March 30, 1951.
2. Leiper to LH, April 12, 1951.

in which there isn't a red figure up near the top somewhere, marked, 'Returns from booksellers.' So congratulations."[3] Many of the books that Hughes ordered he sold in his various speaking engagements. Thus, sometimes through his lecture tours, but certainly in bookstore sales, *Simple Speaks His Mind* compiled a splendid sales record.

The success was attributable in part to advertisements and in other areas to Hughes's own clever tactics. Simon and Schuster ran an ad in the *New York Times* on publication day, April 14, 1950. A week later, at a Simon and Schuster party to celebrate the publication, Hughes proclaimed the value of the book. Leiper wrote to him that she was pleased by his remarks, "particularly what you said about Simple and democracy, and how you hoped your book might lessen that awful gulf that extends through our society." Hughes appeared on television in early May, and Sam Herbert, a New York salesman for Simon and Schuster, told Leiper that Hughes had been "terrific."[4]

Some of the sales tactics were quite innovative. On May 17, Leiper sent a review copy to the *American Journal of Psychiatry,* calling the book "a study of an urban Negro and his daily problems." She went on to inform the review department, "We have been told that psychiatric students and case-workers find the book useful as a guide to the basic causes of many disturbances in Negro patients. We hope you may consider it of interest to your readers." Hughes wrote to Leiper in early August, reminding her that since schools would soon re-open, perhaps the book could be recommended to teachers and librarians on the strength of "Simple's educational, sociological, and literary virtues, and how every human seeking to understand color in our democracy ought to read it—or at least list it for students to read. Marking it 'Easy Study' or 'Laugh While You Learn.' "

Hughes joyfully received news of how his Simple Minded Friend was finding his way into sophisticated academic situations. His friend Arna Bontemps wrote to him:

> You would have liked Ira [De A.] Reid's address to the Fisk students last Thursday. He called it "Mr. Dooley, Mr. Kaplan and Mr. Simple." Shrewdly and most amusingly he showed how each of these fictional

---

3. Leiper to LH, November 15, 1951.
4. Leiper to LH, April 21, 1950; Leiper to LH, quoting Herbert, May 8, 1950.

characters exemplified something very significant in American culture and popular philosophy. He read many quotes, and the students bubbled throughout. He told me afterwards that he was headed for the University of Minnesota where he planned to deliver the same address and that he would continue to use it throughout the year in his popular appearances. A lot of copies of *Simple* could be sold if there were a way to make a tie-in. I have urged Ira to write it up for one of the scholarly journals, and I got the impression that that was in the back of his head.[5]

Having enjoyed a congenial relationship with Reid since the 1930s, Hughes was gratified to see how this respected sociologist was explaining Simple and taking the character to various college campuses. He wrote to Reid at Haverford College, sending him excerpts from reviews of *Simple Speaks His Mind.* In his May 21, 1951, reply, Reid affirmed what Bontemps had told Hughes about the Fisk convocation and went on to thank Hughes for writing a book that permitted such useful discussions across cultural boundaries.

Reid was not the only person bringing Simple into dignified settings. Hughes wrote to Leiper on April 9, 1951, informing her that "New York's Judge Hubert Delaney has been reading the whole chapter of *Simple,* 'When a Man Sees Red,' to his audiences in recent talks in the New York area." Moreover, *Simple Speaks His Mind* had been issued in a British edition by the publisher Gollancz and had received quite a good critical response. Hughes's agent, Maxim Lieber, reported to him that a dramatization of two chapters from the book was performed over BBC from London. The sales records, the interesting uses of Simple for rather sophisticated audiences, and the book's success in England inspired Hughes to expand the terrain. He raised the possibility with his editor:

> Do you think the time is ripe yet to perhaps consider a second *Simple* book? The next one, I think, although still told in the first person and largely conversational, should really be a novel in overall form, telling more of a connected story than before, and leading up to and possibly through a portion of his marriage to Joyce. And perhaps dealing a little less with purely racial situations. As a novel, I think, it would have better sales possibilities.

5. Bontemps to LH, April 2, 1951, LH correspondence, Bontemps file, JWJ.

Hughes admitted that he had already begun slanting his recent columns for the *Defender* toward "a more consecutive story-wise mold." Although he intended to retain relatively short chapters, he hoped to show more coherent transitions from one episode to the next. He knew that the short episodes were successful, having been informed by many New Yorkers that "one of the things they like about the current book is that you can read a chapter or two on the subway on the way to work and not lose your place when you take it up again." Another woman had considered the short chapters an advantage at bedtime, "the chapters being just the right length to read one or two before going to sleep." Hughes added parenthetically to that quotation, "(Which might be a good point for an ad some time.)"

Insisting that he would review the hundred or so columns he had written since the book was published, intending to "weave them into a real story this time with a stronger 'story line' (as Hollywood says) than before," Hughes offered to send Leiper a draft of this second book of Simple episodes. He planned to narrate this more coherent story "primarily in conversation, as formerly, between two friends, only I think with longer narrative sequences here and there from Simple."[6]

His cordial editor at Simon and Schuster did not leap at the offer to issue a sequel to *Simple Speaks His Mind,* but cautioned him in her April 12 reply, "You know how it is, usually, with sequels: for some reason, they're rarely as successful as a first book." However, she liked Hughes's idea of a collection that was more like a novel, so she agreed to take a look at the manuscript when Hughes had compiled it. "Besides, Simple as a character has a real following," she added.

By April 18, 1951, Hughes had the draft assembled. He knew before he mailed it to his agent for delivery to Leiper that it would need revision. He also told Leiper in the cover letter that this second book, which he called *Simply Heavenly,* was *not* a sequel. He expected it to be "a book to stand on its own and to understand it readers need not have read the first book." Hughes suggested to Leiper that, to verify this independent clarity, she give the manuscript to someone who had never read *Simple Speaks His Mind,* someone who could "come to this one fresh, and see how it stands up." Hughes also projected

6. LH to Leiper, April 9, 1951.

even further down the publication road: "And about 1955 we can do the third volume—about Simple and Joyce married and how they raise their kids. Then we'd have a trilogy, *The Saga of Simple.* (I have always wanted to have a Trilogy—it sounds so sort of extensive!!!)" Finally Hughes called Leiper's attention to certain details of the new manuscript:

> You will notice I have put in scarcely a single ! in the new manuscript. Your influence! And nobody *yells* much—even though conversation must now be conducted above television, which creates more racket than juke-boxes. This will probably be the last "conversational" novel, since it is rapidly being drowned out by mechanicals. MacArthur can be heard all over the house today arriving in San Francisco—and in summer I can hardly hear the home folks for the Dodgers coming over the air. The baseball season would be really hard on a "sensitive" author who demanded quiet to work. As the years go on, and more T-V's are installed, Simple will probably have to *yell* the rest of his story. I hope not.[7]

Leiper should have enjoyed a hearty laugh about Hughes's editorial changes. In any case, when Lieber finally delivered the manuscript to her, she was delighted with what she read in the new draft of the Simple stories.

> I was as happy to find Simple again, in *Simply Heavenly,* as I was at the age of eleven to discover Athos (always my favorite of the Three Musketeers) in Dumas' various sequels—*Twenty Years After, Ten Years Later, Louise De Lavalliere, The Death of Porthos, The Vicomte De Bragelonne,* and all the others. Your hero is as charming as ever, and as revealing to his readers of all kinds of facets of life.

In spite of her personal pleasure, she recognized the possible pitfalls of this book. Not only did sequels typically fare worse than first books, but her company was experiencing what she called "the worst doldrums the book business has experienced in a very long time." Those reservations aside, however, she gushed enthusiastically about her personal joy regarding the book. She then said she had sent "the new manuscript, with my blessing, and a number of reports from

7. LH to Leiper, April 18, 1951.

members of the editorial staff, to Mr. Richard Simon—who was, you may remember, one of the enthusiasts when the first Simple book came to us." Having dispatched the book, she said she hoped for the best, because the decision to publish was out of her hands.[8]

With a decision on the second collection of Simple stories still pending, Hughes continued to relay to his publishers any encouraging comments. He shared with Leiper a note from W. H. Wortham, "an uptown real estate man (member of my draft board when I was up for induction)," who encouraged the extension of the Simple tales. Hughes quoted from Wortham:

> "Over and over again we should be able to look forward to new obser-
> vations by Simple annually, to the delight of Americans everywhere. You
> really ought to be able to follow this volume up with many more and I
> think you will be able to do so. Syndicated it could go over delightfully
> and whimsically in white papers, much to the spread of tolerance.
> Whites cannot read Simple without becoming more tolerant."[9]

While another decade would pass before Simple became a regular feature in the "white" press, Hughes and Leiper were encouraged by Wortham's confident predictions.

The draft of the second collection, which Hughes was calling *Simply Heavenly,* overcame the obstacles of the sequel and of the financial doldrums in the publishing industry. By October 15, 1952, Leiper was trying to help Hughes find a more appropriate title for this volume. Tracking Hughes down on tour, and writing to him in care of Margaret Walker Alexander at Jackson State College in Jackson, Mississippi, Leiper offered a viable suggestion:

> You told me, I think (I haven't yet peeked at the end), that Simple and
> Joyce are finally married in this book. Tell me, how does the following
> strike you: *Simple Takes a Wife.* It has the same rhythm as *Simple
> Speaks His Mind,* yet it isn't likely to be confused with the first Simple
> book. Well, let me know honestly what you think of it. I haven't tried it
> out on anyone around here; but no one, I'm afraid, is too enthusiastic
> about the present working title of the script, *Simply Heavenly.* For

8. Leiper to LH, June 6, 1951.
9. Quoted in LH to Leiper, June 11, 1951.

one thing, it doesn't suggest your character, Simple—at least, to us it doesn't.

History proves that Leiper's title indeed gained acceptance. On January 15, 1953, Hughes proudly notified his friends, including prospective Simple critic Arthur P. Davis, that the second collection of Simple stories was more of a continuous story, with more information about Simple's love life. Hughes intended this second collection to read like a novel, largely because he expected a novel to sell better than a collection of vignettes. Indeed, Leiper praised *Simple Takes a Wife* for its coherent flow: "I particularly like the smooth way you have one chapter leading into another. I know, this is nothing new, it was in the script before; but I've just gone over it again, you know, and enjoyed your technical skill in this maneuver."[10] Hughes modestly attributed much of his success in revision to his editor:

> With such thoughtful, helpful, and sympathetic assistance editorially as you give an author, a book is *bound* to come out better. There's no way for it not to. I wish I could publish with you the rest of my writing life. My other publishers have all simply said *Yes* or *No* to a script, and let it go. No help at all! So I really and deeply appreciate the interest you've taken with my two *Simple* books. And I agree with you that in the end it is the little tiny changes that may make a world of difference in the over-all effect of a manuscript. Which is one reason all my prose has at least four or five drafts, and I generally wish there were time for more. Thanks![11]

Hughes and Leiper praised each other profusely—and sincerely—throughout the years of their interaction.

As Simon and Schuster prepared to publish *Simple Takes a Wife*, Hughes celebrated the affordable cost of the book: "The price [$1.95] tickles me, and that is paramount."[12] Having informed his friends about the upcoming second volume of Simple stories, Hughes began to receive congratulations. He felt particularly encouraged by a comment from Arthur P. Davis, the distinguished professor of English who had volunteered to write a critical piece on Simple. Davis wrote,

10. Leiper to LH, January 21, 1953.
11. LH to Leiper, January 22, 1953.
12. LH to Leiper, January 30, 1953.

"I am glad you are bringing out another Simple. In my estimation, *Simple Speaks His Mind* is a fine book—one of the most revealing studies of the Negro to be found anywhere. I have read it twice and have long toyed with the idea of doing a paper on it. Maybe I'll wait now and compare the old and new Simples."[13] Davis's line about *Simple Speaks His Mind* being "one of the most revealing studies of the Negro to be found anywhere" went into Hughes's file of "Comments on 'Simple'" that he copied and sent to Simon and Schuster on February 21, 1953.

Simple Takes a Wife is unique for several reasons. Already noted is the strong sense of coherence in the transition from one episode to the next. Another change is that a strong and important minor character from Simple's family enters the scene: his young cousin F. D. In addition, women gain a more visible and more well-rounded presentation. For example, Simple speaks sensitively about his first girlfriend, Mabel, an older woman who cared deeply about him, and he speaks vituperatively about a flashy young glamour-girl named Cherie. Even the landlady gains the floor long enough to tell a bit about her life. This new emphasis on women, coupled with Simple's fatherly nurturing of young F. D., gives the second Simple book a far more domestic flavor than the first displayed. Much of this collection found its way into *The Best of Simple,* which has remained in print since its appearance in 1961. However, the episodes left out of *The Best of Simple* include several revealing portrayals—particularly those of women—which gave *Simple Takes a Wife* its unique tone. Overall, the depth of character development makes *Simple Takes a Wife* superior to *Simple Speaks His Mind.*

While the coherent flow of episodes did not qualify *Simple Takes a Wife* to be called a novel, it certainly gave the book a pleasant continuity. Excerpted episodes from this volume often depend upon prior or subsequent episodes to reveal their full meaning. For example, "Better than a Pillow" begins with Simple saying, "After that man's dying I got to thinking about myself—suppose I was to die upstairs all alone *by myself* in a lonesome room!" (*Wife,* 17). The reader obviously would wonder, "After *what* man's dying?" This question would not occur to a reader who had just completed the previous episode,

13. Arthur P. Davis to LH, January 29, 1953.

"Empty Room," which describes the death of a roomer in Baltimore.[14] Similarly, "Explain That to Me" begins, " 'I love to be woke up easy,' continued Simple. 'Maybe that is what I liked about Mabel' " (*Return,* 17). The verb *continued* obviously points to a previous discussion, and unless the reader had consumed "Better than a Pillow," she would not recognize Mabel. Many of the episodes display this continuity. The collection is a pleasant and memorable read.

While the sense of continuity is lost upon readers who have not read *Simple Takes a Wife* from beginning to end, the notable character Franklin D. Roosevelt Brown, or "F. D.," is transferred nearly whole from *Simple Takes a Wife* to *The Best of Simple*. This cousin with the "damn-yankee name" was mentioned briefly in *Simple Speaks His Mind,*[15] but his personality is fully revealed in *Simple Takes a Wife*. F. D. enters the scene when he surprises Simple by being in his room one night when he comes home. The landlady permits F. D. to await his cousin's return, and once Simple overcomes his shock and adrenalin, he welcomes his young cousin to Harlem, where he will be Harlemite number "one million and one." F. D. proves vital to the creation of a well-rounded picture of African Americans in Harlem. He is young and idealistic, and he packs energy and industry behind his dreams. On his first day in Harlem, he runs along with an employed fellow to the garment district and gets himself a job. He embarrasses Simple by asking for books to read; Simple discovers that he can only offer comic books and must borrow books instead of beer money from his friend in the bar. F. D. meets and courts an intelligent, attractive, and ambitious girl, and—due to her influence—they both go to college.

The college enrollment episode was not included in *The Best of Simple*. In fact, it resulted from an earlier request from Mozell C. Hill, editor of *Phylon*. Hoping that Hughes could contribute "a special skit, piece, or poem for the special tenth anniversary issue of *Phylon*," Hill noted that the theme of the issue would be "Higher Education Among Negroes: Problems and Trends." As with the special Victory

14. As the episode appears in *Return,* 11, where it does not follow "Empty Room," the editor has created a bridge summarizing the Baltimore roomer's death so that the reader will not wonder after *what* man's dying. "Empty Room" is in *Best,* 103–6.

15. "Confused," *Mind,* 174.

Edition of the *Chicago Defender*, Hill hoped to include in this issue
of *Phylon* articles from "some of the really bigwigs, like Charles S.
Johnson, Franklin Frazier, Rufus Clement, et al., to discuss some of the
more controversial issues in the area of higher education." Hill hoped
that Hughes "could do something that would be not so serious yet
calculated to probe subtly into some of the underlying problems and
situations around higher education."[16] The resulting article, "Simple
Discusses Colleges and Color," features Simple in a discussion of his
cousin Delbert. Hughes selected a "preppy" name for the cousin who
aspires toward college. For *Simple Takes a Wife* Hughes replaces
Delbert, who is never again discussed, with his industrious cousin
F. D. Due to the influence of his college-bound girlfriend, Gloria,
F. D. has decided to apply for admission to college. He shares his
news in this episode.

"Colleges and Color" raises an issue still being discussed in the
1990s: the relative merits of historically black colleges and universities
and of predominantly white institutions. Simple and the foil discuss
the social advantages of HBCUs. However, true to his character, the
foil emphasizes academics, while Simple sees a broader picture. The
foil asserts, " 'At a colored college he can be among his own race and
have a well-rounded social life. Still, I insist, you don't go to college
to dance. You go to get educated.' " Simple begs to differ. " 'If I was
going to college,' said Simple, 'I might not get educated—but I would
come out with a educated wife.' " Simple and the foil agree that social
life would be far more congenial in an HBCU. However, without citing
Up from Slavery or Booker T. Washington, Simple supports one of
the arguments in that book. Simple insists that "mere book learning"
is not all a fellow ought to get from college, and he disagrees with the
foil's conclusion that "the prime purpose of college is education":

> "Do you mean book-learning?" asked Simple.
>
> "Approximately that."
>
> "Then you are approximately wrong," said Simple. "I do not care
> what you know out of a book, you also have to know a lots out of life.
> Life is hard for a colored boy in the manhood stage to learn from white
> folks. If F. D. does learn it around white folks, he is going to learn it
> the hard way. That might make him mad, or else sad. If he gets mad, he

16. Mozell C. Hill to LH, October 4, 1949.

is going to be bad. If he's sad, he is going to just give up and not get nowheres. . . . Facts is, I cares more about F. D.'s heart, anyhow, than I do his head."

Again, never citing Washington's *Up from Slavery,* Simple has invoked two of its three important elements: heart and head. He omits hand. Of course, by finding himself a job in the garment district and by displaying excellence in several sports, F. D. has already shown his ability to develop that aspect of himself.

Simple raises a point against which the foil cannot argue; indeed, learning life the hard way can lead to the anger or depression that has characterized some African American writers, their protagonists, and ordinary people at various stages of our history. The foil, however, does not give up:

> "You imply that there is no fun to be had around white folks."
> "I never had none," said Simple.
> "You have a color complex."
> "A colored complexion," said Simple.
> "I said *complex,* not complexion."
> "I added the *shun* myself," said Simple. "I'm colored, and being around white folks makes me feel *more* colored—since most of them shun Negroes. F. D. is not white. He's not even light, so F. D. would show up very dark in a white college."
> "That would make him outstanding," I said.
> "*Standing out—all by himself,* you mean," said Simple, "and that is just where the 'shun' comes in."
> "You are confusing the issue," I said.
> "I had rather confuse the issue than confuse F. D.," said Simple.

This scene contains the clever play on words that marks the Simple stories at their best, combined with the irrefutable logic that Simple often uses to embarrass the patriotic know-it-alls who spout flimsy platitudes. Simple's wisdom evidently prevails with F. D., since we learn in "Psychologies" that F. D. goes to Lincoln University in Pennsylvania. Simple's wisdom also prevailed with some distinguished readers. Arna Bontemps wrote to Hughes that literary critic Blyden Jackson had given the keynote address for the Fisk University Athletic Banquet, at which football players, basketball players, track team members, and tennis players received awards and new team captains were named. "And what do you think he talked about? *Simple Takes A Wife*. Reviewed the book. Read passages, including the one about sending the nephew to college. Well received. Which, CSJ [Charles S. Johnson] said in follow-up, was a compliment to the Fisk athletes."[17]

Since Lincoln was at that time all male, F. D. would not be attending college with Gloria, who had encouraged him to partake of higher education. Nevertheless, her positive influence is clearly painted in *Simple Takes a Wife*. This volume, in fact, offers broader and more sensitive, honest, and positive images of the women in Simple's life than do any of the other volumes. In these portrayals we see that Simple deeply appreciates the genuine, abiding, sensitive love he has received from some women, and he responds to those women by striving to accomplish his personal best. In contrast, Simple recognizes deceit, exploitation, and disrespect exhibited toward him by other women. He responds to those women with callousness, hostility, and insult. Despite his assertions, Simple categorizes women, but he does not stereotype them. He distinguishes individuals within the categories. Moreover, he recognizes and praises the benefits of support and encouragement from loving women.

"Better than a Pillow," "Explain That to Me," "Baltimore Womens," and "Less than a Damn," four consecutive, smoothly coherent episodes in the second Simple volume, present the clearest available picture of Jesse B. Semple as a young man who made fairly typical mistakes regarding women, and then as a mature man who must live with the consequences of his youthful errors. We meet and appreciate the impact of Mabel and Cherie, two characters whose appearances in *The Best of Simple* are less detailed than in *Simple Takes a Wife*. By presenting the doting Mabel and the flighty Cherie, and by revealing more details about Simple's first wife, Isabel, Hughes helps readers understand why Simple's Virginia childhood led him to his Baltimore mistakes with women.

Simple Speaks His Mind had offered readers a brief introduction to Simple's childhood. His "passed around" existence, his isolation as one who lacked any of the exceptional features that would make

17. Bontemps to LH, no date (ca. May 1953), yellow slip, LH correspondence, Bontemps file, JWJ. "Colleges and Color" is collected in *Return*, 148-51.

him well liked, and his moving recollection of Aunt Lucy's influential "Last Whipping" are all recorded in that first volume. Aunt Lucy's pivotal disciplinary and *caring* whipping—plus her tears—left Simple determined to live a good life. He hoped to remain a source of pride instead of anguish for Aunt Lucy.

However, Simple lacked the self-esteem to enter a fair romantic relationship. His "Feet Live Their Own Life" reveals, "When I did like somebody, I was full-grown and then I picked out the wrong woman because I had no practice in liking anybody before that" (*Best*, 2). Modern analysts and marriage counselors repeatedly indicate how the shortcomings of childhood haunt intimate relationships. Through his relationship with Mabel, Simple may have received the individualized attention he lacked during his childhood. Mabel was his first steady. "Also she was the first woman for which I ever kept a job. . . . I did not give her my money, yet for her sake I kept a job, respectable. Up to that time I had quit and rested any time I wanted to. She settled me down, in fact almost got me housebroke. She were a good influence in my life" ("Better than a Pillow," *Return*, 12).

Mabel was thirty-five when she began shacking up with the nineteen-year-old Jesse. She was a hardworking, church-going woman who had her own problems getting comfortable with a man. Yet, she defends her own right to have somebody special in her life—even if he is younger and even if their living arrangements fall outside the realm of church-approved situations. Her character thus provides a rare contradiction to the restrictive and stereotypical whore/Madonna dichotomy so prevalent in fiction—and in Simple's mind. Her church background would place her in the "good girl" category, but she defends the physical and emotional needs of a "good girl" to live with a man and to enjoy sex with him, without the benefit of marriage. Her character is presented sensibly and sensitively.

Despite her own defense of the "right" to have a man like Jesse, Mabel predicted from the beginning that the relationship was doomed to a short span; she believed the youthful Jesse would not long be content with a woman such as herself. Nevertheless, she cared for him and treated him like somebody special—even making Jesse his first pair of pajamas. Here again, her character is presented as being fully aware of the liabilities of the relationship. Jesse was not *using* Mabel. They both benefited from the relationship. Her gestures of kindness and nurture were offered from her own motivations, not because she had been tricked into envisioning a "happily ever after" future with her man.

By his own admission, Simple sought out this "good influence" by seeking a woman in Mabel's "category" to fill a vital need in his own life. His search began after a fellow roomer in his boarding house in Baltimore died very suddenly one night, leaving behind the hauntingly "empty room" mentioned above. That man's death forced Simple to recognize his own mortality. He began to plan for the way he wanted to die, and particularly he realized that he wanted to be appreciated and mourned. He especially wanted to be missed by one or more women. "Man, I hustled up quick on a stick-close gal before the year was out."[18] Mabel was the "stick-close gal" he found.

Mature Mabel enjoyed merely looking at Jesse, finding him "a good-looking black boy." Mabel filled some of the lonely and empty spaces left from Simple's overcrowded childhood, but she "didn't have what the boys call *class*" ("Explain That to Me," *Return,* 18). A young man, Simple liked Mabel and enjoyed her gentle voice and her soft presence for two years, but he disgraced even himself by leaving her for a young, glamorous playgirl who was worse than Zarita: Cherie.

"Cherie had class—and I paid to gaze upon it. The way the boys I worked with made admiration over her when we passed tickled me no end. She was a beautiful thing to have hanging around on your arm. Daddy-o, she *was* fine, and only eighteen. I was fascinated by that woman. I knowed she was nothing but a playgirl, like Zarita is now, but I didn't care. She was the first sure-enough glamour chick I ever had contact with and I felt like a solid ton." ("Explain That to Me," *Return,* 20)

Even though Simple knew that Mabel was good to him and that Cherie was "nothing but a playgirl," he abandoned Mabel for the gorgeous younger woman. Both Mabel and Jesse fell victim to the appealing looks of their love objects. Yet, both of them also entered these relationships aware of the liabilities.

18. "Better than a Pillow," *Return,* 11. One might also note the deathbed scene captured in Hughes's poem "Sylvester's Dying Bed," in which "All the womens in town / Was gathered round me" (*Selected Poems of Langston Hughes,* 38).

Mabel satisfied Simple's childhood yearning for personal attention. Unlike any of his guardians, except Aunt Lucy, Mabel made him feel important and valued. She worried about him getting enough sleep. She made sure he had good food to eat. In a word, she mothered him. However, she accommodated his needs so much that she failed to defend her own dignity and self-worth. Mabel tolerated Simple's late hours and his overnight absences rather than confronting him. Even when she realized Simple was betraying her, she wept and threw things, but she never hit him. *Simple Speaks His Mind* had already revealed in "Last Whipping" how Aunt Lucy's tears had led Jess to change his behavior. Similarly, "Blue Evening" showed how deeply moved Simple had been by Joyce's gentle response to finding Zarita's birthday party in full swing in his room. Simple's character consistently responds to women's tender concerns. Mabel's tenderness touched Jess and left a lifelong impression upon him, but it could not hold him to her in a monogamous relationship. As she read the manuscript for *Simple Takes a Wife,* Leiper liked the way Hughes had written the Mabel story, and she wrote to him about Simple's behavior that "after all, very young people *are* relatively heartless," but she also liked the way Hughes had "underline[d] slightly his later contrition."[19]

A particularly striking aspect of the imagery Hughes selected for the Mabel story is his consistent use of an ocean metaphor, which he allows Simple to express:

"Do you want me to tell you what that woman was like? Boy, I don't know. She was like some kind of ocean, I guess, some kind of great big old sea, like the water at Coney Island on a real hot day, cool and warm all at once—and company like a big crowd of people—also like some woman you love to be alone with, if you dig my meaning." ("Better than a Pillow," *Return,* 12)

Readers well acquainted with Hughes's works recognize a familiar metaphor in that "great big old sea," but here it gains a new dimension by its comparison to Mabel. Simple continues his use of the imagery. When Mabel finally confronts him at the Morocco Bar, she appears suddenly and looks him "dead in the eyes." He explains his reaction

19. Leiper to LH, January 21, 1953.

to her unexpected arrival. "What did I say? Nothing. I were struck dumb. I was not scared. But it was like a wave had washed over me. I was confused" ("Explain That to Me," *Return,* 21).

Simple tells how Cherie screamed, jumped up, and ran past Mabel out of the bar. He attempted to maintain a masculine bravado in his verbal confrontation with Mabel, since his "bar-friends" could over-hear every word. Mabel remained low key, however. Then, when she did "scream," it was silent: "Then all of a sudden her eyes screamed. Not a sound came out of her mouth, but her eyes screamed." Simple ducked and dodged as Mabel splintered glass objects "each place from where I had just dodged." The bartender put her out, and Simple told his barfly friends that he would not take their suggestion to pursue Mabel and "slap her head off," because, he said, "That old has-been don't mean a thing. She's just my used-to-be. She don't mean nothing." Then, when Mr. Macho Simple went to the men's room and bent down to wash his face, "It seemed like the floor was slipping out from under me in there, like sand does at Coney Island, when a big old wave goes sucking itself backwards into the ocean, pulling out from under your feet, water and sand from under your feet. I was sick when I bent over that washbowl to run the water. Explain that to me, daddy-o. I was sick as hell." In a deeply moving narration, Simple has consistently compared Mabel to an ocean. He has recalled both the soothing qualities and the unsettling power of this element of nature. Such beautiful and memorable figurative speech is a distinctive feature of *Simple Takes a Wife.*

Although Simple parted from Mabel in order to date Cherie, the "fine" and classy eighteen-year-old playgirl proved unworthy of Jesse's money or attention. In fact, she is the one woman Jesse sometimes wishes he had hit. "Cherie were really no-good—like Zarita. Except that Zarita will drink you up for fun, whereas Cherie drunk you up only for money" ("Two Loving Arms," *Best,* 142). When he quit Cherie, he quit all women for a while. This abstention, Simple reports, "is not good for a fellow. After he gets through working hard all day every man ought to have a little honey in the evening" ("Baltimore Womens," *Return,* 23).

When he ended his celibacy, Simple met and courted Isabel, who became his first wife. "Then I met Isabel, coffee-brown, fine-hipped, young and dizzy, with gold hoop earrings in her ear, sharp as a tack, jack! . . . Isabel dressed down, and was built, man, built! I loved to tell her, 'Baby, latch on my arm and let's walk down the street this evening' " ("Baltimore Womens," *Return,* 23-24). Obviously Simple forgot the lessons he should have learned from Cherie and once again succumbed to a woman's style. He even insisted that Isabel quit her night job "so she could be home when I come and we could go out sporting together" (24). He still needed a woman whose principal appeal was physical.

Despite his wife's attractive appearance, however, the unforeseen Great Depression created a financial calamity that Jesse could not overcome and that his marriage to Isabel could not weather: as his jobs ended and he found new jobs to replace them, each new one paid him less. Meanwhile, Isabel wanted more support from her man. She imposed the ultimatum, "take over or take off," and Simple walked out ("Conversation," *Best,* 16). He moved to Harlem and drank heavily, "trying to wear that woman off my mind. I had found out by then that she did not really care a thing about me, only what I had in my pocket" ("Less than a Damn," *Return,* 28). While he may have married the wrong woman, he retained enough self-worth to leave when his wife valued his income more than she valued him.

Observe that Simple never objected to financially supporting his wife. The problem was that the depression depleted the income he could earn. Simple upholds many double standards about women, but he certainly appreciates the need of a woman in the 1940s to ascertain the earning power of her potential mate. He elaborates on his theory in his musings about his Cousin Minnie, whom he introduces in the third collection, *Simple Stakes a Claim,* which is discussed in Chapter 7.

Readers get a different economic philosophy when Simple's land-lady, Madam Butler, gains her moment in the spotlight in "Nothing but Roomers." This episode mentions Simple's neighbor, *Ezra* Boyd, and notes that Simple has been living there for seven years. The landlady offers information about her own economic priorities:

"I was working in a tobacco barn when I was fourteen. I first married when I was sixteen and started buying a house. This man is my third husband. This house is my fourth house. And this house I swear I am gonna keep. Neither husbands nor mortgages is gonna take this house from me. I handles this business myself now. This property is in my own name—and all the papers. Losing husbands and losing houses is what has been my education. Now I say, 'To hell with husbands—I am going to hang onto this house!' I'll tell any woman, a roof over your head is better than a husband in your bed! A good woman can always get a man, but a house costs money." (*Return*, 181)

As Simple has reported the story, he has told his bar buddy what Madam Butler says she will tell any *woman*. Thus, ironically, in the male-to-male dialogue between Simple and the bar buddy, the reader learns a woman-to-woman secret of economic success and business priorities. Indeed, in this telling description, the landlady sounds very much like the fiercely independent and outspoken Madam Alberta K. Johnson, of the "Madam to You" poetry series Hughes included in *One Way Ticket* (1949) and reprinted in *Selected Poems*. Simple's landlady is currently married, but she certainly does not take marriage to be a necessarily permanent arrangement: "From now on a husband might share my bed, but not my bankbook. Oh, no! I have learned my lessons. When a woman wants to get ahead, she cannot tie a millstone to her feet. Most men is millstones" (*Return*, 182).

When the usually flat and static landlady tells her story, she emerges—albeit briefly—as a woman who has survived more than one failure, of marriage and of real estate. Her strict rules in the rooming house suddenly have reason behind them, and readers can now at least understand her rather caustic chastisement of Jesse when his habits fail to uphold the standards of her house—or her income requirements.

Experience has forced Madam Butler to become pragmatic. Her decision to hold on to real estate more tenaciously than she holds on to a man has not prevented her from marrying her third husband. She has not rejected men, but she has learned lessons from her first two marriages. "Nothing but Roomers" provides the only forum for her autobiographical discourse, and Simple never again discusses the information she has revealed. Therefore, the conversation does not seem to have left any discernable impact upon him. It has not influenced his opinion of her, nor has it altered his habits of paying his rent. The episode should leave an impact upon *readers*, however. In this story, the otherwise moody or apparently cranky landlady explains her reasons for placing such a high value on her house. She demands the rent—even padlocking doors to get it—because she has seized her own destiny. She intends to keep that house. She demands certain standards of behavior because she has decided to evict any roomers who might threaten her goal. Maybe she even allows Joyce to walk in on Simple when he has been invaded by Zarita's birthday party in the previously discussed "Blue Evening" because she wants Joyce to know *before* marriage that Simple is fooling around. Having lost two husbands, she knows the pain and financial complications associated with divorce. She might be "butting in" to save Joyce some trouble—or even to jar Simple back into acceptable limits of behavior. Thus, in this rare spotlight upon Madam Butler, Hughes presents a black woman who has taken action to accomplish positive achievement in her own life.

These portrayals of Mabel, Cherie, Isabel, and Madam Butler do not supplant Joyce's significance in Simple's life. In fact, as the title indicates, Simple and Joyce marry. As a sales tactic, Hughes made certain that he withheld the marriage from the newspaper column, thereby requiring fans to buy the book to find out how the marriage occurs. This "might be a point for the ads in the Negro press: *Read How Joyce Gets Simple at Last,*" Hughes suggested to his editor.[20]

Fully cognizant of the emphasis on women, Hughes sought to publish portions of *Simple Takes a Wife* in women's magazines. Hoping to help maximize sales, he asked his new literary agent with Harold Ober Associates, Ivan von Auw Jr., "Do you think it would be worthwhile to make a condensation of the book, selecting the straight story chapters, and leaving out the race-argument or incident chapters, for possible magazine use?" His agent sent copies of Simple stories to *Today's Woman, Collier's, Woman's Home Companion, Ladies' Home Journal,* and *McCall's,* but he failed to attract a publisher.[21] Despite these failures with women's magazines, *Simple Takes a Wife* received glowing praise in the press. As with *Simple Speaks His Mind,* Hughes's British publisher, Gollancz, agreed to offer this second volume. Gollancz wrote "a little squib" for the book jacket: "This is a

20. LH to Leiper, March 2, 1953.
21. LH to Ivan von Auw, November 10, 1952, and von Auw to LH, March 2, 1953. Rampersad, *Life of Langston Hughes,* vol. 2, 195–96, discusses the political conservatism that chased Maxim Lieber out of the United States in 1951. Hughes guarded his political image for the sake of his literary career.

diamond of the purest water: a novel about the character described by the press of two continents as 'great' and 'immortal.' "[22]

One reason for the new emphasis in *Simple Takes a Wife* on women and emotional characterization, instead of the more prevalent emphasis on political events and attitudes in *Simple Speaks His Mind,* is the politically repressive climate of the mid-1950s. As the McCarthy era reached its peak, Hughes found himself in the midst of the notorious "witch hunt" for Communists. In fact, on March 26, 1953, Hughes was called to give his testimony before the House Committee on Un-American Activities. He read from portions of the episode "When a Man Sees Red," from *Simple Speaks His Mind.* The senators asked him questions about when and why it was written.

> I replied that in my opinion the chapter indicated clearly that Americans had freedom of press, speech, and publication, and the right of which we are all proud to freely criticize any branch of our government or any elected persons. And that this chapter was written just after, and grew out of, an incident that occurred in the Un-American Committee when a member of the Committee called a Negro witness a name which I could not repeat on the air (the hearing being televised) but which came under the heading of "playing the dozens" to Harlemites, namely talking badly about someone's mother. This incident greatly shocked Negro citizens and others of good will. And many translated it into terms of unfairness toward members of our race. So, in his imagined satire on the Un-American Committee the fictional character, Simple, was simply voicing his criticism which reflected a general community feeling. After this answer, the McCarthy committee did not pursue the subject further.[23]

Although some writers and actors pleaded the Fifth Amendment to avoid testifying, they sometimes forfeited their careers. Hughes clearly wanted to continue to earn his living as a writer, but he did not wish to endanger any of his past associates—or himself—with damaging testimony. He wanted to clarify the true value of his writing and to place into proper perspective those works that had raised the suspicions of the investigators. In his biography, Arnold Rampersad

---

22. Quoted in von Auw to LH, May 12, 1953.
23. Letter sent to over one hundred people, explaining Hughes's testimony before the committee, Hughes MSS, JWJ.

details the anguish that this experience caused Hughes.[24] Hughes guarded his career and consciously de-emphasized potentially explosive political nuances in his writing. The more guarded exploration of race in *Simple Takes a Wife* is evident in "Apple Strudel," in which a white coworker brings to Simple an apple strudel that his wife baked and sent "for a present for you and your girl." The gesture did not melt Simple's heart, although he appreciated the kindness.

> "I said, 'Thank you,' because I knew he meant well. He would also like to do well. Still and yet, he is one of the very ones who will argue with me most about how the Negro problem is improving, beat me down that things is getting *so* much better, how we got so many white friends in America. Just because he gives me an apple strudel, does he think I can give everybody in Harlem a slice?
>
> "I wish I could. To tell the truth, I really wish we could."

As he prepared the manuscript, Hughes commented to his editor about the value of this episode: "I hope that last line of the *Strudel* chapter comes across. What Simple means is that he wishes he could share this evidence of 'white' kindness with all of Harlem, since he feels it doesn't happen to many Harlemites often."[25] This closing line and the interpretation once again touch on an issue that typifies Hughes's works: all whites are not hostile to blacks. However, the lesson also relates to an issue very current in racial discussions of the 1990s: when the benefits of employment, education, or wealth become available to *some* African Americans, should that then end all discussion of the lack of benefits that prevails with many others? Can an advantaged African American "give everybody in Harlem a slice" of the American "pie" of opportunity?

His care in treating racial issues resulted in a delightful award; *Simple Takes a Wife* won the 1953 Anisfield-Wolf Book Award in Race Relations. His friend Arna Bontemps considered the award an "exciting and richly deserved recognition of his excellency Jesse B." Hoping that the $1,000 award might speed Simple's transformation into theater, Bontemps observed, "Quietly, steadily, one step at a time,

24. Rampersad, *Life of Langston Hughes,* vol. 2, 209-21.
25. LH to Leiper, January 22, 1953.

Simple is moving into the folklore of our period. I'm proud to have been one of the first to have hailed him."[26]

Perhaps because he was nudged by Bontemps or encouraged by the Anisfield-Wolf award, Hughes did work toward bringing Simple to the stage. He gave his play the title he had tried to give his second collection of stories, *Simply Heavenly.* Hughes wrote a few articles describing the passages of Simple from newspaper column to book to stage, and these articles detail complications galore. He reported in the *New York Herald Tribune* that soon after he created Simple he began to hear of people reading his columns aloud at parties, club meetings, and public programs in widely scattered places. "Then I heard of little dramatizations of some of the episodes at Hampton and on other college campuses. In Harlem Alice Childress adapted the character into an amusing little revue." Other readers of the Simple episodes began to dramatize the character, so quite naturally Hughes needed to prepare his own script. However, he found theater to be the most challenging venue for his character.

In the first place, Hughes found it "much simpler and easier to write a book and see it through the printer's than it is to write a play and follow it through production." Too many people try to influence a play, contrasted to the few substantive suggestions an author receives. "What suggestions a sympathetic editor in a publisher's office may offer are usually few and of minor importance. But the suggestions which everyone offers who looks at a play script are generally many and major, requiring a great deal of time, trouble, and thought to consider."[27] On his own, Hughes determined to produce audible laughs among theatergoers, thereby causing producers and directors to consider his work "good theatre." To that end, he "made the characters and situations in 'Simply Heavenly' as amusing as I knew how."

The tight structure and visual presentation of the play required Hughes to condense and clarify the actions that had been coming and going in his Simple stories since 1943. Unlike any of the collections of

26. Rampersad, *Life of Langston Hughes,* vol. 2, 234; Bontemps to LH, March 27, 1954.

27. "You're Simple if You Want to Write a Play," Hughes MSS #3851, JWJ. Written for the Dorothy Killgalen column, sent to Dave Lipsky, September 25, 1957.

stories, *Simply Heavenly* begins with character notes. Before seeing any of the action, the audience is informed that all the characters are "ordinary, hard-working" residents of Harlem who use the bar as "a neighborhood club."

For the play, Hughes gave the foil a name, "Ananias Boyd," a different Boyd from the "Ezra" Boyd mentioned in *Simple Takes a Wife*. As does Ezra, this Boyd lives in Simple's rooming house. Thus, many of the conversations Simple has with the foil in the barroom of the books and newspaper columns, he has with Ananias Boyd in his rooming house in the play. Yet, like the foil, Boyd frequents Paddy's Bar and is trying to be a writer. He has money more frequently than other bar regulars in the play due to his G.I. benefits. The foil in the book and column was not a veteran.

The character notes also clearly specify that Zarita is *not* a prostitute. We understand that Simple is dark and slight, Joyce is tall and brownskin, Zarita is good-looking, and Madam Butler is large and fat. All of these physical characteristics have wandered onto the page in the stories, but they are presented up front in the play.

To maintain variety and interest on stage, Hughes introduced more bar patrons. For example, Melon hotly pursues Mamie—a sort of female counterpart of Simple in her approach to racial pride. (Hughes's liabilities as a male interpreting a female emerge in the "Say *no* when you mean *yes*" scene [2.1].) Arcie appears as Bodiddly's sherry-drinking wife.

Character development takes interesting twists for the sake of the stage. Obviously, to enact the dialogue of the stories would result in tedium. Thus, for greater drama and comedy, interactions that Simple had merely narrated in the stories are acted out in the play. An unfortunate by-product of this revision is that the intimacy of the man-to-man dialogue is completely disrupted. Lines in the stories that had previously been assigned only to Simple are delivered in the play by Miss Mamie ("chitterling passer" 1.3), Bodiddly ("set up the bar—this far—from Mamie to me" 1.3), and other characters. Simple shares and dramatizes his dream of commanding white troops with supportive coparticipants Arcie, Hopkins, and Melon (2.9).

The play also redistributes lines to Joyce, Melon, and Hopkins that were previously assigned only to the foil. Joyce hears the "Last Whipping" episode while visiting Simple in the hospital (1.4) and hears the explanation of *I was* versus *I were* (1.6); Melon visits Simple in the hospital after his night in the rumble seat with Zarita (1.4); and Hopkins the bartender hears details about the progress of the funds for the divorce (1.5) and the description of Simple's unsuccessful efforts to contact Joyce following Zarita's disruptive birthday party (2.4). Thus, more characters in the play listen and respond to Simple's philosophies and his verbal tendencies toward rhyme. Although he remains the main character, he seems less remarkable in the play because he is clearly just one of the "ordinary, hard-working" Harlem residents who frequent Paddy's Bar.

Zarita has moments on stage in which she offers her own perspective on things without Simple's interpretation. She never receives such an opportunity in the stories. When Simple, having paid his third of the divorce costs, resists her charms and leaves the bar before midnight, Zarita describes his new condition and reflects on her own desires. "He's getting domesticated. You know, Arcie, I wish someone would feel about me the way Simple feels about Joyce, and she about him, even if they do have their ups and downs. I guess a little trouble now and then just helps to draw people together. But you got to have somebody to come together with" (2.1).

Zarita also reveals a caring and generous side of herself that differs greatly from the "user" persona she exudes in the stories. While she is portrayed as a sponge in the stories, in the play she offers the jobless Jess ten dollars and daily dinners. She also explains her motivation for bringing her birthday party to his room. "Knowing you wasn't working, thinking maybe you'd be kinder embarrassed to come to my place for my birthday and not bring a present, I brought the party to you. Meant no harm—just trying to cheer you up" (2.4). Any inkling of such thoughtful qualities is missing in the stories.

As it was in *Simple Speaks His Mind,* Zarita's birthday party scene is crucial to character development in the play. However, the sadly narrated episode from "Blue Evening" becomes quite an event on stage, including, as Hughes specifies in the stage directions, "all the bar customers and as many strangers as desired to make the staging lively" (2.3). And it clearly is lively. For example, when Zarita's purse opens, spilling all its contents, one of the items Bodiddly helpfully holds up is a red brassiere. When Joyce appears, holding a bundle of laundry she has washed for the unemployed love of her life, the drama of her pain is muted by the comedy of the drunken pianist, who calls out "Slappy slirthday!" and "Happy slirthday!" and by the unsinkable Mamie, who leaves with a huffy "I been throwed out of better places than this." The words and actions of the other characters did not emerge in the narrated version of the story, but they rival the words and actions of the principal characters in the humorously staged dramatic version.

Simple's pain and the significance of Joyce's indignant departure are conveyed in his posture and language after all the guests have left, Boyd last, closing the door behind him. Simple wipes the incriminating lipstick off his cheek, "throws the handkerchief on the dresser and sinks down on the bed, his head in his hands" saying "Oh, my God! . . . Oh, my God! . . . My God! . . . Oh, God" (2.3). Both the dejected posture and the dearth of words help to project the absolute misery in which Simple finds himself.

In short, the play captures much of what was important in the stories, but the stage and Hughes's desire to make everything "as amusing as I knew how" led to numerous distinctions in the play. As Hughes recalls and as the manuscripts attest, "the play" fails to account for all the forms, lengths, and revisions of the manuscript that eventually was passed down as *Simply Heavenly*. From initial conception to its final form on stage, it took Hughes about four years—roughly from *Simple Takes a Wife* to *Simple Stakes a Claim* (from 1953 to 1957).

> When I first put Simple into play form myself, it was a straight comedy. The producers holding the option, however, suggested making it a musical, so I rewrote it and inserted twenty songs. Meanwhile these showmen went broke and allowed their option to run out. The producers who took the next option had entirely opposite ideas, so working with a new director of their choice, the play underwent a third drastic revision. Still no production came about.[28]

As Hughes reports, "along the way several producers and directors had their hands on the script at one time or another. Each man or woman who touched it had different ideas for changes, cuts, additions, or new scenes." Hughes, of course, was quite well prepared to add new scenes. "Since the play was derived from my Simple books— 'Simple Speaks His Mind' and 'Simple Takes A Wife' with a bit of

28. "Simple's Long Trek to Broadway," for the *New York Herald Tribune*, from the 4th and Final Draft, August 2, 1957, Hughes MSS #3570, JWJ.

the latest one, 'Simple Stakes a Claim,' in it, too—I had plenty of material to dramatize." With boyish glee he admits, "I had fun letting the directors think I am a fast writer."[29] Being a fast writer was not sufficient to bring Simple to the theater. The next director with whom Hughes worked broke away and moved to London. Finally, with a fourth director, *Simply Heavenly* as we now have it became a reality. "Over a period of years then, from a comedy to a musical comedy, to a comedy with music 'Simply Heavenly' evolved."[30]

Hughes apparently enjoyed adding the songs to his script. He worked with a congenial composer, David Martin. With that collaborator, he said, "Songs are the most fun." In fact, Hughes may have gone overboard in his addition of songs: "Originally a comedy without music, 'Simply Heavenly' at one point in its evolution, had twenty numbers. But then it would have lasted as long as 'The Ice Man Cometh' so I eventually kept only the best songs. The others went back into the files, maybe for future Central European productions, where spectators eat between the acts and like shows to be longer."[31] A favorite producer, Stella Holt, shepherded Simple to Broadway. However, neither Holt nor Hughes especially wanted Broadway rather than a smaller, more intimate theater.

> In May of this year [1957] Stella Holt, the able executive of the Greenwich Mews, presented it at the auditorium of the Order of the True Sisters on West 85th Street. There it opened to wonderful notices and ran successfully through the hottest Spring that New York had known in years. However, no sooner had we opened than folks started saying, "You ought to take it to Broadway."
>
> But Stella Holt said, and I agreed, "Why Broadway? With such business in hot weather, in cool weather we can run here for years." And such were our simple intentions. We were happy in 85th Street, the neighborhood seemed happy with us, and there we intended to stay. But the Fire Department decided otherwise. From balcony to backstage, a dozen ancient building violations were discovered. Four days before what would have been our 50th performance, we were closed up, and all our weekend audiences turned away. Since no other off-Broadway haven could be found to house "Simply Heavenly" we

29. "You're Simple if You Want to Write a Play," Hughes MSS #3851, JWJ.
30. "Simple's Long Trek to Broadway."
31. Ibid.

were *forced* to Broadway. We come now to the Playhouse, fortunately a charming little intimate theatre ideally suited to our Simple play. About the Playhouse there is a friendly feeling like Patsy's Bar, so we don't mind moving. And since on Broadway union musicians are required, we are now *forced* to have an orchestra—which adds additional gaiety to David Martin's music. "It is an ill wind that bodes nobody good." And as Simple once said, "Something is always happening to a man, especially if he is colored." In Simple's case, the Fire Department kicked him right square to Broadway.

The 1957 opening of *Simply Heavenly* on Broadway coincided with the publication of the third volume of Simple stories, *Simple Stakes a Claim.* Hughes delighted to see the show on "The Great White Way." "The tickets to 'Simply Heavenly' are no longer sold across a table as they were uptown. And I can stand on Broadway and look up to see the name of my show all lighted up. Lucky, I guess! Book writing is nice, peaceful—a quiet occupation. But I believe I'll write another show—even if I do tell young folks who want to be playwrights, 'You must be simple.' "[32] Despite the complications and despite his complaints, Hughes was very pleased to see his Simple Minded Friend on Broadway. He was also pleased to complete his desired trilogy of Simple books. As usual, however, the pathway to the finished *Simple Stakes a Claim* was fraught with complications.

32. "You're Simple if You Want to Write a Play," Hughes MSS #3851, JWJ.

7

Simple Claims the Best

THE THIRD COLLECTION of Simple stories had been destined as early as 1951, when Hughes assembled and revised the episodes for *Simple Takes a Wife*. Even then the author anticipated a third volume, greatly desiring a trilogy. At that point, Hughes projected that the third volume would continue the saga by focusing upon Simple's life as a married man and perhaps as a father.[1] Another possibility for the third volume was suggested by Arna Bontemps, Hughes's close friend, a sincere critic of his work, and one of Simple's earliest fans. When Bontemps read in the *Defender* about Simple's Cousin Minnie, he immediately recognized her value in fiction and wrote to Hughes:

> Minnie is the universal skeleton in the closet of the striver. God's wrath indeed! If she survives in Harlem, she may be just what is needed to bring together a third volume of the Simple saga. She could, conceivably, figure in an over-all drama in which Simple 1) discovers Harlem, 2) settles down (takes a wife) and 3) tries to rescue his relatives who have lingered behind in the South. Let's have more of Minnie! Soon!![2]

However, the third volume as it emerged neither hinged on Minnie nor showed Simple's life as a married man. Instead it took on a heavy-handed political tone.

Considering Hughes's practice and experience, one would think the third collection of Simple stories should have been easier for him to compile and edit, and that it should have moved more quickly through the publishing process. However, this was not the case. As

---

1. LH to Maxim Lieber, April 16, 1951, JWJ.
2. Bontemps to LH, January 30, 1956, JWJ.

Arnold Rampersad details in the second volume of his biography of Hughes, life had become hectic for the author. Hughes was juggling numerous publishing obligations—having just completed his seven-and-one-half-pound draft of *I Wonder as I Wander* and *A Pictorial History of the Negro in America,* with Milton Meltzer—with a variety of public appearances, always mindful of the precarious opinion of the red-baiting public. The sociopolitical climate had grown more intense, and having survived under the scrutiny of the McCarthy committee, Hughes wanted to express his concerns regarding the state of the union.

Facing these numerous obligations and feeling strongly that his serious editorial voice should be heard, Hughes resorted to the collect-and-publish method he had unsuccessfully attempted with *Simple Speaks His Mind.* He hastily assembled some of the stories he had cut from *Simple Takes a Wife,* along with a variety of other early columns, many of them using his own nonfiction editorial voice rather than the Simple technique. These he collected into a book, which he tentatively called "How to Integrate without Danger of Intermarriage & Other Simple Recipes for Salvation, by Langston Hughes with interventions by Jesse B. Semple." The title tells the story. Hughes was offering his own opinions, with "interventions" by Simple. This collection, in its initial draft, was *not* a sequel to the previously published Simple books. Instead, it merely assembled Hughes's columns.

The worst consequence of this attempt is that it forced Hughes to find a new publisher for Simple. On August 25, 1955, when he offered the concept to his editor at Simon and Schuster, he defended the "column collecting" by citing the need for such a book:

> I have frequently had letters from readers asking if my column were available in book form. Since the *Simple Books* have come out, I now refer them to those books. It might however be that a selection of enough of my columns to make a short book to sell for $1.—and dealing entirely with various phases of the race problem, might be pertinent to our times—somewhat like Lillian Smith's recent small book on race relations. There has been no such book lately so far as I know, written by a Negro. So it might have a sale.[3]

3. LH to Maria Leiper, August 25, 1955, JWJ.

He went on to emphasize the focal topic of this volume as he currently envisioned it: "At the moment, the main thing I like about this idea is the title—'How to Integrate without Danger of Intermarriage.' "

From the beginning, Maria Leiper, whom he repeatedly called his favorite editor, discouraged this idea. She had seen the column-collecting draft of *Simple Speaks His Mind,* after all, and she knew the amount of revision that had gone into the published version of that edition. She agreed to look at his project, but she cautioned him about the dangers of column-collecting: "As you must know, we are all eager to publish as many good Langston Hughes books as possible; but sometimes a collection of columns, no matter how fine they are individually, will not hold up well as a book."[4] However, Hughes would not be deterred.

In his cover letter to Leiper, Hughes detailed a four-pronged raison d'être for this collection: (1) to "focus attention on some of the problems" both whites and blacks had with integration; (2) to "provoke, shock, amuse, or otherwise intrigue more people into thinking more deeply on these problems"; (3) to reveal the kind of opinion that is prevalent in the Negro press, "but which seldom reaches a wider public in pure, unslanted, and unadulterated form"; and finally (4) to allow fans of Simple in book form "a chance to meet him . . . in his natural journalistic habitat along with the *other* kinds of articles between which he is ever so often placed" in the *Chicago Defender.* Hughes also highlighted the extremely flexible dimensions of his proposed book. "Any columns may be dropped—or more added—as feasible. There are available 52 weeks times 13 some-odd years—around 700 columns filed away since my first appearance in the *Chicago Defender* in the early '40s."[5]

Hughes had already changed his mind about which columns to include—but not about the concept—when he actually sent the text to Simon and Schuster on September 28, 1955. At that time he deleted from his original manuscript "Hold Tight! They're Crazy White," one of the more biting World War II columns, and "Letter to White Shopkeepers," a heavy-handed lecture to white merchants whose businesses had been vandalized or looted during the 1943 Harlem

4. Leiper to LH, August 29, 1955.
5. LH to Leiper, September 28, 1955.

Riot.[6] These stories had value for *Chicago Defender* readers, but they lacked that intimacy and entertainment value that endeared Simple to so many readers.

The nonfiction columns he sent in that draft included discussions of New York City, colored hotels, public profanity by African Americans, and the use of stocking caps by black men, to name a few of the topics. Many of these columns had elicited exuberant praise from his *Chicago Defender* readers. In fact, some of these observations remain quite fascinating, such as his notation of the "Dear Old Southland" as "The Land of the Positive Negative": "If you ask a clerk in a drug store if he has any soap, he is likely to say, 'I *sure* don't.' Ask a student if he has finished his class assignment and the answer is likely to be, 'I *sure* haven't.' Ask anyone if he has seen the latest Marilyn Monroe picture. If not, the answer will be, 'I *sure* didn't.' Southerners are very positive about their negatives, which adds a quaint verbal charm to the language." Those well acquainted with colloquialisms in the South will confirm the continuing validity of this observation. However, it hardly ranks with Simple's best episodes. Ultimately, the draft he sent in September 1955 deserved the veto it received from Simon and Schuster.

His editor replied about one month later, breaking the news to him in her characteristically gentle manner. "I'm sorry—we just don't believe we can sell enough copies of 'How to Integrate' to make publication worthwhile." She went on to wish Hughes success as he submitted the manuscript to another publisher. "I can't help hoping another house will disagree with us as to the possibilities, and do well with it.—I'd have loved to see us do it, though."[7]

As he had done with the first collection of Simple columns, Hughes optimistically sought another publishing house, writing to Theodore S. Amussen, vice president of Rinehart. Hughes was already under contract with Rinehart at this point; he was busy editing his efforts toward his second autobiographical volume, *I Wonder as I Wander*. Rinehart had elected an option for three of Hughes's books, so "How

6. For a discussion of "Hold Tight! They're Crazy White," see Chapter 2. For "Letter to White Shopkeepers," see discussion of the Harlem Riot in Chapter 3.

7. Leiper to LH, October 27, 1955.

to Integrate" would be their second book. His letter to Amussen explained the value of the book in essentially the same manner as he had explained it to Leiper. Once again he pointed out the completely flexible size of the project and emphasized the need for an African American voice in book form regarding "integration and its problems and puzzlements. . . . The new James Baldwin book, *Notes of a Native Son* (which I'm reviewing for the *Times*) is an excellent collection of literary essays, very good indeed, but hardly covers this field."[8]

Hughes could not have known at the moment he appealed to Rinehart to accept this collection that the company was soon to become one of his least favorite publishers. Hughes could compare Rinehart with other publishers regarding promotion of new releases he had authored. His hectic pace and his multiple projects had resulted in his birthing of more than one new book at a time. He was solidifying the third volume of Simple stories while he was the proud author of a highly acclaimed pictorial history with Crown Publishers, a fourth juvenile history with Franklin Watts, and his second autobiographical volume with Rinehart. His complaints about Rinehart concerned promotional copies never being sent, the cost of the copies, promotions in general, and editing costs.

A Pictorial History of the Negro in America, written with Milton Meltzer, first appeared in 1956.[9] However, Crown publishers accepted Hughes's suggestions and took their own initiative to interest the public in the *Pictorial.* Hughes complained to his agent that he had appeared on three uptown radio shows arranged by Crown for the *Pictorial,* and, although he naturally seized the opportunity to mention the second volume of his autobiography, none of the stations had received *I Wonder as I Wander* from Rinehart.

A concurrent publication, *The First Book of the West Indies,* was the fourth in a series of juvenile histories Hughes had written for another publisher, Franklin Watts. The first three were *The First Book of Negroes* (1952), *The First Book of Rhythms* (1954), and *The First Book of Jazz* (1955). To highlight his frustration with Rinehart,

8. LH to Ted Amussen, November 21, 1955.

9. The fifth revised edition of *A Pictorial History of Black Americans* was published by Crown in 1983, and *A Pictorial History of African Americans,* by Hughes et al., is forthcoming from Crown.

Hughes quoted to Ivan von Auw a portion of a letter Watts had written him: "If all authors were as competent, as good guys, and as zealous in promoting their books as you are, all of us would make more money. I do appreciate your suggestions." Both Crown and Watts notified him that they had received numerous letters "from prominent persons to whom it was sent," reported Hughes, but "nary a note from Rinehart's! . . . not even *one* interview, not *one* radio show, not a single thing of any sort publicity wise has come my way from their office." Hughes concludes his lengthy and detailed complaint to his agent with his usual optimism and resilience, and with a feigned indifference: "So I'm just curious as to what's their story? Not that it worries me any—or I crave more things to do, for Crown has kept me busy every day for the last two weeks, and tomorrow have arranged a library forum. But I am curious? Can you shed any light?"[10]

Whether or not von Auw shed any light, the publisher eventually revealed that Hughes would have to prepay for all those "comment copies" he had requested be sent to prominent people. Other publishers had furnished some of these copies at no cost to the author or had charged such expenses against future royalties. Rinehart proved extremely difficult on this point.

Besides the negligence in publicity and the trouble about review copies, Hughes also suffered from alteration-of-galley proof costs with Rinehart. Having received yet another bill from the publisher, Hughes paid it, but asked for clarification. The project this time was the third collection of Simple stories, containing no nonfiction editorials, except two used as the foreword. As he sought to see *Simple Stakes a Claim* to completion, he expressed his frustration with Rinehart directly to the company:

> In answer to your note of July 18th, I am enclosing my check for $17.68 for author's alterations. Since the galley proofs seemed in better shape than usual to me, I am rather curious to know what the excess alterations were, if someone would be so kind as to tell me. . . .
>
> At any rate, whenever copies are ready, I'd like to have 50 mailed to me at the above address. And if you will let me know how much that will be, I will send my check now—well in advance—since you probably recall what happened regarding *I Wonder As I Wander.* The

10. LH to Ivan von Auw, November 29, 1956.

copies I had ordered of that book to be sent to friends and relatives did not go out until a month or more *after* publication date—and no one in the office seemed to know what was holding them up. Until finally someone informed me that I was expected to pay for them in advance. This I would not have minded doing, had I only been so informed— although in 25 years of publishing, I'd never had such an experience with any other publisher. But now that I know, I'll confirm this order for fifty (50) *Simple Stakes a Claim* by sending my check ahead as soon as your office tells me the amount.[11]

Although his letters to Rinehart retained his characteristically pleasant tone and cooperative spirit, his letters to his literary agent, Ivan von Auw, complained bitterly about Rinehart's failure to promote *I Wonder as I Wander* and their refusal to mail out the copies Hughes had requested for friends who had promised to publicize his latest autobiography.

I am really a bit puzzled about Rinehart's promotion (or lack of it) at least in relation to the Negro market and Harlem, and their apparently paying no attention *at all* to any of the numerous lists, memos, and suggestions re publicity and promotion which I sent them—at their own request. For example, not even Carl Van Vechten (who was at the top of my list for a comment copy) had received a copy until I asked about it two or three times—and he's known to write and talk about ANY Negro book at the drop of a hat. . . . Another puzzlement: So far as I know, not a single Harlem radio commentator received a copy of *I Wonder*.[12]

These letters of inquiry, letters indicating payment of bills, and letters of complaint shared only with his agent were written by a breathlessly busy Langston Hughes. In 1957 he was at work on several projects at once, as he would continue to be for the rest of his life. Besides the new Simple collection, he was preparing translations of Gabriela Mistral for Bernard Perry, who was now with Indiana University Press, and he was revising his script of *Simply Heavenly* for production on stage. Thus, his taking the time to send these many letters indicates his deep dissatisfaction with Rinehart. Clearly he felt undervalued

11. LH to Miss Reese of Rinehart, July 20, 1957.
12. LH to von Auw, November 29, 1956.

and disrespected in Rinehart's promotional treatment of his second autobiographical volume and of his orders for personal copies. Had he anticipated the unwillingness of both Simon and Schuster and Rinehart to present the collection of columns he first submitted as "How to Integrate," and had he anticipated the book as being a third collection containing only Simple episodes, he surely would have preferred to remain with Simon and Schuster. However, eager to gain more mileage from the existing columns and hoping to minimize his own labor, Hughes unwittingly chose an even more difficult route, which uprooted Simple from his genial publishers at Simon and Schuster.

Yale University's file of correspondence between Hughes and Rinehart does not include documentation of when and how Rinehart persuaded Hughes to create a third volume of Simple stories from the column collection he sought to publish. However, Leiper approved of Rinehart's publishing the collection of entirely Simple stories. Hughes wrote to tell his agent, "Maria Leiper, before she flew to Europe, says it's O.K. for Rinehart to publish the *How to Integrate without Danger of Intermarriage* as an all-Simple columns book, which is what Sandy and Ted suggest. So let's contract it, if they wish, and I can give them a revised manuscript by Labor Day."[13]

Thus, Hughes returned to the tried and true method of shaping a whole from its parts. He included a couple of the episodes deleted from *Simple Takes a Wife* along with a portion of one that appeared in that book, and he revised the episodes borrowed from the *Defender*. Nevertheless, with *Simple Stakes a Claim* he created a different kind of Simple book. Although he could not include the non-Simple columns, in which he used his own editorial voice, Hughes still retained a far more politicized volume than he had offered with either of the two preceding collections. Biographer Arnold Rampersad notes this distinction: "Langston spoke again through Simple on the question of civil rights—this time more comprehensively—when he quickly finished work on his third collection of columns, 'Simple Stakes a Claim.' Unlike the earlier volumes, this would be 'essentially a topical book,' as he explained to Carl Van Vechten, with less emphasis on his hero's personal adventures, especially his love affairs, and

13. LH to von Auw, July 16, 1956.

more on his claim to democracy." Hughes declared this parenthetical addition to the title when he personalized the book jacket of Van Vechten's copy: "*Simple Stakes a Claim* (in democracy)," he wrote in the green ink that had become his trademark.[14]

However, even as he sought to discuss serious issues of democracy, he also wanted to defend and extend his own penchant for humor. Hughes retained two of the non-Simple columns in this third collection and published them as the foreword to the book, entitled "Let's Laugh a Little." This foreword combined "Nothing Like It" and "Let's Laugh a Little" from *Defender* columns of June 19, 1948, and November 6, 1943. With his suggestion to "laugh a little," Hughes confronted the "serious" Negro publications that refused to acknowledge the value of "laughing to keep from crying"—that blues ethos incorporated into most of Hughes's work. Although it is far less prevalent in this third collection, there is humor in the Simple stories of this volume. In "Mississippi Fists," for example, the foil seems amused that Simple defends his southern home state, Virginia, as being less harsh than Mississippi. However, when the foil asks why so many Negroes stay down South, Simple replies: "Why does a pig stay in his pen? Answer—because his slop is there" (*Claim,* 154). However, this same episode is about Emmett Till—decidedly not a funny topic.

Van Vechten praised this third collection, and he noted its distinct change of tone:

> This Simple is different from that of the other two books. He is
> more serious and he indulges in a good deal of race talk whereas his
> predecessor mostly indulged in conversation about ladies or at any rate
> females. The only prominent Lady in the present work is Cousin Minnie.
> Cousin Minnie is a delightful diversion and I, for one, would like to
> meet her again. Joyce comes back occasionally, but not intensively.
> Your preface [the Foreword] takes some of the sting away from the race
> talk with its constant insistence on the villainy of the white man, but
> not too much of it, and white men innocent of misbehavior towards
> black brothers will read some pages with burning cheeks, thank God.

14. Rampersad, *Life of Langston Hughes,* vol. 2, 264; Van Vechten's copy of *Simple Stakes a Claim* is in the James Weldon Johnson Collection at the Beinecke Library, Yale University.

I loved the book myself, Langston, and I hope it will show some ofays the way.[15]

He adds as a postscript: "Copies of SSAC should be sent to every congressman and senator."

Despite the foreword and some humor in the episodes, *Simple Stakes a Claim* is far more polemical than humorous. Instead of extending the saga, Hughes retreated to more didactic discussions. Joyce is mentioned in only a few episodes and participates in even fewer. The original topic, integration, occupies a large chunk of space. "With All Deliberate Speed," for example, begins with Simple's dangerous reference to race mixing on the highest levels:

> "Some of them Dixieland governors have been damning race-mixing ever since time begun, allowing as how God made everybody separate. Then, after nightfall, them governors themselves start mixing as hard as they can. Why, I went to school with a governor's son who were colored on his mother's side. Them governors talk against intermarriage, but don't say a word about intermating, which amounts to practically the same thing—and there is many a yellow Negro to prove it. You are kinder light-complexioned yourself." (*Claim,* 67)

Having devoted many works in numerous genres to the mulatto theme, Hughes was merely dipping his pen into familiar ink. Not one to promote interracial marriage, however, Simple proposes an easy solution in "The Atomic Age," which had previously been the title story of the manuscript "How to Integrate without Fear of Intermarriage":

> "White folks always seems to be worried so about intermarriage," said Simple. "Why I do not know. All a white girl has to do to keep from marrying a Negro is to say, 'No.'"
> "That problem really has a simple answer," I agreed.
> "Nobody can make a woman marry a man, white or colored, so the answer is just a plain and simple, 'No.' But me, I got a great many other things to worry about besides intermarriage. And I already got a wife

15. Carlo [Carl Van Vechten] to LH, August 18, 1957. *Ofays* is pig Latin for "foes" and was a colloquial term referring to white people. Although Van Vechten was white, he felt comfortable using black slang.

on my hands, chocolate-brown and sweet-all-reet, so intermarriage is no problem to me, not Jesse B., at all." (*Claim,* 81)

This same theory made perfect sense to Hughes, as he demonstrated in both the Simple dialogues and his nonfiction editorial columns. His highlighting of this topic for his working title also shows his characteristic wit. While the United States quaked in the aftermath of *Brown v. Board of Education,* even liberal whites who were willing to integrate schools were challenging each other with "the" question: "Would you want your daughter to marry one?" Hughes allows Simple to mock the question in a wonderfully warm and amusing way.

The heavy-handed political oration in this volume is exemplified by "Four-Way Celebrations" and "Be Broad-Minded, Please!" In "Four-Way Celebrations" Simple suggests White History Week to follow Negro History Week. He suggests that during White History Week white folks celebrate "the day they bought the first Negroes off that slave ship in Jamestown and started us out working for nothing in this here country and have been trying to keep us working for nothing, or little of nothing, ever since" (*Claim,* 171). Simple would also have whites unveil a monument to Jim Crow during White History Week, and would have white children spend one day pretending to be colored while the colored children pretended to demonstrate democracy. As the foil says to Simple, "Nothing you say sounds funny to me" (*Claim,* 173).

On the heels of "Four-Way Celebrations" comes "Be Broad-Minded, Please!" in which the foil says that Simple is not a full citizen of the United States. The foil, who usually modifies and softens Simple's harsh and race-centered assertions, this time tells Simple, "If you were a full citizen, there would be no need of the N.A.A.C.P. running to the Supreme Court all the time to try to consolidate your citizenship. You are a COLORED citizen" (*Claim,* 175). Simple complains about white immigrants being able to arrive in the United States and get better jobs here than the average Negro. The foil and Simple actually share their perception, but not their reactions to what they perceive:

"Still and yet, you mean to tell me a Hungarian what has been here a half hour is worth more than me?"

"I am colored just like you," I said, "so why are you hollering at me? Did I create this condition?"

"You take it too calm," said Simple. "You must be an Uncle Tom."

"Do not call me out of my name," I said. "I see no use to get excited about obvious facts. Everybody knows that any white refugee can expect a better job in America than the average Negro." (*Claim,* 176)

A less pedantic, but still highly political, story is "Cellophane Bandannas," in which Simple wonders why the "high-brow, educated, political double-talkers of the Negro race" (*Claim,* 126) wear their invisible bandannas on their heads. The bandanna symbolizes the "handkerchief head," or spineless, sycophantic Negro commonly called an "Uncle Tom." Simple claims to recognize these simpering supporters of white power, even when their handkerchiefs are invisible, saying, "A bandanna is a bandanna even when you can see through it" (*Claim,* 127). Pointing out as an example a man at the end of the bar who has hovered over a ten-cent glass of beer arguing for two hours about events in Hungary, Simple says, "he's got too much education to know how to use it. His predilect is for the intellect. . . . He ought to be talking about what is going to happen in Harlem where he is."

The foil then acts to further Hughes's original purpose in the "Here to Yonder" columns, calling Simple an isolationist who needs to realize that while local problems are important, so are international ones. However, Simple knows what he wants to do. "I want to deal with the local ones first, otherwise, I won't be living to deal with no others" (*Claim,* 129). In his lengthy explanation of the things that deserve immediate attention, Simple mentions exactly the kinds of concerns that Hughes has expressed in his nonfiction editorials:

"I do not know anybody way over there in Hungary. If Uncle Sam would just stop worrying about Hungary and start spending half of that money in Harlem, instead of on Hungarians, we could tear down all these crowded old houses and build new ones—then I would have a place to live. We could tear down all these little old ugly schools—and there wouldn't need to be three shifts a day for our children. We could have more garbage trucks to collect the garbage so the streets wouldn't look like pigpens. And we could clean up all them dumps along the river front and make parks for the kids to play. Why, we could even tear down this bar—and make it over to look just like the Stork Club."

"You have gone from the sublime to the ridiculous now," I said.

"I have gone from Hungary to Harlem, that's all," said Simple, "which you and that joker at the end of the bar would both understand if you would take off your cellophane bandannas." (*Claim,* 130)

Having previously called his bar buddy "one of the biggest but-and-if-men I know," and an "Uncle Tom," Simple advances his criticism one step further, by suggesting that his friend is one of those "highbrow, educated, political double-talkers of the Negro race" who wear invisible bandannas.[16]

Simple does not actually discredit the crisis in Hungary—"Yonder" —but he does suggest that some of the issues in Harlem—"Here"— including less than sanitary conditions and young people with insufficient recreational and educational opportunities, could result in his own untimely death. Dead, what could he do about Hungary or anyplace else? Simple's logic again defies contradiction.

In these heavily political episodes, Simple's domestic squabbles and marital adjustments take a backseat. His discussions of insincere friends of African Americans ("Duty Is Not Snooty"), the value of a foreign language in beating Jim Crow policies ("Puerto Ricans"), and the media's penchant for publicizing only the negative side of black life ("Name in Print") all occur without any reference to Simple's wife, Joyce. Although Simple does tackle the issue of violence against women when his cousin Minnie enters the dialogue, he addresses few other women's issues. Furthermore, in this volume, his political conversations generally do not involve women in the dialogues.

Thus, when one notes that Joyce is mentioned in only thirteen of the forty-three episodes, Hughes's switch from the cordial character-emphasis of *Simple Takes a Wife* becomes evident. Ironically, however, when Hughes reviewed *Simple Stakes a Claim* to select stories for *The Best of Simple,* he included only fifteen stories from that third collection, and of the fifteen he chose, Joyce is mentioned in eight and Minnie dominates two others. The episodes involving women, therefore, seem to have been among those he ultimately considered his best.

An interesting peccadillo occurs in *Simples Stakes a Claim.* "Puerto Ricans" was written without the quotation marks throughout that typically signal dialogue between Simple and the foil, almost as an entry in Simple's journal (*Best,* 216–18). One might even think the

16. Simples calls his bar buddy "one of the biggest but-and-if men I know" in "Let the South Secede," *CD,* June 26, 1943, and "Uncle Tom" in "Be Broad-Minded, Please!" *Claim,* 176.

episode is narrated by the foil, except for the "daddy-o" and "ain't" sprinkled in, and the announcement that the speaker would create a series of comics called *Jess Simple's Jim Crow Jive*. An earlier episode, "A Veteran Falls," similarly involved no comments from the foil, but it was written in the quotation marks, which suggests that Simple was narrating this entire story to someone (*Best,* 49–52). None of the correspondence for this volume indicates why "Puerto Ricans" lacks the usual punctuation.

The biggest innovation and the most successful feature of the third volume of Simple stories was—as Arna Bontemps had predicted—Cousin Minnie. Minnie appears in four episodes, all of which are included in *The Best of Simple*. She is more than a liability to Simple as he strives to achieve home ownership and a stable married life, although she *is* "a begging relative" (*Best,* 220). Minnie is an assertive woman who gets what she wants in life—and doesn't get much of it by the sweat of her brow. She is feisty like Zarita, but she does not charm men with her looks. In fact, Simple sometimes marvels that she charms men at all. When the foil asks how Minnie looks, Simple replies, "Like the junior wrath of God" (*Best,* 205). When he expounds, Simple reveals his awe and respect for that certain something Minnie uses on men. " 'Minnie is also homely, squat, shot, beat and what not,' said Simple, 'yet there is something about that chick that mens admires. To tell the truth, if Minnie were not my cousin by blood—as well as by fooling around—I might kinder like her myself. Minnie is not pretty, but she is something else not pretty—which is I do not know how to explain by sight—but which must be good' " (*Best,* 232). When Simple cautions her about her ruthless exploitation of men's paychecks, warning that she might get "a good old New York head-whipping if she don't watch out," Minnie insists that she can take care of herself, which Simple believes (*Best,* 232). She admits that she prefers a man who warns before he attempts violence. Other men, she says, "just haul off and hit you." She has no doubt about how she would respond if a man hit her without warning: "Cousin Jess, I would phone you to come and go my bail, because I would be in jail, and the man would be in Paradise." She goes on to explain her theories regarding women who face the threat of battering.

"If ever some man was to hit me, Jesse B., I would wear my
ladyhood like a loose garment, with my sleeves rolled up. Bad man

or no bad man, as sure as I am setting on my anatomy this evening, I would be setting on it tomorrow, too. When push comes to shove, Jesse B., I am one woman who can take care of myself, married or unmarried. Listen, I learned long ago that when a man slaps a woman, that is the time for a woman to make a stand—the very first time she gets slapped. If she don't the next thing you know, that man will hit her and knock her down. If she lets him get away with that, next thing, he will kick her—slap her first, kick her, then stomp her. Next thing he'll cut her. If a man gets away with cutting a woman and she don't stop him, he will shoot her. Yes, he will! If a woman lets a man slap her in the beginning, he is liable to shoot her in the end. I say, stop him when he first raises his hand! My advice to all womens is to raise theirs, too! Raise your hand, women! Protect yourself—then you won't have to bury yourself later! That's my theory."

The foil, hearing Simple repeat Minnie's theory, admits, "you won't have to worry about your Cousin Minnie's physical well-being while she is in New York," and this shows quite a leap in perception from the foil who had called women "frail" and "helpless" just one page earlier (*Best,* 236, 235).

Minnie is another in Hughes's long line of capable, assertive women, although she is more sensual and fun-loving than the equally able Madam Butler, Simple's former landlady. Whereas Madam Butler earns her own way in life, Minnie mooches—perhaps having received her name due to that trait and the Cab Calloway song, "Minnie the Moocher." Whereas Zarita attracts men with her attractive physical appearance, Minnie attracts men with her charm. Minnie's behavior is more respectable when she reappears in the fifth book, *Simple's Uncle Sam.* She has arrived in *Simple Stakes a Claim,* however, and has staked *her* claim on Harlem and on the readers of the Simple stories.

Minnie's inclusion helps to bridge the gap between the "good girls," such as Joyce, and the "bad girls," such as Zarita. Whereas Joyce has no use for bars, and she will not allow Simple to enter her rented room unless he leaves the door open a crack, Minnie drinks as much as Simple does. Clearly Minnie knows what she wants from men and she is not the least bit hesitant to use her charms to gain her desired goals. Unlike Zarita, Minnie gains access to the audience's ear, and in Hughes's works, nearly any character who is given a voice can gain some empathy from the audience.

While Simple and some readers may lose respect for Minnie because of her heavy drinking, one and all learn to respect her intelligence and resourcefulness. Her firm belief in the American dream may not be realistic in the face of the economic realities of Harlem, but even Simple succumbs to Minnie's quest "to stay up North in freedom" (*Best,* 209). Thus, she contributes to the underlying discussion of political realities for African Americans, but she also brings important women's issues to the fore. The public could benefit by adopting her obduracy about women refusing to allow themselves to be battered. Minnie is indeed a vital new addition to the Simple saga.

Simple Stakes a Claim received excellent reviews, and it arrived in print at the auspicious moment when *Simply Heavenly* was (briefly) on Broadway. Thus, the play and the third volume shared each other's publicity. Hughes helped to create publicity stunts for both ventures, suggesting an autographing party at the theater and other events. He continued to be haunted by the record of silence Rinehart had established with *I Wonder as I Wander,* but, happily, Rinehart publicized *Simple Stakes a Claim* to his satisfaction.[17]

Once again the British publisher Gollancz accepted the Simple stories for publication. Expecting publication of the British edition in 1958, and hoping for a London production of *Simply Heavenly,* Hughes hoped to see 1958 as "Simple's year in England."[18] Unfortunately, the expensive and complicated process of theatrical production made Simple's moment on the British stage a liability more than a boon. Moreover, *Simple Stakes a Claim* did not receive critical favor in England. Simple also arrived in other international locations, with *Simple Speaks His Mind* being translated into Danish (1954) and German (1960).

After tangling with his misbegotten *How to Integrate,* Hughes had published his long-desired trilogy of Simple books. He had not yet discussed Joyce and Simple as parents, but the trilogy for which he had once only hoped finally existed. When Hill and Wang corresponded with him on another matter, coincidentally raising the possibility of publishing a collection of his poems in their American Century series, Hughes seized the opportunity to speculate about the

17. LH to von Auw, September 14, 1957.
18. LH to Miss Davis of Rinehart, October 16, 1957.

collected episodes of Simple. First, he responded warmly to their proposal, promising to find out whether Knopf would permit him to republish some of the poems already included in *Selected Poems*. He also mentioned other published poems not included in *Selected Poems* whose rights had reverted to him which might be included in such a collection. Finally he proposed including "some new and hitherto unpublished poems." Hughes then redirected their American Century offer into the Simple direction: "Another idea might be to do a paperback omnibus of my Simple stories—selected from *Simple Speaks His Mind, Simple Takes a Wife* (Simon and Schuster) and *Simple Stakes a Claim* (Rinehart). These books have had a very wide sale to Negro readers (among others) and high school and college students like their humor, the teachers their social commentary. And both publishers are agreeable to such an idea." Lawrence Hill responded immediately, expressing interest in the play version of *Tambourines to Glory* and in further exploring the possibility of the Simple book. "My partner is at present on vacation; when he returns we will discuss your suggestion of an omnibus volume of your selections from your delightful Simple books," he wrote. The publishers did not leap at the opportunity, but they kept open the possibilities.[19]

Seven months later, on October 22, 1960, with his hopes still high, Hughes sent Hill and Wang the German translation of Simple, illustrated by Bernhard Nast; the *Simply Heavenly* programs; and his own biographical sheet. When he met with them on October 25, he took them the three Simple books and a copy of his *Selected Poems*. After the meeting he wrote to his agent:

> Hill and Wang would also like to bring out a sort of Simple omnibus composed of selections from all three Simple books (2 Simon and Schuster, 1 Rinehart) with perhaps a subtitle like "The Best of Simple" so for this I have made the enclosed tentative selection, to be cut down to suit their book size, the enclosed being a little over, but containing the best and least dated chapters and maintaining the Simple-Joyce story line from the first book through the third.[20]

Two days later, on October 27, he sent the play *Simply Heavenly*.

19. LH to Lawrence Hill, March 31, 1960; Hill to LH, April 1, 1960.
20. LH to von Auw, October 25, 1960.

Still having no definite confirmations from the publisher, Hughes wrote to Lawrence Hill on November 7 to thank him for a Sidney Bechet book he had received and to inform him that he was on his way to Nigeria "for a week for the inauguration of my classmate, Azikiwe, as Governor-General." He added with almost boyish glee, "Let me know about Simple by the time I get back, please, sir."

When Hughes returned from Nigeria the news about Simple was what he had hoped for:

> We have now definitely decided to do your one-volume selection from the Simple books. Arthur Wang will, by the time you receive this letter, have approached your agent about the terms for the new edition. We will probably publish it with the next batch of American Century titles in August or September. I would also like to look into the possibility of getting some or all of the illustrations used in the German edition to use in ours, this is provided that the cost is not too great.[21]

So, within eight months, Hughes essentially negotiated his own deal. Hill contacted him first as a sort of editorial commentator, writing in care of Knopf. Once the correspondence came directly to his home, Hughes redirected Hill's initial inquiry about a poetry edition and urged the collection of Simple in addition to the poetry. Also, Hughes nominated the illustrator, having been quite satisfied with Nast's work in the German edition of Simple. *The Best of Simple* represented some of his fastest Simple work, from concept to printed book. Since this edition required almost no new writing or revision, Hughes finally enjoyed the luxury of selecting existing Simple episodes for collection.

The Hill and Wang correspondence files in the James Weldon Johnson Collection fail to reveal who or what may have influenced Hughes in his selection of stories to include in the collection, and manuscript copies of *The Best of Simple* are missing. We have only his reference to "the enclosed tentative selection," which he hoped would contain "the best and least dated chapters" and maintain the progression of Simple's relationship to Joyce from *Simple Speaks His Mind* through *Simple Stakes a Claim*. However, Arthur Wang recalls that Hughes selected the episodes himself, without influence by the publishers.[22]

21. Lawrence Hill to LH, November 15, 1960.
22. Arthur Wang, telephone interview with author, June 28, 1993.

The absence of editorial suggestion becomes quite significant since the omnibus collection omits the episodes from *Simple Takes a Wife* that had been most sensitive to women, and it also avoids the hot issue of interracial marriage. On the other hand, Hughes included from *Simple Stakes a Claim* all the Minnie episodes and almost all the episodes featuring Joyce, and he omitted the political orations.

In total, Hughes selected seventy episodes from the three previously published volumes for the omnibus edition. The largest portion, thirty, came from *Simple Takes a Wife*. Keeping in mind the narrative flow of the episodes, one would not be surprised to see that many consecutive episodes are preserved in chunks. The second largest selection, twenty-five episodes, came from *Simple Speaks His Mind.* From the third collection, *Simple Stakes a Claim,* he chose only fifteen stories. Eight of these feature either Joyce or Minnie, and none of these fifteen includes the excessively polemical episodes dwelling on Hungary or Emmett Till.

The correspondence as preserved at Yale University reveals that a congenial relationship existed between Hughes and the publishers and staff at Hill and Wang. This warm relationship led to a smooth and rapid publication of the omnibus edition. By early April 1961 the production process had begun. Wang wrote to Hughes with a few suggestions:

> We are sending in the *Simple Collection* for cast off and composition and it has occurred to us that you might care to write a brief introduction—of 1,000 words or fewer if you wish. It would I think help to make the book a bit more timely and interesting if you would write your introduction and explain the reasons for your selections.
>
> As I understand it, Ivan von Auw was going to get in touch with you about a dedication to the present volume. There were three dedications, of course, to the three volumes, and it seemed to us that you might care to dedicate the present volume separately.[23]

The only new writing Hughes contributed to *The Best of Simple* was the foreword, "Who Is Simple?" He also sent a new dedication, "To Melvin Stewart, *Broadway's genial Simple.*" Hughes also

23. Wang to LH, April 3, 1961.

attempted to give the collection a clever title, offering as possibilities: "Simply Splendiferous," "Simple Digs the Scene," "Simple in the Saddle," "Simple Wraps It Up," "Simple Has His Say," "Simple's Spectorama," "Simple in the Sun," "Simple's Shebang," and "Mister Simple." Arthur Wang received all that Hughes sent, and while he and Lawrence Hill were "delighted" with the foreword, which they felt "hits the spot," they flatly rejected Hughes's list of potential titles, explaining, "We feel that we should call the book *The Best of Simple.* Anything else, Mr. Simple, etc. will make the book sound like a fourth in the series. Our title, lacking in glamour, is more representative of the book. Unless we hear a loud 'No!' from you we'll proceed."[24] Thus, the title *The Best of Simple* was suggested and insisted upon by Hill and Wang.

Arranging the episodes in the same order as they had appeared in the previous volumes, and arranging the selections from the three volumes chronologically as they were published, Hughes produced a relatively coherent saga that takes the reader from Simple's Virginia childhood to his married life with Joyce. The courtship and the dilemma with the divorce are retained, and cousins F. D. and Minnie pop in at the appropriate times, F. D. while Simple is single and Minnie after he is married. Whereas the original books had themes or seasons to divide them into sections, *The Best of Simple* offers no divisions. Hughes only changed a few words for the fourth collection, most of these the names of places or references to specific politicians. For example, "Ma Frazier's griddle" (*Wife,* 97) was changed to "Jennie Lou's griddle" (*Best,* 125). This probably reflected the closing of "Ma Frazier's," and Hughes wanted to keep the episodes from being dated. This omnibus edition provides an extremely convenient way to meet Simple. It continues to elicit laughter from readers, as well as the nods of agreement with those jewels of wisdom preserved in the episodes.

Hughes's agent wrote encouragingly: "Apparently the initial reception of the 'Simple' book is very good indeed." Hughes seemed quite satisfied with the edition, and he sent inscribed copies to the

---

24. Title suggestions are in "Miscellaneous," UNCLE SAM Folder, Hughes MSS, JWJ (these titles were offered for *The Best of Simple,* so they are in the wrong folder); Wang to LH, April 21, 1961, LH correspondence, Hill and Wang file, JWJ.

special people in Simple's life: John Sengstacke and his wife: "Simple's fosterparents . . . who have sheltered him all these years in the *Defender*"; Maria Leiper: "Simple's Godmother . . . who introduced him to the world"; Metz Lochard: "Simple's genial Godfather, under whose auspices he first met the world via the *Defender*"; Anne Louise Davis: "who so ably guided Simple from print to footlights"; Melvin Stewart: "to whom this book is dedicated—with all my gratitude for so wonderfully bringing Simple to life in the theatre"; David Martin: "who first gave Simple songs to sing"; Josh Shelly: "who first set Simple up in show biz"; Ruth Jett: "who first put Simple on stage"; Stella Holt: "without whom Simple might never have made his theatrical bow"; Alice Childress: "whose 'Just a Little Simple' first made him come alive"; Kenneth Manigault: "Harlem's first live Simple"; and Claudia McNeil: "who made 'Simply Heavenly' a sparkle."[25]

As a consequence of the successful omnibus, Hughes received an offer to record these stories on an album. He explained the offer to von Auw, "Folkways Records would like to make a tie-in of their Melvin Stewart recording of 'Simple' monologues with the Hill & Wang book, *The Best of Simple,* using the same title on the record. Concerning this I have referred them to Lawrence Hill."[26] While the original offer asked for Melvin Stewart, the Simple from Broadway, to read, Hughes himself ultimately recorded the audio versions of the stories.

The success of this omnibus edition is witnessed by its remaining in print since its first publication. Spelman College recommended it as part of its Freshman Reading List for several years, and it is included as a text for various courses. Many bookstores keep *The Best of Simple* in stock, and—as of the 1992 imprint—the book is in its thirty-sixth printing. What an extraordinary literary history for an average fellow from Harlem.

25. Von Auw to LH, August 9, 1961. Notations of inscriptions, "The Best of Simple," Hughes MSS 146, JWJ.
26. LH to von Auw, October 7, 1961.

8

Simple's Last Moves

PERHAPS ON THE STRENGTH of the immensely successful *The Best of Simple,* Hughes gained some confidence about Simple's value. Having remained with the *Chicago Defender* for fifteen years, Hughes began in 1957 to be more vocal about lapses in payment and other unsatisfactory arrangements there. Simultaneously, the *New York Post* began to court him, beginning with a biographical piece by African American columnist and fiction writer Ted Poston. Shortly after publication of the biographical article, the *Post* contracted to publish some of the Simple sketches. "That's a real break," Arna Bontemps applauded.[1] Thus, the move to the *Post* began in 1957, but Hughes continued writing the column for the *Defender,* too, for several years to come.

As discussed in Chapter 7 with regard to his difficulties with Rinehart, Hughes displayed inordinate patience, even in the face of unjustified rudeness and exploitation of his writing skills. However, his correspondence gives some clue that he was not a man of steel. In early 1962, he ceased sending columns to the *Defender.* Bontemps mentioned to his friend on February 6, 1962, that he had missed Hughes's column in the *Defender,* but that he noted the newspaper had carried a statement saying that Hughes was on vacation and would return to his accustomed place soon.[2] However, that announcement reflected optimism by the newspaper rather than reality. Hughes informed a friend at the Afro-American Newspapers that the absence signaled a change: "The *Defender* is no longer carrying my column. Strike difficulties apparently cause them to be unable to pay for it for the past six months—but I wrote for them anyway up until January 1. Would the *Afro,* by any chance, be interested in a Simple

---

1. Bontemps to LH, November 29, 1957.
2. Bontemps to LH, in Nichols, ed., *Letters,* 431.

column? Alfred Duckett, Vital Information Press, 143 Fenimore Street, Brooklyn 25, New York, is now handling the placing of my Simple material for me."[3] A key to Hughes's longevity and productivity as a writer was his resilience. He promoted his own work, created some of his own opportunities, and rose up from each setback with determination to succeed the next time. In addition to courting the Afro-American Newspapers, Hughes also had a "socko" Simple column reprinted in *Jet*.[4]

In mid–1962, however, Hughes began writing a regular column for the *New York Post,* a development that Bontemps called "the most exciting news." The official arrangements were completed by the end of 1963, when Paul Sann, executive editor of the *Post,* wrote to Hughes:

> Now that relations have been severed with the syndicate which was handling your column, I trust that this letter may serve as the necessary agreement covering our new relationship. We would like to go along on the same basis as before, with the understanding that your column is to be carried in the *Post* one day a week, subject to a 15-day cancellation notice on either side, at the rate of $15 per week. I don't believe that we need any more formal contract.
>
> While we are on it, I would like to tell you how happy we are that you are back in the paper at long last.

Hughes agreed to the terms as stated and added that he was "delighted to be back in the paper again."[5]

Obviously, Simple had been exposed to and appreciated by white audiences ever since *Simple Speaks His Mind* was published in 1950. However, when the Simple columns jumped from the homogeneous audience of the Negro press into the diverse audience of the *New York Post,* the weekly columns became vulnerable to a much wider range of audience response. Fans' sentiments continued to range from love to hate, but whereas the *Defender* readers who contacted the author tended to write relatively brief and often handwritten letters,

3. LH to Carl Murphy, Afro-American Newspapers, March 22, 1962.
4. Bontemps to LH, August 19, 1962.
5. Bontemps to LH, June 4, 1962; Paul Sann to LH, December 13, 1963; LH to Sann, December 14, 1963.

much of the mail directed to Hughes in care of the *Post* came in lengthy typewritten missives.

Some of the *Post* readers were encountering Hughes for the first time, which is almost unfathomable considering he had been publishing for more than thirty years. Although the *New York Post* in the 1960s had a bit less of the tabloid look and feel than it does in the 1990s, it certainly appealed to a vastly different audience than had frequented the black press. Imagine Maya Angelou writing a weekly column for the weekend edition of *USA Today* in the mid-1990s and being challenged by some women readers for having too pristine a view of sexuality. The *Post* response was that surprising.

A few of the complainers wondered about Hughes or the scope of his writings in such a naive way that Hughes must have been extremely amused or deeply irritated. To the readers who signed their names and gave their addresses, however, he responded. He patiently explained his motives and tried to help readers distinguish between his character Simple and himself.

> I am sure . . . that you do not really believe I am unaware of the sensitivity of other minority groups to their own problem elements. My character, Simple, however, like many other provincial hemmed-in ghettoized folks, thinks that *his* problems are peculiar only to himself. To ascribe to him (Simple) a broader point of view, would be out of character. But certainly I, as author, know better—as I am sure you know I know, and as expressed in many of my previous *Post* columns.
>
> My column is now over twenty years old, syndicated in other papers long before the *Post* began to print it. During the War and both before and after that period, many columns were anti-fascist, anti-Hitler, deploring and protesting the Germany gas-ovens, etc., praising the Warsaw uprising, etc., so writing-wise, that is where I was—while the ovens were working in Hitlerland, the lynchropes were swinging in Dixieland. Neither pleasant to contemplate.[6]

Thus, in letters of reply to his readers, Hughes kindly reviewed his columns and defended his own broad view of global events and human history.

While some readers lamented Simple's parochial opinions, others berated him in the most sincerely flattering way: they copied him.

6. LH to Mrs. Kapnik, April 4, 1963.

Several Simple clones are preserved in the correspondence received through the *New York Post* and in the *Post* columns. "Complicated Cohen" was sent in by a reader on March 23, 1964. Patterned after the dialogues between the Hughes persona and Simple, this alternate buddy is the exact opposite: "Complicated." This imitation is the exact opposite of sincere flattery; it berates Hughes for failing to appreciate the woes that have befallen Jewish people:

> Complicated Cohen shook his very intelligent head and said Oy! That Mr. Langston Hughes, he went on to say, sure is simple, isn't he? And so selfish! All he can think of is Negroes. How about Puerto Ricans? How about the Chinese? And remember what was done to the Japanese on the West Coast during the late Unpleasantness in Europe? Hum?
>
> Dear Mr. Hughes, please get the hell off that single track and give us something a little broader in scope. We really are tired of reading about nothing but the hard lot of the Negroes. Other peoples have a hard time, too. What about them? Huh, Mr. Hughes?
>
> On second thought, Mr. Hughes, why the hell don't you stick to poetry, which you do so well?
>
> I quote from memory: "That Justice is a blind goddess we poor are wise; her bandage hides two festering sores that once were eyes."
>
> Pretty close, Mr. Hughes? It's the best my memory can do after twenty years of crud.
>
> Please, Mr. Hughes, write us some more poetry, will you, huh?

Although this reader enjoyed Hughes's poetry well enough to keep it memorized—almost verbatim—for twenty years, he refused to grant Hughes an author's prerogative to focus upon a topic of his own choice.

Another imitation appeared in the January 29, 1965, column—a new Simple created and sent in by Sallvatore Russo, a white cab driver. The cab driver is the "simple" friend, and the rider is the foil. The cab driver expresses his irate reactions to a Hughes column, which is exactly the way the Simple Minded Friend interacted with Hughes in the earliest *Defender* columns. His passenger tries to calm him, reminding him that Hughes "has to write something in his column—otherwise he'll be fired." The cab driver, however, wants Hughes's columns about taxi drivers to represent the drivers themselves. "Why doesn't he write and ask the cab industry to give us protection devices for our cabs, so that we can go anywhere in the five boroughs without being afraid? They gave us a ten cent raise. Big deal! A half cent goes to the company, five cents goes for benefits, and four and a half cents goes to us." Indeed, Russo's cab driver sounds quite a bit like Simple might sound if he drove a taxi.

Thus, many of the readers, especially the Jewish ones, resented Hughes's race consciousness and his failure to allow other voices with other views to speak for themselves. As suggested in Chapter 1, the challenge of audience has influenced many African American writers. Having been created in the black press, the earliest Simple stories escaped criticism and scrutiny by most nonblack readers. His readers may have disliked certain things about him, but they seldom regretted his ethnocentrism. Readers in the *Post* were very different.

The difficult criticism that greeted Hughes's *Post* column may not have reflected either the publication or the nonblack readership so much as it reflected the times: the mid-1960s had grown serious. The Black Pride movement had led to large "afro" hairstyles, African dashiki clothing, clenched black fist jewelry, militant slogans, angry protests, political upheaval, and even violent demands. As in any other politically charged period in history, humor lost its sheen. Recall that in the 1940s, Simple emerged as one of the few humorous offerings during that serious decade. By the mid-1960s, twenty years later, Hughes had grown weary of the public outcry about his character.

The outcry was not reserved for Simple alone, however. A 1962 article in *Jet* quoted comedian Willie Lewis saying that "people are getting too serious." The article went on to describe the kinds of changes that African American comedians were making to accommodate more sophisticated audiences. "The new popularity of Slappy White, Jackie (Moms) Mabley and Nipsey Russell—and the sudden rise of Dick Gregory—is growing evidence of the maturity of today's theater and night club audiences, and their entertainers. Instead of only joking about sex habits, skin color and 'down home,' Negro comedians are talking about integration problems, politics and world affairs."[7] It is indeed ironic that these "changes" could have been used as the table of contents for the first collection of Simple stories—or even for the stories from their beginnings in the *Chicago Defender.*

7. Larry Still, "Sophisticated Audiences Force Negro Comedians to Change," *Jet,* February 22, 1962, 58.

While he was not a comedian, Hughes cared deeply about humor. He had never used Simple or any of his other creations as a stereotyped betrayal of his people. Nevertheless, the times had created different audiences for Hughes, with different expectations. Thus, Simple did not have as favorable a reception as the 1960s wore on. As early as the August 17, 1963, syndicated column, Hughes was asking his readers, "Should Simple Be Put Away?" In this column, he quoted an anonymous reader who wrote to ask, "Why do you continue to perpetuate the stupid, ignorant, offensive character you call Jess Semple?" The reader went on to describe himself and to expound upon the reason for his complaint:

> I am a Negro and I can find no one who talks in his idiom although I live in Harlem and go to the usual places. I doubt if you live among your people, or you would have realized this long ago. The people talk in harsh, bitter, and angry terms. They are not "funny" and no one laughs at the things they say. Where is this simple "Jess Semple" you create? I say he is dead and died with all the other Uncle Toms like him.[8]

Hughes defended Simple by discussing the mentality of this type of reader:

> This letter expresses a type of Negro opinion regarding folk expression which is not new. When the Fisk Jubilee Singers first carried the Negro spirituals around the world in 1871, there were other Negroes who were horrified that these "slave songs" were being offered as a part of Negro culture. . . . Even the great Mahalia Jackson is outside the pale of appreciation for some colored listeners—who a few years ago did not appreciate Leontyne Price, either, when she sang in "Porgy and Bess." Now that Miss Price is a part of the Metropolitan Opera, however, "Oh! Ah! Ah-aa-aa-a! She's wonderful!"

Hughes went on to mention his own poetry and how it had suffered harsh criticism. However, he defended his perception of the average man in Harlem:

> I know there are many persons who prefer the formal arts, the academic arts, over the folk arts—which is their privilege. But there are

8. *Post* Fan Letters, May 29, 1963, LH correspondence, JWJ.

also many Simples in this world—millions, in fact—from Lenox Avenue in Harlem to Soho to Montmartre to the Bund in Shanghai. And they do not speak the school-book languages of their lands.

But they are not stupid (albeit sometimes confused) and they are human—often wonderfully warm and human—and sometimes wise. "Look at that gal shake that thing," writes the Atlanta poet, Julian Bond, "Everybody can't be Martin Luther King Jr."[9]

Bontemps congratulated Hughes for his method of responding to the anonymous letter-writer who didn't like Simple. "The anti-folk element is becoming vocal again. They are ashamed of Mahalia and Ray Charles. Down with them!" When Bontemps mentions that the "anti-folk element is becoming vocal" *again,* he brings to mind Hughes's trademark "The Negro Artist and the Racial Mountain," in which Hughes disparages the cultural preferences of "the Nordicized Negro intelligentsia."[10] Calvin Hernton condemned the same type of cultural elitist responses to Hughes's folk poetry during the 1960s:

> By some perverse twist of logic, rather than seeing Hughes's folk genre poems as a literal affirmation of black folk and life and art, during the 1960s some of the Black Arts politicians said the blues were "counter-productive" to the "revolution," and they trashed Langston Hughes as an "uncle tom" because of his faithful renditions in the blues idiom of our people. The detractors labeled as "reactionary" in Hughes's poems nothing less than that which has sustained the masses of African Americans through the centuries.[11]

Hughes's hostile *Post* readers must have missed his foreword to *Simple Stakes a Claim,* in which he cautions the "serious" journals and magazines to retain the valuable sense of humor that had sustained African Americans throughout their tortured history in this continent. Perhaps worse, these readers seemed oblivious to the poetry Hughes had written.

9. *Post,* August 17, 1963. (Author's note: I am pretty sure that Bond did not put that *Jr.* at the end of that line, the last word of which should rhyme with *thing.*)

10. Bontemps to LH, September 6, 1963, in Nichols, ed., *Letters,* 466; LH, "The Negro Artist," 162.

11. Calvin C. Hernton, "The Poetic Consciousness of Langston Hughes from Affirmation to Revolution," 3.

The poem "Puzzled," in *Selected Poems,* describes Harlem as being "on the edge of hell" and its residents as growing angry and restless with "The old *Be patient* / They told us before." "Elderly Politicians," in *The Langston Hughes Reader,*[12] succinctly criticizes those who would compromise racial progress for personal gain:

The old, the cautious, the over-wise—
Wisdom reduced to the personal equation:
Life is a system of half-truths and lies,
Opportunistic, convenient evasion.
  Elderly,
  Famous,
  Very well paid,
  They clutch at the egg
  Their master's
  Goose laid:
  $$$$$
  $$$$
  $$$
  $$
  $

Hughes probably felt that his works spoke for themselves. He knew that his stance and his writings had reflected a wide range of African American reality and that he had not exaggerated humor. His entire body of writing attests to his desire to distinguish racist, unthinking whites from those who feel goodwill toward other races. His international travels had sensitized him to the common bonds of people all over the world, and his works—particularly his original column entitled "Here to Yonder"—had reflected that awareness. Almost in "round two" of the witch hunts, Hughes found himself once again having to testify before a committee. This time, the hunt was for the 1960s brand of correctness, and this time the committee was the readers of the *Post.*

Dedicated to answering his letters, and determined to preserve an accurate image of himself as writer, Hughes continued to defend himself, separately, to one after another of the disgruntled readers

12. "Puzzled," *Selected Poems* (1957), 191; "Elderly Politicians," *Lanston Hughes Reader* (1958), 130.

willing to identify themselves. To the "Committee for Racial Pride" he wrote:

> I am sure you know (if you know my books at all) that as long as I have been writing and fighting for race pride, the presentation of black beauty, and the achievements of Africa, past and present, I would hardly be deserting that standard now.
>
> In one short newspaper column, it is not possible to present fully each time every complete side of whatever the subject may be, as I know you realize. So sometimes a theme is misunderstood—as when I once had Simple say, "When Linda Byrd Johnson goes to Howard . . ." I got several letters asking if the President's daughter was registering in Howard, a colored school! What was meant as a fictional and humorous jive was taken quite seriously by some people.[13]

How interesting that while black radicals found Simple too silly, too full of laughs at a time when "no one laughs," many white readers, especially those identifying themselves as Jewish, found Simple (or Hughes) too bitter. Hughes must have tired of the multiple negatives his columns drew, and he must have been tremendously grateful for the praise during that time.

In fairness to the African American protesters, however, one should notice that Simple's dialect in some of his *Post* appearances had grown to sound less educated than it had sounded in the beginning. For example, in one of his final episodes, "Repairs," Simple explains that humans are like houses, in need of repair:

> "For instant, if the boys play football, they liable to break a collar bone. If the girls ride horseback in Central Park, they liable to get throwed head over heels and break their neck. If they ski, they sure to break an ankle. And if they go out eight in a car after a party, they bound to speed—then WHAM! Crash! Kids scattered all over the highway—and them that lives is in need of repairs.
>
> "Looks like right now American white folks have got the notion that it be their Christian duty to repair the whole world, right or wrong, everywhere from Santo Domingo to Vietnam, even if they have to kill off half the people to cure them of what Americans think ails them."[14]

13. December 10, 1964, *Post.*
14. November 19, 1965, *Post.*

The subject-verb disagreement strikes the ear as less natural and more stereotypically "ignorant" than had been the case with Simple in his previous twenty years of existence. The cause of such a loss of a familiar style remains to be uncovered. One might even speculate as to whether a helpful secretary or typist had been given too free a rein in assisting with or preparing the column. Fortunately, however, even though poor stories such as "Repairs" appeared more often in the final years than in the earlier years, even at the end, most of the stories retained the appropriate "Simple" style and wisdom.

During his turbulent *Post* period, Hughes created his final volume of Simple stories. With the political climate becoming more serious, and with patriotism being diluted with "Flower Power" and "Black Power," Hughes again gave Simple a fairly political forum, although not nearly as political as *Simple Stakes a Claim* had been. Fortunately for him, his final volume of Simple stories was the fastest to move from typescript to publication. In February 1965 Hughes wrote to Lindsay Patterson, a much younger African American writer whom Hughes had mentored and assisted in recent years:

> Since I already have in process of being copied, nearly enough "Simple" columns for a book, I would like to *eliminate* at least half (or two-thirds) of these *remaining* columns that I have not myself read over or revised. So I would be delighted if you would put your critical acumen to work on them, and help me to weed out those least interesting. Another's judgement is always good to have.
>
> I'd say the most useful criteria for judging this particular material would be Humor and Timeliness. Those columns that seem *least* humorous, most dull, and the least timely in subject matter should come out at once. So put them into the *Omit* class.
>
> Into the *Doubtful* class, I'd say put those that are repetitious of material already in the better ones, but in a less interesting way—but which contain paragraphs or phrases that might be incorporated into the better ones on similar subjects, if used at all. Also *Doubtful* would be those whose subject matter has little contemporary application.
>
> Into the *Best* category, put those columns that are either humorous, poetic, or very timely in application. I'd say the *ten to twenty* (10–20) columns out of this lot that you yourself like the best, and would publish were you yourself a publisher. Since I already have enough columns revised and being copied to make a small book, I do not need too many more from this lot to fill a sizable volume. So you can be *really selective* as to the ones you'd put into Class A's envelope. . . .

> On all or any of them, please draw a line along margin wherever there are *dated passages,* in whatever of the three categories they are found, so I can cut or change those parts, if the rest is used. . . . If you come across columns that seem to you might be combined to make longer chapters (by putting two or three together—by writing new bridges, of course) these you might clip together—or otherwise indicate your thinking.[15]

Hughes remained conscious of the same factors that had guided his collections of Simple stories since the 1940s: avoiding anachronistic usages, emphasizing timeless humor, and minimizing repetition. Yet, for no other volume of stories does the correspondence reveal Hughes so overtly soliciting the editorial selection of another person. Had he begun to question his feel for the tastes of the audience?

Since he was already working with the congenial editors at Hill and Wang, Hughes simply introduced the idea of a new Simple volume in a cover letter to them with a draft of approximately thirty episodes. Within weeks, Arthur Wang expressed his delight with the idea. Seven months later, the book was off the press.Hughes sent his first draft of *Simple's Uncle Sam* to his agent, Ivan von Auw; to his publisher, Arthur Wang; and to Adele Glasgow, a friend who sometimes assisted him with typing, on February 23, 1965. He considered the draft of thirty typical stories "a sampler of partial contents." As he had done with each previous collection, he told his publisher that the final book could easily be expanded, because approximately one hundred more columns existed from which additional selections could be made. Since this volume followed the omnibus edition drawn from three existing books, Hughes clarified that none of these episodes had been published in book form before. These episodes had come from the *New York Post* and *Chicago Defender,* plus two pieces previously published in the *Saturday Review.*

Despite Hughes's disclaimer, *Simple's Uncle Sam* begins with "Census," a revised combination of two favorites from *Simple Speaks His Mind* that were also reprinted in *The Best of Simple.* For the attentive census taker, Simple lists all the things his feet have done ("Feet Live Their Own Life") and adds his "final fear" of dying before

15. LH to Lindsay Patterson, February 4, 1965, LH correspondence, Schomburg Center.

his time. However, as a joke, he tells the census taker he expects to "ugly away." Much to Simple's dismay, the census taker records the answer without cracking a smile. In the new ending for the combination of these hyperbolic lists, Simple wonders if that man really thought him homely enough to "ugly away."

After the introductory episode and its several familiar passages, the other episodes of *Simple's Uncle Sam* take the reader to new territory, much of it humorous in the way the first two volumes had been. The barbs of wisdom remain, however, forcing readers to see the world as Simple sees it. As with *Simple Stakes a Claim* and *The Best of Simple, Simple's Uncle Sam* contains no divisions between episodes. The forty-six stories include some chronological order, though. For example, another of Simple's cousins, Lynn Clarisse, enters the Harlem scene and later moves to Greenwich Village. Cousin Minnie resumes her place at the various bars of Harlem, but she later participates in the Harlem Riot of 1964 and eventually faces a serious health problem. Otherwise, Simple continues his pattern of assessing both the news and the local happenings from his own special perspective.

In "Coffee Break," which originally appeared in the *Post,* Simple complains that his boss is "talking about THE Negro. He always says THE Negro, as if there was not 50-11 different kinds of Negroes in the U.S.A." (*Return,* 102). Simple's complaint rephrases a crucial point Hughes has expressed in his works from the beginning, especially in *Not without Laughter* and all the Simple stories: one of his greatest contributions to human rights is his graphic revelation that there is no monolithic "African American."

To exemplify one of the "50-11 different kinds of Negroes in the U.S.A.," *Simple's Uncle Sam* introduces Lynn Clarisse. Educated at Fisk University, she is an avid reader, a fan of theater, and an activist for voter registration. The foil is so shocked that he playfully asks her, "Are you really colored?" Lynn Clarisse proudly points out her "darker than dark brownskin" complexion and reminds Mr. Boyd—by name—that Fisk University "has one of the best libraries in the country" (*Return,* 58).

Cousin Minnie reappears in *Simple's Uncle Sam,* continuing to seek "a boy friend who means business" (*Return,* 42). While Arna Bontemps encouraged Hughes to use Minnie heavily in the third Simple collection, we do not see her full power until this final collection. In it, Minnie tells many stories, but significantly she narrates her own episode for the first and only time in "Nothing but a Dog." She is allegedly telling this story to Simple, but in the same way that the foil was often left out of Simple's narrations, in this story Minnie does all the talking; her cousin never says a word.

Having established in *Simple Stakes a Claim* that she can take care of herself, Minnie proves in the final collection that she will also defend her rights and privileges. Although she prefers to let other people earn their own living and earn *her* living, too, in the final collection "Minnie will even work to keep her head above water" (*Sam,* 69; *Return,* 75). At one point in "Self Protection," Simple recounts about how this working woman rejected exploitation. Minnie kindly offered her boyfriend, Rombow, some of her own hard-earned money to go "sporting" on New Year's Eve. Rombow got drunk and tried to send Minnie home, while keeping *her* money to continue his celebrations. When he raised his voice and "upped his hand at Cousin Minnie . . . Minnie squatted. The blow went over her head. When Minnie come up, the nearest beer bottle were in her hand. With this Minnie christened, crowned, and conked Rombow all at once" (*Return,* 52). Simple did not completely approve of her tactics:

> "It would have been more politer—and cheaper, too—had Minnie hit him with something that did not contain good alcohol," said Simple. "Or if she had screamed and throwed a glass. But Minnie did not scream. She just up and knocked the man out with a bottle. Should not a lady settle things in a more gentler manner? Maybe even faint first?"
>
> "Your concept of the word 'lady' evidently comes from remote romantic sources," I said. "Gentle ladies in the days of antiquity never had to face the problems Minnie has to face. In fact, the whole conventional concept of the word 'lady' is tied up with wealth, high standing, and a sheltered life for women. Minnie has to face the world every day, in fact, do battle with it."
>
> "True," said Simple, "to remain a lady, Minnie often has to fight. It is not always easy for a colored lady to keep her ladyhood." ("Ladyhood," *Return,* 55–56)

The foil raises an important distinction between the romantic notions of delicate, sheltered, helpless "ladies" and the realistic lives of hard-working, self-protecting "women"—especially African American women.

While Minnie knows how to protect herself from men who fail to respect her, she cannot protect herself from being injured during a riot. "Wigs for Freedom" details her participation in the Harlem Riot of 1964. In the common pattern of twentieth-century urban race riots, this one was precipitated by a white policeman who shot a young African American boy. In the same way that Simple had earlier rejected the unseen leadership of Dr. Butts, Cousin Minnie rejects her so-called leaders, whom she suspects are ashamed of their own people. "Telling me to be cool. Huh! I'm too hot to be cool—so I guess I will just have to lead my own self—which I dead sure will do. I will lead myself" (*Return,* 124).

Neither can Minnie protect herself from a tumor. She withholds the news of her medical condition from Simple until the weekend before she goes for surgery. At that point, she informs him that her surgery "might not take like vaccination. If it do not take, I am gone to Glory." Minnie leaves the bar without telling Jesse in which hospital she would have her surgery. As Simple says, "Minnie would borrow money from me at the drop of a hat. Yes, she would. But I guess she don't want to borrow sympathy" (*Return,* 204). Minnie has emerged in two volumes as a lovable woman with faults. Her illness and possible death leave the reader feeling sympathetic.

Simple's Uncle Sam rebounds from the nearly relentless political haranguing found in *Simple Stakes a Claim.* It reestablishes Simple as a well-rounded fellow who is willing to help a cousin in need and able to struggle with a budget, who will challenge his boss or the United States Postal Service—which ought to put more Negroes on stamps. Simple demands that the world pay attention to African Americans. When the foil points out that "Negroes are only about ten percent of the American population," Simple replies, "But we raise ninety percent of the hell." As Simple dreams of seeing his own face on a space-stamp, "designed to fly off into orbit," the foil closes the book with the advice Hughes gave throughout his literary career: "Dream on, dreamer, dream on" (*Sam,* 180).

J. Saunders Redding, in his review of *Simple's Uncle Sam,* officially declared that with this volume Simple had taken his place among "the great folk hero-gods in the American pantheon." Hughes did not proclaim any godlike status for Simple, but if he remembered his own 1941 article, "The Need for Heroes," he might have agreed that

Simple was among those "Negro heroes and Negro heroines—who may or may not always speak perfect English but who are courageous, straightforward, strong; . . . whose words and thoughts gather up what is in our own hearts and say it clearly and plainly for all to hear." As part of his own publicity program, and perhaps to address those tiresome critics who attacked his column for excessive humor or the lack thereof, in the *Post* Hughes emphasized Simple's universality to promote *Simple's Uncle Sam:*

> Simple had thousands and thousands of Negro readers before the white public discovered him. Now he is known around the world, because the books in which Simple appears have gone into many editions in the United States and been translated in numerous foreign languages.
>
> When I am, as author, speaking at writers conferences, or giving advice to young writers, particularly Negroes, some of them sometimes say, "Why be Negro writers? Why not write just about people? Why limit ourselves?" in their seeking to achieve a sort of integrated universality, I say that a fictional character can be ever so ethnic, ever so local and regional, and still be universal in terms of humanity. And I give Simple as an example. He is a Harlemite whose bailiwick is Lenox Avenue, whose language is Harlemese, and whose thoughts are those of Harlem. Yet in print Simple is known on the Boulevard Saint Michel in Paris, in Soho in London, on the Unter den Linden in Berlin, and I expect on the Ginza in Tokyo since some of his stories are in Japanese. Folks in far off lands identify with him.
>
> When readers identify with Simple, I imagine they identify with him first as a man, another human being, rather than as a *colored* man. But when he is in a book, he is after all merely a fictional man. Readers can close the book and put it on a shelf and, if they wish, forget about it, having used it to pass away a bit of literary time, accepting it for what it is on paper. But Simple as a *real* man, a living Harlemite, cannot be put away on a shelf anywhere anymore in these parlous days and times. Every day nowadays he says something real from the front pages of the newspapers. I, as a creative writer, do not believe in trying to keep up with the daily headlines. But since my character Simple whom I write about is an avid news reader, radio listener and TV watcher, I have to keep up with him. So in his new book, "Simple's Uncle Sam," published this week, I find that his comments which I have transcribed run up to the latest riots, and he is concerned with such current American dilemmas as Birmingham and Selma, as well as the old and puzzling

problem as to just how closely is he, a colored American, related to Uncle Sam.[16]

Notice that Hughes emphasizes Simple's responses to the riots and to the confrontations between Negro protesters and the forces of Jim Crow law and order in Selma and Birmingham. Simple fully recognized that some things were not the least bit funny. Yet, Hughes also highlights the global appeal of this Harlem resident. If Simple had merely harangued without humor about racial oppression, surely the readers in other nations would have joined Americans in tuning him out.

Audiences listened to Simple, however. The international publication of Simple, and the range of nations in which he has been published, is really quite astonishing. Translations of Simple have been issued in—among other places—Czechoslovakia, East Germany, England, France, the Netherlands, and South Africa. Hughes emphasized the power of ethnic specificity to reach people of ethnic diversity.

To identify with Simple, international readers had to encounter more than an African American protagonist. They encountered a protagonist from an oppressed community, one who conversed with a more privileged member of the same community. In 1950 William Gardner Smith, a reporter for the *Pittsburgh Courier,* urged black writers to render their tales authentically, "to convey suffering without romanticizing," thereby reaching all people.[17] Without the intervention of the foil, Simple might not "convey suffering without romanticizing." The foil, with questions, challenges, interventions, and frequently with agreement, helps to voice readers' doubts and concessions regarding Simple's narrations. Indeed, by echoing the original aims of the "Here to Yonder" column, the foil helps Simple relate his own suffering to the suffering around the globe. Such a link may have helped Simple to become universally appreciated. On the other hand, when Simple and the foil agree, the unseen other, the "establishment," becomes the butt of their jokes. Society's foibles, not those of the average man, become the subject of ridicule. Thus, once

16. J. Saunders Redding, review of *Sam,* 172; LH, "Need for Heroes," 185; LH, October 29, 1965, "Simple Again" (folder says "Simple's Birth"), *Post* file, JWJ.

17. Smith, "The Negro Writer: Pitfalls and Compensations," 76.

again, readers around the world can delight in a kind of victory when both the severely oppressed and the privileged oppressed agree that the ruling powers deserve scorn. Hughes's characters and his scenes are all black, but their strength in the face of adversity is universal. Thus, as he proved, "any Negro can write about anything he chooses, even the most narrow problems: if he can write about it forcefully and honestly and truly, it is very possible that that bit of writing will be read and understood, in Iceland or Uruguay."[18]

Of course, in order to be read in other nations, the works had to be translated. Therefore, one must consider the complex and challenging task of translating the Harlem slang that distinguished Simple from the foil. To encourage international publishers, Hughes sometimes recommended previously successful translators. His publishers and agents appreciated the special affinity he had developed with translators who could render his works into other languages without damaging their unique Hughesian touches.

For a different perspective on Simple's universality, readers should recognize the favorable critical responses to these multiple translations of the Simple stories. The entire Fall 1985 issue of *The Langston Hughes Review* treats the subject of Langston Hughes in translation. Included in this issue are Harry L. Jones's discussion of Simple in Danish and Soi-Daniel W. Brown's discussion of Simple in German. Later issues of *The Langston Hughes Review* provide Michel Fabre's comments on the French reception of Simple, and a small news service report mentions amputees in Kartoum, Sudan, who appreciate the Simple stories.

The Danish translations of Simple emphasize common bonds. Jones reports that Michael Tegn, in his translation, considers Simple "the universal little man who has intelligence enough to see the disparity between a society's preachments and practices, and who is articulate enough to express his personal dilemma and frustrations at the difference." Jones goes on to credit Hughes with the necessary beginning: "Had not Hughes himself created a universal outsider, an Everyman, if you will, Tegn would not have been able to render Simple as such."[19]

18. LH, "The Negro in American Culture," 90–91.
19. Harry L. Jones, "Simple Speaks Danish," 24, 25.

Similarly, Brown assesses Hans Rogge's German article, "Die Figur des Simples im Werke von Langston Hughes." Brown finds that Rogge "recognizes the reason for the popularity and success of Hughes's Simple stories: Hughes's mastery of dialogue and ability to make demands on the American public and government in an apparently naive and innocuous manner."[20] With both the Danish and the German interpretations, Simple's complaints about the United States and its racism translate into other concerns that oppressed individuals express regarding their own alienation from government. However, the endearing aspect of Simple is that he can register his complaints without beating the establishment upon the head. With humor, with exaggeration, with fantasy, and with logic, Simple makes his points clear in many languages.

Michel Fabre summarizes the French response to Simple. "To gauge the scope of [Hughes's] literary reputation in Paris, one need only go through the varied, but unanimously laudatory remarks of French critics—of every ideological affiliation—when *L'Ingénu de Harlem,* a collection of selected Simple stories, was published the Spring of 1967."[21] Given the radical political extremes in France, such acclaim attests to Hughes's own varying perceptions of leadership ideologies. Fabre also highlights comments from Dahomean and Ethiopian writers who attested to the authenticity of Simple.

The amputees in the Sudan were recipients of Islamic justice. Their crimes warranted losing a hand or a foot. Yet, despite their being on the other side of the world, they enjoyed reading Simple. They could relate their own penalization to Simple's oppression; in Simple's survival perhaps they saw their own pattern for laughter in the face of trouble.

Thus, Hughes's success has taught subsequent generations of writers valuable lessons about universality. While the literary establishment once associated broad human values that were not limited to one place or time period only with such Western classics as Shakespeare's *Romeo and Juliet* or Jane Austen's *Pride and Prejudice,* we can now trace both critical and popular appraisals of the Simple tales and find the same praise being offered to Hughes's portrayal of this

---

20. Soi-Daniel W. Brown, " 'Black Orpheus': Langston Hughes' Reception in German Translation (An Overview)," 35.

21. Michel Fabre, "Hughes's Literary Reputation in France," 26.

everyman from Harlem. Hughes's last collection of Simple stories, *Simple's Uncle Sam*, began as did his first, *Simple Speaks His Mind*, with Simple's litany of hardships, particularly those revealed through his feet; it ended as did no other volume—with that signature phrase, that code word that evokes Langston Hughes, *dream:* "Dream on, dreamer, dream on." This time, however, the admonition was not to "Hold fast to dreams" or to "Gather . . . / One handful of dream-dust / Not for sale."[22] This time, the foil, the Hughes persona, has the last word. He responds to Simple's enthusiastic fantasy of his own face on the first space-stamp with the patronizing response of one who hears but cannot even begin to believe.

As those closing words in *Simple's Uncle Sam* suggest, Hughes's dreams of Simple had begun to fade by the time this last volume reached the bookstores. He had begun collecting and polishing episodes for it in late February 1965; it was published seven months later, and he stopped writing the column in December 1965, only three months after the book came off the press. The sixty-three-year-old Hughes wrote to Joe Rabinovich, assistant managing editor of the *New York Post,* announcing that, effective December 31, 1965, he would no longer write his column. He promised to send two additional columns to complete his contract. His initial explanation for ending the column cited the range and number of his other projects and the extent of his upcoming travels:

> I expect to be going to Paris before the end of the year as my show, "The Prodigal Son," is scheduled to open there at the Champs Elysées Theatre on December 21; and the proofs of *The Best of Simple* in translation, and an *Anthologie de la Poésie Negro-Américaine* which I edited will be ready for me to read and correct in early January. Then at the end of March I go on a rather extended tour of Africa. So it would be difficult to write a weekly column while travelling about so much.

Hughes thanked Rabinovich for the courtesies extended to him, and he said he had "greatly appreciated having a column in the *Post.*" In his reply, Rabinovich expressed his regret at Hughes's resignation, saying that his column had "consistently been one of our more readable and

22. "Hold fast to dreams" is from "Dreams," *The Dream Keeper* (New York: Knopf, 1932), 7; "Gather . . . dream dust" is from "Dream Dust," *Selected Poems,* 75.

worthy features and we have been quite proud of it." While wishing Hughes success in his upcoming ventures, he also pleaded "that when your spring projects are completed you reconsider the situation? If you should decide to resume the column I am sure we can make a more satisfactory arrangement."[23]

Meanwhile, things with the Associated Negro Press, which had syndicated Hughes's columns, went downhill. Hughes terminated the relationship with them at the same time that he left the *Post*. Writing to Alfred A. Duckett, Hughes politely explained his frustrations:

> I am sure it must seem almost as absurd to you as it does to me that the Associated Negro Press International has been allowed to continue to syndicate my weekly column to numerous newspapers without paying me one penny whatsoever for several months. According to my records, the last payment you sent me was in January, 1965. By now, I figure ANPI owes me at least a thousand dollars. Therefore, I request that after the end of this month, December, 1965 (the end of the current year) you no longer submit my column to any newspapers.
>
> As of this month, I shall discontinue sending you copy beyond the four articles needed to complete 1965 publication in compliance with this 30 day severance notice. Therefore, I would very much appreciate your informing the newspapers serviced by your syndicate that after the end of December, they will no longer be receiving my column, and that they should not, without my personal permission in writing, reprint any of my work as such further publication would render them liable to infringement of copyright. I have alerted my attorneys and literary agents to this effect as of the above date.[24]

The genial and resilient Hughes was tired. He was tired of being financially exploited by the black press he so dearly loved. He was tired of having to explain the breadth of his political and artistic expressions. He was tired of having to defend his Afrocentricity and his respect for all humankind. When Hughes warned of possible legal actions, he was revealing a professional fatigue that Alfred Duckett must have taken seriously. Nevertheless, Hughes increased the effectiveness of his message by copying it and mailing it directly to

23. LH to Joe Rabinovich, December 10, 1965; Rabinovich to LH, December 14, 1965.
24. LH to Alfred Duckett, December 1, 1965.

editors of all the newspapers in which his columns appeared: the *Baltimore Afro-American* (and affiliated newspapers); the *Chicago Defender* (and affiliates); the *Pittsburgh Courier* (and affiliates); the *Norfolk Journal and Guide* (and affiliates); and even *Mohammed Speaks*. This last publication may surprise a reader or two, but indeed an occasional Hughes column—including Simple—appeared in the newspaper dominated by photographs and messages from "the Honorable Elijah Mohammed." While the *Mohammed Speaks* editors selected only topics that fit their own editorial preferences, they did sporadically include the Hughes columns.

Over a year after he ended his column, perhaps relieved with the absence of the weekly deadlines, but certainly missing his regular audience, Hughes again wrote to Joe Rabinovich of the *Post*. He sent along a clipping of interest, and he reflected on his pleasure at having been associated with the *New York Post*. He also revealed—perhaps more honestly—more of his reasons for terminating the weekly column:

> Sometimes I wish I were writing for the *Post* again; and people keep asking me where is *Simple*. But so "out of joint" are the times, and currently so confusing is the racial situation, that were Simple to attempt to express the opinions of the average Harlem "man in the streets" right now, he wouldn't be considered as amiable as he used to be, nor the dialogue as balanced. I am afraid that tolerance is running downhill at a rapid rate and the situation is a difficult one to kid. And irony, satire, and humor are so easily taken amiss these days, both uptown and down. For the sake of my own peace of mind, I'd just as leave not be a columnist any more. I never was by nature very argumentative my own self.[25]

Once called "Shakespeare in Harlem," Hughes had resorted to a phrase of the Bard to express how the shifts in public taste had contributed to his exit from the newspaper: "so 'out of joint' are the times," he wrote.

The final episode of Simple's saga appeared in the December 31, 1965, issue of the *Post*. In "Hail and Farewell" Simple announces the reason for his departure from the Harlem scene: "I am going to the suburbans":

25. LH to Joe Rabinovich, January 7, 1967.

"Joyce has saved enough money to make a down payment on a house, that's what's happening. You know my wife always wanted a house. She is now going to make a down payment," said Simple. "The first week of the first of the Year, 1966, my Joyce—who controls the budget and our Carver Savings Bank book—which is *not a joint* account—is having the cashier make out a certified check to this real estate agent who has done sold my wife a house so far away from Harlem you have to get off the train at the dead end of the subway then take a bus to get to our street, then walk three blocks after that to reach this house which my wife is making me buy. I will be shovelling snow, stoking the furnace and putting washers in sinks for the rest of my natural life."

Joyce has finally accumulated enough money to make the down payment on the house she has always wanted. Simple, who knows he can't win an argument against Joyce, has agreed to move to the suburbs, although he heartily regrets leaving. "I had rather have a kitchenette in Harlem than a mansion on Long Island or a palace in Westchester. A lawn with grass to mow and leaves to rake is the *last* thing I want. And God knows I do not like to shovel snow."

Simple has focused on the physical labor associated with home ownership, but the whiteness of the snow represents the final insult to this man who offered a toast to Harlem. "Joyce says we will be the first Negroes in the block." Simple does not welcome the potential violence from indignant white neighbors, nor does he like the high expectations Joyce will impose, so that he and Joyce can "show white folks we can keep a house up as well as anybody else."

Most importantly, though, Simple will leave behind all the pleasures he celebrated about Harlem. "I do not want to move out of Harlem. I will miss Harlem, Seventh Avenue, Lenox, the Apollo and the Palms, also this little old bar in which I am now drinking. I will also miss my friends—and you." He emphasizes his feelings at the end of the column:

"Life to me is where *peoples* is at—not nature and snow and trees with falling leaves to rake all by yourself, and furnaces to stoke, and no landlords in earshot to holler at downstairs to keep the heat up, and no next door neighbors on your floor to raise a ruckus Saturday nights, and no bad children drawing pictures on the walls in the halls, and nobody to drink a beer with at the corner bar—because that corner in the suburbans has nothing on it but a dim old lonesome street light on a cold old lonesome pole. And to get to Harlem from where you live you have to walk to a bus line, then ride to a subway line, then change at Times Square for the *A* train to Harlem. Friend, when I move to the suburbans, I am gone. So bye-bye-bye-bye! Goodbye! Yes, Jesse B. Semple is gone." ("Hail and Farewell," *Return,* 212-15)

Indeed, with those words, Langston Hughes allowed Jesse B. Semple to end his engagement with the newspaper-reading public. Simple quit the scene because Hughes quit the newspaper columns. Born in the weekly column setting, Simple also bid the public "farewell" when that setting was eliminated from Hughes's literary domain.

Simple's Curtain Call

WHAT REMAINS AFTER ONE examines *Simple's Uncle Sam* are the Simple stories never included in any collection. Some of them, such as "Repairs," cited in Chapter 8, are inferior in style or tedious in theme. Those stories mercifully rest, nearly abandoned, in the archives of various libraries. Other episodes, however, continue to breathe life into Simple and his supporting cast. Among these worthy but uncollected stories we find some highly political episodes, along with more of the otherwise missing testimonials to the strength of women. The most entertaining and noteworthy of these uncollected episodes, together with rather obscure stories from *Simple Speaks His Mind, Simple Takes a Wife, Simple Stakes a Claim,* and *Simple's Uncle Sam,* have recently been collected in a new edition of Simple stories, *The Return of Simple.* These, like Faith Berry's *Good Morning, Revolution,* offer dimensions of Simple that Hughes did not highlight as "the best"—or just did not have time to offer in book form, due to his death. Hughes died on May 22, 1967—less than two years after *Simple's Uncle Sam* was published.

Among the newly collected episodes is "Africa's Daughters," which was really ahead of its time. Feminist and Afracentric women will rejoice (pun intended) to see that Joyce is a Pan-Africanist. She wants to attend " 'The First Conference of African Women and Women of African Descent,' which I read in the 'Defender' is to be held in Ghana in July." Ever conscious of her budgets and her goal of owning a home, she admits, "If my club does not send me, I might not be able to go—in the flesh. But I will be there in spirit." Among the issues Joyce wants to address is a woman's right to prevent sexual harassment:

> " ' . . . no woman needs to make her body a part of her job, like too many women have had to do in the past. I BELONG TO ME is the new

slogan for black women. I SHALL BE FREE! the new slogan for black
women. EQUAL JOBS AND EQUAL RIGHTS FOR MEN AND WOMEN,
BLACK OR WHITE is our new slogan.'
  " 'I am glad you include equal rights for mens, too,' I grinned.
  " 'Keep on laughing,' said Joyce, 'but she who laughs last is always a
woman.'
  "I wiped that grin off my face, because I could see that Joyce was
getting serious." (*Return,* 169)

Feminists can point with pride to Joyce's assertions of women's rights.
What an important addition to her portrait as the culture-starved
middle-class striver.

"African Names" is derived from three *Defender* episodes: "Bull
Session at the Bar," "Simple's Stumbling Block," and "Let's Take Back
Our African Names." Simple tells tall animal tales, then decides he
wishes he had a truly accurate name, recalling his Indian and African
ancestry, such as "Buffalo Horn Yusef Ali Congo" (*Return,* 172). Anyone who ever doubted Simple's identification with the motherland
can put those doubts to rest.

Other topics considered in these previously uncollected episodes
include animal rights ("Money and Mice"), birth control ("Population
Explosion"), and some portions of the homeless population ("Help,
Mayor, Help!"). Simple waxes tender, and he speaks out against psychological child abuse: "Grown-up peoples should not get mad with a
child, even when they aggravate you. We is too much bigger and too
much older than children to get mad at them. Children has nowhere
else to live except with grown peoples, and when you get mad with
children, you make them feel like you do not want them any more"
(*Return,* 211). The "out of joint" times and the hostile mail from
readers who judged Hughes by a single column rather than by forty
years of writing may have made Hughes the columnist feel, like a
child with angry parents, that the newspaper readers did not want
him any more.

Indeed, the Simple technique and the Simple perspective continue. Actress and poet Ruby Dee has devised a few "Simple" stories of
her own. She explains her reasons for creating these stories: "Simple
just wouldn't leave me alone. It was as if he wanted to keep on
expressing himself after Langston left him and all of us. He'd come
to me and say, 'Hughes can't walk out on me like this after all our

years together. I wasn't finished talking yet!' That's how I came to write the Simple stories, 'To Pig or Not to Pig' and 'Honkies Is A Blip.' I hope Langston approves." Langston, no doubt, would approve. Ruby Dee advances the marriage into the more comfortable—or uncomfortable—stages where the "in love" glow has faded to a "how to live together" smog:

> "I am in the doghouse now," said Simple. "Let me take that back. The truth of the matter is that I am under the doghouse, if I am not the mangy dog."
> "Why's that?" asked the bartender.
> "Well, the other day I brought home some pork chops and Joyce started in on me. Made me so mad yak yakking about this and that, and that if I don't lay off my pork chops, I'm gonna get a case of cholesterol, turn to worms and die with a heart attack."
> "Lots of people are giving up the hog and trying to eat less meat altogether. Raw food seems to be the big thing now," ventured the bartender.
> "Now you bad as Joyce," said Simple. "What I look like walking up to a raw cow and taking a bite."
> "You know I don't mean raw cow. Although some people do eat raw cow. Of course, it's all ground up with onions and spices. It's called steak tartare. However, I was referring mostly to raw vegetables."
> "Refer on," said Simple. "Like I told Joyce, I do not like and will not eat raw vegetables or any other kind of rabbit food. I know I'll die from something, so it may as well be from something I love like pork chops."[1]

While Ruby Dee has patterned new episodes directly upon the tried and true Simple method, other writers keep Simple alive by expanding or innovating upon the techniques.

In his second book of allegorical essays to discuss racism in America, *Faces at the Bottom of the Well,* noted law professor and activist Derrick Bell evokes the dialogue and debate characteristic of Hughes's Simple stories. In chapter 1, "Racial Symbols: A Limited Legacy," the protagonist (a Bell persona) laments "the contradictions of civil rights representation" as he dashes into a limousine waiting to deliver him

---

1. Ruby Dee, *My One Good Nerve: Rhythms, Rhymes, Reasons,* ix, 39.

from one lecture to another. The driver, a dark-skinned, thin African American, probably in his late fifties, is named Jesse B. Semple.

Fully aware of his namesake, the driver proudly announces "that's been my name all my life, and I'm not about to change it." He goes on to explain, "My mother loved Langston Hughes. Our family name was Semple, and it was a natural to name me Jesse B. If you know the character, you also know why I'm sure not sorry about the name." The rest of the chapter appears to ignore Hughes's creation and concentrate on Bell's dialogue between himself and Semple. However, the entire scene deconstructs the Simple setting. Bell deliberately avoids telling the driver his own identity, thereby becoming the anonymous "I" of the Simple dialogues. This time Mr. Semple avidly reads books, a direct contrast to the newspaper aficionado Hughes created. The result of both sets of reading materials is the same, however. Both of these Semple men are "race men," but both tend to sound excessively negative.

This Semple of the 1990s reads voraciously and widely, including history, psychology, and fiction in his recommended list. He echoes his namesake in chiding the achievers who fail to act. "Aware don't make it, man! You got to be *with* it, like the rappers. I bet you don't even listen to their music unless one of the groups gets tossed in jail for bodacious language. But read what John Edgar Wideman says about them. He makes my point." With that last point, this new Semple hands Bell *Breaking Ice: An Anthology of Contemporary African-American Fiction* and urges him to read MacArthur Award–winner Wideman's preface. This new Mr. Semple discusses the Emancipation Proclamation, Jesse Jackson, the Martin Luther King Jr. holiday, and Michael Jordan. He says he wants his symbols off the shelf and "in action, embarrassing white folks and mobilizing black folks to take themselves seriously." For his own philosophy, he borrows from Toni Morrison's novel *Beloved,* espousing the advice Denver imagines her grandmother giving her as she braces herself to leave her house to get help for her sick mother: know that there is danger and no defense, and then go on. Thus, Bell has employed a man with a literary name who draws upon a different fictional character to voice what is his own central theme in the book: "racism is an integral, permanent, and indestructible component of this society." Yet, Bell asserts that we must move beyond any despair which that pronouncement might engender. "In these perilous times, we must . . . fashion a philosophy that both matches the unique dangers we face, and enables us to recognize in those dangers opportunities for committed living and humane service." In other words, "know it, and go on." Bell, in his marvelous montage of ideas, indirectly credits Hughes's Simple as a forefather of that philosophy. After all, did Simple ever deny the existence of racism? the horror of racism? the injustice of racism? Never. Simple saw life as it was, replete with discomfort. Yet he demonstrated that he could "know it, and go on."[2]

As demonstrated by these recent works by Ruby Dee and Derrick Bell and with the new collection of Simple stories, *The Return of Simple,* Simple may have bid the world "hail and farewell" in December 1965, but he lives on.

Critical attention to Simple lives on, as well. This work has broken some ground, but it remains far from comprehensive. A full study could be devoted to Simple in translation. Feminist criticism will offer new ways of looking at Joyce, Zarita, Minnie, Mabel, Madam Butler, and other women in these stories. John T. West III has suggested that the Simple stories need to be evaluated as essays, in the tradition of Joseph Addison and Richard Steele. Such essays tended to have roots in journalism, not literature. Indeed, the whole journalistic angle deserves a full exploration. Linguistic analysis has been applied to the stories to a limited degree, but particularly as one measures the language of Simple in its less grammatical form in the later years, thorough analysis may shed additional light.

As literary criticism and popular tastes cycle back to a more human-centered focus, levels of appreciation and the numbers of critical studies focused upon Simple should escalate once again. Much remains to be appreciated and criticized about Jesse B. Semple.

2. Derrick Bell, *Faces at the Bottom of the Well: The Permanence of Racism,* ix, 16-17, 21, 28-29, 195; Toni Morrison, *Beloved* (New York: Knopf, 1988), 244.

"Here to Yonder" Columns, 1942–1949

THE FOLLOWING IS A LIST of Langston Hughes's "Here to Yonder" columns as they appeared in the *Chicago Defender* from 1942 to 1949, including their dates, individual titles, categories, subjects, and, if republished, where they appeared, new titles, or into what story they were incorporated.

These abbreviations were used for the categories:

NF = Nonfiction   F = Fiction, not Simple
S = Simple   P = Poetry
Wonder = I Wonder as I Wander

All Simple stories below that were published in the book-length collections appear in *Simple Speaks His Mind* unless otherwise indicated. No subject description accompanies published Simple stories.

Date	Title	Category and Subject
1942		
Nov. 21	Why and Wherefore	NF: racial injustice
Nov. 28	Maker of the Blues	NF: tribute to W. C. Handy
Dec. 5	Child of Charm	NF: tribute to Josephine Baker
Dec. 12	Jokes on Our White Folks	NF: foolish racism; army, Red Cross regulations
Dec. 19	He'd Leave Him Dying	NF: racism wastes lives
Dec. 26	Rationed Xmases	NF: autobiographical

Continued on next page

Date	Title	Category and Subject
1943		
Jan. 2	no column	
Jan. 9	Music at Year's End	NF: music and economics (compare *Ask Your Mama*)
Jan. 16	No Half-Freedoms	NF: historical and current criticism
Jan. 23	Hotels Non-Deluxe	NF: poor service in colored hotels
Jan. 30	Ask for Everything	NF: criticism, challenge to blacks
Feb. 6	The Duke Plays for Russia	NF: freedoms, travel-type report
Feb. 13	Conversation at Midnight	S: Nazis vs. Jim Crow
Feb. 20	Wives, War and Money	S: money problems
Feb. 27	My Friend Wants to Argue	S: Nazis
Mar. 6	The Red Army	NF: Russia (*Wonder*)
Mar. 13	Time Now to Stop, Actors	NF: Hollywood and stereotypes
Mar. 20	Further Comment on Hollywood	NF: challenge to actors
Mar. 27	What You Can Do about Blacks	NF: suggestions to Hollywood
Apr. 3	Don't Be a Food Sissy	NF: travels, foods
Apr. 10	A Young Lady Lectures	NF: tribute to Margaret Walker
Apr. 17	Jews, Negroes and Hollywood	S: responds to earlier columns
Apr. 24	Bad Southern Cop	NF: bad cop seems as bad as Hitler
May 1	Mugging	NF: mentions Simple; criticizes black crime
May 8	Plays for a Negro Theater	NF: criticism of black companies acting white plays
May 15	Ode to My Simple Minded Friend	P: humorous poem showing the joys of their arguments

Date	Title	Category and Subject
May 22	America after the War	NF: freedoms, mentions Red Cross
May 29	The World after the War	NF: freedoms, challenge to all
June 5	God, War, and Swing	NF: Don't violate church songs
June 12	After the Accident	F: humor; Amelia, the jealous wife; Nancy, the flirt "Heaven to Hell" in *Laughing to Keep from Crying*
June 19	Key Chains with No Keys	NF: current criticism; economics and racism
June 26	Let the South Secede	S: southern racism
July 3	On Leaping and Shouting	NF: tribute to Pearl Primus; regret Jim Crow
July 10	Letter to the South	NF: direct address to whites; problems of Jim Crow life
July 17	Get Together, Minorities	NF: pure Americans and racism; Red Cross blood
July 24	If Dixie Invades Europe	NF: Red Cross blood; Russia not fascist like racist U.S.
July 31	On Missing a Train	NF: autobiographical, funny
Aug. 7	Saturday Night	NF: sounds of a Harlem street (compare *Montage of a Dream*)
Aug. 14	Letter to White Shopkeepers	NF: Harlem Riots; direct address to whites; jobs, profits (used in "Ways and Means")
Aug. 21	Suggestions to White Shopkeepers	NF: continues from week before (used in "Ways and Means")
Aug. 28	Simple Looks for Justice	S: Harlem Riots; Simple's role (used in "Ways and Means")

Continued on next page

Date	Title	Category and Subject
Sept. 4	What to Do Now	NF: challenges for blacks
Sept. 11	The Detroit Blues	NF: Detroit riots; fascist Jim Crow
Sept. 18	Are You Spanish?	NF: Jim Crow fascism; prejudice against black passengers on trains
Sept. 25	Things That Amaze Me	NF: factual incidents of racism; Jim Crow blood
Oct. 2	On the Positive Side	NF: reader's poem; Hitler worse than Jim Crow
Oct. 9	Simple and the Landladies	S: oppressive landlady; mentions Mr. Boyd ("Landladies")
Oct. 16	The Snake in the House	NF: Indirect address to whites; Jim Crow
Oct. 23	Gall and Glory	NF: Jim Crow army training
Oct. 30	The Failure of Education	NF: how higher education failed to teach attainers how to act for humanity's benefit
Nov. 6	Let's Laugh a Little	NF: (used in foreword to *Claim*)
Nov. 13	Simple and the Darak Nuance [*sic*—"Dark"]	S: uncharacteristic economic analysis from Simple
Nov. 20	The Power of Poetry	NF: Du Bois's poetry; blacks' being "terrific subjects"; poetry can't do everything to change bad situations
Nov. 27	Simple and the Late Date	S: Johnnie Bell is late and Simple doesn't want to discuss it
Dec. 4	Questions and Answers	NF: news snippets
Dec. 11	Equality and Dogs	S: compares black and white dogs and people ("Equality and Dogs")
Dec. 18	Photographs from Teheran	NF: end Jim Crow; Stalin, Roosevelt and Churchill

Date	Title	Category and Subject
Dec. 25	Books Are Friends	NF: make good Christmas gifts
1944		
Jan. 1	Happy New Year	S: foil talks most; Four Freedoms
Jan. 8	Can You Spell 'Maneuver'?	NF: a writer full of race pride; humor
Jan. 15	Bad Is Wrong	NF: cussing in public
Jan. 22	Cussing Is Damning	NF: cussing in public
Jan. 29	Riding West in Style	NF: travelogue; bedroom coach
Feb. 5	Airliner to Oklahoma	NF: travelogue; amazed at speed and complications of air travel
Feb. 12	Second Anniversary: Fort Sill USO	NF: friendly folks at Lawton
Feb. 19	Jeeps, Bands, and Bulls	NF: Langston University
Feb. 26	Hey, Doc! I Got Jim Crow Shock!	NF: southern training camps can drive Negroes NUTS
Mar. 4	Doc, Wait! I Can't Sublimate	NF: Jim Crow ruins Four Freedoms; some blacks explode
Mar. 11	Hold Tight! They're Crazy White	NF: domination complex needs psychological help
Mar. 18	At Long Last, Thanks	NF: travel; Japanese people courteous in hotels
Mar. 25	Center of America: Fort Riley	NF: travel; Midwest cordial
Apr. 1	no column	
Apr. 8	Huachuca Bound	NF: travel; air travel not racist
Apr. 15	Arizona—Land of Sunshine	NF: travel; love for Arizona
Apr. 22	Cotton to A Cappella	NF: spirituals moved from cotton fields to concert halls
Apr. 29	Share—and Share Alike	S: whites should ride Jim Crow (see "Duty Is Not Snooty," in *Claim*)

Continued on next page

Date	Title	Category and Subject
May 6	Dixie to Golden Gate	NF: people should help others to rise
May 13	Race Leaders and Jazz	NF: need black-written books on Jazz
May 20	A Worthy Drive for Funds	NF: United Negro College Fund
May 27	Travel Is Broadening	NF: travel: Dallas, Phoenix
June 3	Simple Sees *Othello*	S: mentions *Native Son;* choking white woman
June 10	Walter White's First 25	NF: praise and criticism
June 17	Invasion!!	NF: segregation wastes energy and morale
June 24	On Women Who Drink You Up	S: ("On Women Who Drink You Up," *Return*)
July 1	Random Thoughts on Nice People	NF: "nice" DAR barred Marian Anderson; many care only about gratification of their own needs
July 8	On Being Black	S: don't say 'Negro' or 'brown'
July 15	Army of Liberation	NF: Russian Army not segregated like U.S. Army
July 22	Theater in Washington	NF: actors should follow Paul Robeson's example, refusing Jim Crow bookings
July 29	Dark Glasses at Night	S: explains strategy of shading eyes at night
Aug. 5	Capt. Josephine Baker	NF: strange paradox: when some blacks succeed in breaking color bars, others get mad
Aug. 12	Simple and the Elections	S: vote for *Mrs.* Roosevelt (compare Oct. 14, 1944)
Aug. 19	Over-Ripe Apple	NF: Hitler's ideas must be defeated

Date	Title	Category and Subject
Aug. 26	Unsung Americans Sung	NF: W. C. Handy's book, a musical-historical anthology
Sept. 2	Too Good a Time	S: (used in "After Hours") buddy can't sympathize with Simple's hangovers
Sept. 9	A Great Music Festival	NF: travel
Sept. 16	Not So Simple	S: ("Nickel for the Phone")
Sept. 23	Theaters, Clubs, and Negroes	NF: white patron hoped seat not beside Negro; Zanzibar seats blacks on border of room
Sept. 30	Concerning Colored Hotels . . . Again	NF: need for chain of decent colored hotels (see Jan. 23, 1943)
Oct. 7	A Mighty Fine Letter	NF: San Francisco motorman hires Negro conductors; some whites are good
Oct. 14	Mr. Dewey and Me	NF: can't vote for *Mrs.* Dewey's Texas (see Aug. 12, 1944)
Oct. 21	On Combing Hair	NF: humor; phrases echo Simple (e.g., *hurrah's nest, circus Ubangi*)
Oct. 28	The Disadvantages of Race	S: can't gamble because blacks must behave better than whites (used in "Possum, Race, and Face")
Nov. 4	Your Brother's Keeper	NF: admonishes cussers, vote sellers, and careless journalists to do right
Nov. 11	On Human Loneliness	NF: in dentist's waiting room, on battle front
Nov. 18	One Is Mine	NF: strength of Negro vote—better if more vote
Nov. 25	Simple's Rainy Day	S: he would not save money even if he *could*

Continued on next page

Date	Title	Category and Subject
Dec. 2	Fifty Young Negroes	NF: sailors guilty of mutiny; "white folks tried them"
Dec. 9	Simple in the Hospital	S: ("High Bed")
Dec. 16	Books for Christmas	NF: suggested titles to buy
Dec. 23	Simple's Merry Christmas	S: ("Simple Santa," *Return*)
Dec. 30	Simple and the Second Coming	S: (used in "Simple Prays a Prayer")

1945

Date	Title	Category and Subject
Jan. 6	not available on microfilm	
Jan. 13	Simple and the Law	S: ("The Law")
Jan. 20	Congressman Adam Powell	NF: tribute; biographical
Jan. 27	Colored Lived There Once	NF: restrictive covenants and the quality of housing
Feb. 3	The Animals Must Wonder	NF: about racism
Feb. 10	Negro History Week	NF: meaning of celebration
Feb. 17	Simple Pins on Medals	S: ("Simple Pins on Medals") retitled "Simple on Military Integration," *Best*
Feb. 24	Will It Be Jim Crow, Too?	NF: after the war
Mar. 3	Simple on Race Relations	S: ("Race Relations")
Mar. 10	Nazi and Dixie Nordics	NF: same kind of racism
Mar. 17	Fair Play in Dixie	NF: same wishes as "Simple Pins on Medals"
Mar. 24	The Purple Heart	NF: no color line in death
Mar. 31	It's a Barn	NF: huge house he visited
Apr. 7	Youth Meets the Elders	NF: youth in Knoxville's Triad Clubs raise hard questions for elders
Apr. 14	Simple Wants to Be Genius	S: to improve his social standing
Apr. 21	The Song Writing Game	NF: cautions young writers
Apr. 28	My Day	NF: young researcher requests LH to describe typical day
May 5	My Nights	NF: autobiographical, funny

Date	Title	Category and Subject
May 12	The Fall of Berlin	NF: current events
May 19	Simple's Last Whipping	S: ("Last Whipping")
May 26	A Minor Miracle	NF: travel: Hotel Gotham in Detroit, black owned, managed, and staffed, is great
June 2	Adventures in Dining	NF: blacks may and should eat in white diners
June 9	Simple in the Dark	S: ("In the Dark")
June 16	Simple and the NAACP	S: (used in "Ways and Means")
June 23	War and a Sorry Fear	NF: War might end without whites having learned enough
June 30	America's Most Unique Newspaper	NF: a Negro paper, the *Union,* in Cincinnati
July 7	"Noblesse Oblige"	NF: well-educated blacks must show consideration to all
July 14	Here Comes Old Me	S: ("Here Comes Old Me," *Wife*)
July 21	Simple Starts at Rock Bottom	S: Bilbo, Rankin, Eastland going to Hell
July 28	This Snaggle-Tooth World	S: foil talks most; Simple wants *one* job
Aug. 4	Nerve of Some White Folks	NF: domestic, global racism
Aug. 11	A Wedding, a Song, an Aviator	NF: Adam Powell and Hazel Scott; other news items
Aug. 18	Simple and the Atom Bomb	S: ("Serious Talk about the Atom Bomb," in *Return*)
Aug. 25	V-J Night in Harlem	NF: loud and lively, but incomplete; racism remains
Sept. 1	Ballad in Black and White	NF: recommends Gwen Brooks's "Ballad of Pearl May Lee," from *A Street in Bronzeville*

Continued on next page

Date	Title	Category and Subject
Sept. 8	Laughing at White Folks	NF: similar to "White Folks Do the Funniest Things," in *Common Ground,* Spring 1944
Sept. 15	Simple's Selfish Peace	S: (used in "Simple Prays a Prayer")
Sept. 22	The Mother-Foulers	NF: cussing in public
Sept. 29	The Origin of Mother-Foulers	NF: racial prejudice
Oct. 6	"Deep Are the Roots"	NF: Broadway play mixes sex and race
Oct. 13	Simple's Final Fear	S: (used in "Final Fear")
Oct. 20	Art and Integrity	NF: politicians lie, but artists should not
Oct. 27	"North, South, and the Army"	NF: (used in "Income Tax") black taxi driver won't transport southerner because of ill treatment at a Mississippi military training camp
Nov. 3	Simple's Indian Blood	S: ("Family Tree")
Nov. 10	Simple Speaks of Shouting	S: it's helpful, not high-toned
Nov. 17	Too "Too" Artistic Entertainers	NF: critical of hush-hush policy in clubs
Nov. 24	Black Is Fine	S: "all black is fine—but mine," e.g., tuxedo, gloves
Dec. 1	Simple and Cosmic Time	S: past can ruin future, i.e., Isabel ("Final Fear")
Dec. 8	Christmas Books	NF: recommends books as gifts
Dec. 15	The Great State of Texas	NF: praises Melvin Tolson
Dec. 22	Simple's Christmas Wish	S: for possum (used in "Possum, Race, and Face")
Dec. 29	New Years I've Known	NF: travel comparisons

Date	Title	Category and Subject

1946

Date	Title	Category and Subject
Jan. 5	Simple Views the News	S: whites own the world (used in "Possum, Race, and Face")
Jan. 12	Planes versus Trains	NF: cheaper, faster, no Jim Crow
Jan. 19	Simple and the Fur Coats	S: ("Letting Off Steam")
Jan. 26	California Boom Town	NF: travel
Feb. 2	Countee Cullen	NF: tribute to poet, friend who died so young
Feb. 9	Simple and the GI's	S: black GI's kept overseas longer and missed out on jobs; whites were deferred
Feb. 16	Travelogue	NF: tour schedule for LH
Feb. 23	Weather in the West	NF: travel
Mar. 2	Into the South	NF: travel
Mar. 9	St. Joseph to Memphis	NF: travel
Mar. 16	Mississippi	NF: travel
Mar. 23	Simple and the Secret	S: would reveal atom bomb secret to Selassie
Mar. 30	Encounter at the Counter	NF: travel and Jim Crow
Apr. 6	Art and the Heart	NF: travel
Apr. 13	Resolving Ain't Solving	S: (see "Simple Pins on Medals") let's solve problems, not just pass resolutions
Apr. 20	The See-Saw of Race	NF: some progress, some woe in race relations
Apr. 27	Simple and the Heads	S: greasy head on clean Easter suit
May 4	Posing and Imposing	NF: some rude folks impose to get recommendations
May 11	Humor in the Mails	NF: columnists not funny, public is (see Nov. 6, 1943)

Continued on next page

Date	Title	Category and Subject
May 18	Simple's Psychosis	S: ("Simple's Psychosis," in *Return*)
May 25	Cleveland—A Good Town	NF: travel
June 1	The Soviet Union	NF: first of series (see *Wonder*)
June 8	The Soviet Union and Jews	NF: continues series
June 15	The Soviet Union and Color	NF: continues series
June 22	"On Whitman Avenue"	NF: recommends play
June 29	The Soviet Union and Women	NF: continues series
July 6	Simple Sees Double	S: ("Seeing Double")
July 13	Summer Ain't Simple	S: ("Summer Ain't Simple")
July 20	The Soviet Union and Health	NF: continues series
July 27	Simple and the Country	S: (used in "Wooing the Muse")
Aug. 3	Faults of the Soviet Union	NF: continues series; why LH still prefers the USA
Aug. 10	Light and the Soviet Union	NF: concludes series
Aug. 17	Simple on Commentators	S: ("Question Period")
Aug. 24	New York	NF: travel; first of series
Aug. 31	New York and Us	NF: continues series; relative freedom from Jim Crow
Sept. 7	Sights of New York	NF: continues series
Sept. 14	Manhattan's Cultural Sights	NF: continues series
Sept. 21	New York to the Nation	NF: continues series; tribute to *Opportunity*
Sept. 28	Simple's Vacation	S: ("Vacation")
Oct. 5	Simple and Harlem	S: ("A Toast to Harlem")
Oct. 12	409 Edgecombe	NF: names in the news; tour guide in New York
Oct. 19	Greenwich Village Negroes	NF: names in the news
Oct. 26	Simple's Landlady's Dog	S: ("No Alternative")
Nov. 2	Simple Late at Night	S: ("Conversation on the Corner")
Nov. 9	Letter and Answer	NF: replies to reader's question about "no race prejudice in Russia"
Nov. 16	Little Bad Habits	NF: manners, courtesy
Nov. 23	Simple Shivers	S: war hurt black soldiers "in their souls!"

Date	Title	Category and Subject
Nov. 30	Low Down I.Q.	NF: manners, courtesy
Dec. 7	A Veteran Falls	NF: apparently true incident; never mentions Simple ("A Veteran Falls")
Dec. 14	Simple and the Dance	S: Joyce dances to African music at Simple's apartment; landlady protests
Dec. 21	*Street Scene*	NF: LH's involvement with this play
Dec. 28	Christmas Wishes	NF: suppose Santa were a cosmic magician

1947

Date	Title	Category and Subject
Jan. 4	Happy New Year to Mexico	NF: we have Jim Crowed Mexican visitors; Mexico good place for blacks to visit
Jan. 11	Simple after the Holidays	S: Simple, Joyce argue over each other's friends (used in "Letting Off Steam")
Jan. 18	At Long Last	NF: his play "Mulatto" 1930; now "Street Scene" opens, Jan. 9, 1947
Jan. 25	Simple and the Year Gone By	S: Simple is down, doesn't care about global unrest
Feb. 1	Adventures of the Road	NF: travel; humor (LH left his butt print in a tub)
Feb. 8	South Bend's Smart Young Men	NF: praises taxi drivers who organized group
Feb. 15	Dear Old Southland	NF: compares U.S. to Spain, France, USSR
Feb. 22	Little Journeys	NF: at Atlanta University for the semester; urges heroism in black novels
Mar. 1	Simple Lets Off Steam	S: (used in "Letting Off Steam")

Continued on next page

Date	Title	Category and Subject
Mar. 8	Simple, Soaring, and Sleeping	NF: I = LH, asks Simple what to buy with salary from Atlanta Univ. position
Mar. 15	Simple's Income Tax	S: ("Income Tax")
Mar. 22	untitled	NF: Hull House in Chicago
Mar. 29	Here to Yonder Sure Enough	NF: LH sounds like Simple; wishes United Nations "would take a trusteeship over the South"
Apr. 5	Spring	NF: shoppers in Atlanta and NY
Apr. 12	New Worlds for Us	NF: Asia hates whites; new opportunities for blacks
Apr. 19	Simple and the High Prices	S: ("Simple and the High Prices," in *Return*)
Apr. 26	Simple Sees Red	S: ("When a Man Sees Red")
May 3	Week-end Reveries	NF: wishes to be at Fisk and in Atlanta at the same time
May 10	Freight	NF: do white doctors consider Negroes freight?
May 17	One Old, One New	NF: reviews books, Motley, Yerby, Du Bois
May 24	A Writer's Mail	NF: received 313 letters in Apr.
May 31	Sorry Spring	NF: $400 million for "democracy" in Greece and Turkey, while 31 lynchers in Greenville, S.C., go free
June 7	Simple and the Seasons	S: ("Spring Time")
June 14	Time Flies! Me, Too!	NF: travel
June 21	Simple's Un-Americanism	S: since racism is American, Simple is eager to face Rankin's Un-American Committee

Date	Title	Category and Subject
June 28	Just Thinking	NF: if born again, would want name *Robinson* or *Johnson*
July 5	Simple's Domestic Problems	S: (used in "Conversation on the Corner")
July 12	The Rest of the World	NF: their problems = yours
July 19	Harvest of Words	NF: Yerby, Motley, *Fields of Wonder*
July 26	Church, Theater, and Gospel Songs	NF: Hughes likes sweet gospel; church has invaded theater and vice-versa
Aug. 2	Bad Apples in a Nice Barrel	NF: dirty mouths, dirty streets
Aug. 9	This Summer: 1947	NF: scraps of news
Aug. 16	Simple Woos the Muse	S: (used in "Wooing the Muse")
Aug. 23	Simple Dines Out	S: "Summer Ain't Simple"
Aug. 30	The Death of Bilbo	NF: so racist that he pulled others together
Sept. 6	Simple and Jackie	S: (used in "Matter for a Book")
Sept. 13	Are You a Communist	NF: Equal rights supporters labeled "communist"
Sept. 20	Wallace Speaks	NF: Henry Wallace; Russia
Sept. 27	Simple Writes a Book	S: (used in "Matter for a Book")
Oct. 4	Heroes	NF: Dorie Miller should be featured in movie; also John Brown
Oct. 11	Simple Begs to Differ	S: bootleg (parts in "A Letter from Baltimore"; "Seeing Double"; "A Toast to Harlem")
Oct. 18	Too Noble for Nobility	NF: DAR, Truman, churches—broad fronts
Oct. 25	Simple and Temptation	S: ("Temptation")

Continued on next page

Date	Title	Category and Subject
Nov. 1	Celebrities' Mail Bag	NF: famous Negroes should answer their mail; LH tries to answer each person at least once
Nov. 8	More about Letters	NF: People write asking for money, pen pals, help with parole, recommendations; one woman irate about famous black men marrying white women.
Nov. 15	Dear Old Southland	NF: reprinted by request from Feb. 15, 1947
Nov. 22	Simple at the Bar	S: ("Something to Lean On")
Nov. 29	Holiday in Jamaica	NF: begins series: travel; color line almost nonexistent in Jamaica
Dec. 6	The Colors of Jamaica	NF: continues series
Dec. 13	untitled	NF: continues series: praises race pride in Jamaica
Dec. 20	The Girls of Jamaica	NF: continues series (compare poem "Harlem Sweeties," in *The Poetry of the Negro,* describing the range of feminine beauty)
Dec. 27	The Foods of Jamaica	NF: continues series

1948

Date	Title	Category and Subject
Jan. 3	Trip around Jamaica	NF: continues series
Jan. 10	Nuances of Jamaica	NF: continues series: streets, houses, street cart vendors all have names
Jan. 17	Music in Jamaica	NF: continues series: restraint in dance and music may reflect British influence
Jan. 24	Simple Rocks a Rocket	S: (used in "High Bed")

Date	Title	Category and Subject
Jan. 31	Politics in Jamaica	NF: continues series: contrasts Manley and Bustamante to Adam Powell Jr.
Feb. 7	Simple and the License	S: (compare "Family Tree")
Feb. 14	Simple at the Party	S: ("Party in the Bronx," in *Wife*)
Feb. 21	Simple Plays with Fire	S: Deedee was married; Simple was dreaming
Feb. 28	Simple Down Under	S: foil never speaks (compare with "After Hours" and article "Down under in Harlem," in *New Republic*)
Mar. 6	The Sunny South	NF: paradise—except for Jim Crow; bitter tone; LH wishes atom bomb would wipe all whites off the dining coach
Mar. 13	Sex! By Heck!	NF: teach facts of life
Mar. 20	Our White Folks: Shame!	NF: links race-hating and red-baiting.
Mar. 27	Our White Folks: So?	NF: asks whites if they will act to end Jim Crow
Apr. 3	Our White Folks: Boo!	NF: if Russia scares whites, tells them to compare Russia to U.S.—same injustices
Apr. 10	Richest Hill on Earth	NF: Butte—mineral rich, but full of Jim Crow
Apr. 17	Simple Gets Confused	S: ("Confused")
Apr. 24	Game Preserves for Negroes	S: ("There Ought to Be a Law")
May 1	San Francisco	NF: travel; little Jim Crow
May 8	Ten Thousand Beds	NF: ("Ten Thousand Beds," in *Langston Hughes Reader*)

Continued on next page

Date	Title	Category and Subject
May 15	A Thorn in the Side	NF: fears attacks on Negroes
May 22	*Trial by Fire*	NF: an excellent play, LH recommends
May 29	*Story of the Negro*	NF: by Arna Bontemps, would make a good gift
June 5	Silver Lining	NF: travel, California
June 12	Simple and the Rosenwald Fund	S: foil talks most; Simple regrets not receiving money from now-defunct organization
June 19	Nothing Like It	NF: could be Simple talking; celebrates the black press
June 26	Colored and Colorful	NF: more on the black press
July 3	Simple and the Lingerie	S: ("Lingerie")
July 10	Simple Spins a Yarn	S: Simple tells a fictional story about the democracy kids and the convents
July 17	Simple Goes on Record	S: Cousin Mabel sold all his jazz oldies; he needs I. W. Harper this time—not beer
July 24	Those Little Things	NF: whites claim to know Negroes, but they fail to know about stocking caps and "Daddy"
July 31	Beware of Basements	NF: things perish there—autographed books, letters
Aug. 7	Simple's If	S: troubles in the world; no beer tonight
Aug. 14	Simple Betrayed	S: by Humphrey Bogart; mugged after movie, Joyce beat muggers, not Jess
Aug. 21	Dumb, Dumber, Dumbest	S: dumbest white has better chance than smartest black

Date	Title	Category and Subject
Aug. 28	Simple and His Sins	S: ("Simple and His Sins")
Sept. 4	Simple after Hours	S: (used in "After Hours")
Sept. 11	Too Noble for Nobility	NF: reprinted by request from October 18, 1947
Sept. 18	Simple Thinks He's Simple	S: ("Right Simple")
Sept. 25	Silver Lining	NF: reprint, but column does not say so, from June 5, 1948
Oct. 2	Harlem's Bitter Laughter	NF: Red Cross blood, other Jim Crow treatment
Oct. 9	Notes at Summer's End	NF: prefers writing books to writing radio scripts
Oct. 16	Have You Ever Thought about What Will Happen after Doom's Day?	NF: [Format of paper has changed. Third section added. Now a two-column feature, with new photo. Followed by Mary McLeod Bethune's column.] Africa would probably be left to rise up after doomsday
Oct. 23	Simple Brings Condemnation on Himself	S: about interracial marriage (see Nov. 8, 1947, for a Simple remark)
Oct. 30	Simple Says Some Folks Don't Have a Moral Right to a Dog (Don't Let Your Dog Curb You)	S: people who cheat or lie must beware; even dogs can detect phonies (*Montage of a Dream Deferred* uses the phrase "don't let your dog curb you")
Nov. 6	U.S. Likes Nazis and Franco Better than Its Own Negroes	NF: Red Cross blood; poverty and color
Nov. 13	Being No Vegetarian, Simple Wants, Gets Meat, but How!	S: Joyce serves a meatless dinner
Nov. 20	Being Black Isn't So Bad, in Fact, It's Fun, Says Langston	NF: it provides jobs for lawyers and columnists

Continued on next page

Date	Title	Category and Subject
Nov. 27	Simple's Cousin Slick Gets the Cure from Sister Clarina Ray	S: Slick gets into religion strictly for easy money (prefigures *Tambourines to Glory*)
Dec. 4	Stray Cats in Cold Weather Need a Good Samaritan in the Cement City	NF: Neighborhood woman is a good mother to stray cats
Dec. 11	Simple Is No Patron of Arts; Loves Music He Can Understand	S: Simple asks why culture can't be in English
Dec. 18	Childhood Memories of Good Old Home-Made Fudge, Penny Candies	NF: Begs readers for homemade fudge, pull-taffy, molasses popcorn balls
Dec. 25	Brownskin Cards, Sepia Dolls, All Mean a Merrier Christmas	NF: Hollywood, unlike art, hasn't stopped the caricatures of Negroes

1949

Date	Title	Category and Subject
Jan. 1	Simple and the Clerk	S: ("A Ball of String")
Jan. 8	Words to Remember: Stein's	NF: cites Nannie Burroughs; whites have detracted from LH's contributions
Jan. 15	Simple on Recession	S: next depression to be called recession
Jan. 22	Simple Talks at Random about Some Mean People in the South	S: Simple is "jumping from one subject to another like a drunken flea"
Jan. 29	Without a Word of Warning Simple Discloses His Creative Self	S: poems, which the foil cringes to hear
Feb. 5	A Portent and a Warning to the Negro People from Hughes	NF: trial of NYC Communists foretells fate of blacks; Hitler attacked Communists first, then Jews
Feb. 12	James Weldon Johnson Collection Source of Contemporary History	NF: lists some holdings; founded in 1941

Date	Title	Category and Subject
Feb. 19	Simple Listens to a Bar-side Speech on Contrary Democracy	S: foil talks about contradictions in professed democracy
Feb. 26	Poetry Buys a Ticket for Little Trip South during History Week	NF: travel
Mar. 5	Democracy is Not a Theory at Black Mountain College	NF: integrated, labor-sharing college gives no degree, has no classes, 1-4 teacher to student ratio
Mar. 12	It Is Criminal to Refuse Any Person Food Who Has the Cash	NF: Hazel Scott was refused service in Pasco, Washington
Mar. 19	Friend Simple Makes Startling Discovery about Other People	S: White folks filibuster rent controls but rush to pass super secret spy bill
Mar. 26	"Troubled Island": The Story of How an Opera Was Created	NF: first opera written entirely by blacks and given a major presentation by an organized opera company
Apr. 2	"Troubled Island": Story of Great Dreams, Tragedy	NF: gives story line of opera
Apr. 9	Friend Simple's Philosophy: Let Other Fellow Do the Figuring	S: a medium checks Simple's numbers
Apr. 16	Joyce Says, "It's Just Matter of Taste"; Simple Gets Jealous	S: ("Jealousy")
Apr. 23	Culture: A Real Diamond Never Has to Force Itself to Sparkle	NF: "A genuinely learned man does not use his learning to humiliate others"
Apr. 30	Simple Contemplates Crossing the Ocean and Coming Back a Foreigner	S: Foreigners get more chances to earn financial success ("For the Sake of Argument")

Continued on next page

240   Appendix A

Date	Title	Category and Subject
May 7	Contemplations on Two Movies, Three Books and a Danger	NF: movie and book reviews
May 14	Simple Swears Off Pyramids; Finds Them Hard Work and Very Dangerous	S: no profits, in debt because of pyramid scheme
May 21	Simple Thinks Liberals Need a Mascot Like the Demos and GOP	S: ("Liberals Need a Mascot," in *Return*)
May 28	With Money, Love Is a Sweet Orange, without It's a Lemon	S: Isabel vs. Joyce; "What Could Be Better" poem used in "Wooing the Muse"
June 4	Old Ghost Was Once a Howard Man But That Was Long, Long, Long Ago	F: ghost tells rich lady to give to United Negro College Fund
June 11	From the International House, Bronzeville Seems Far Away	NF: true ivory tower at Univ. of Chicago, and truly international
June 18	Things I Like about Chicago I Like, and What I Don't, I Don't	NF: travel
June 25	Chicago's Southside Has Wealth of Negro Talent in the Arts	NF: mentions Drake and Cayton, Brooks, Charlemae Rollins
July 2	Old Ghost Revives Atavistic Memories in a Lady of the DAR	F: ghost of Blind Boone at piano makes rich lady boogie despite her hatred
July 9	Simple Says with Four Feet He Could Have Stood in More Places	S: ("Feet Live Their Own Life")
July 16	Old Ghost Has Three Little Words for the Grand Dragon of the Klan	F: Dr. Green "re-reading for the 18th time" Bilbo's book is told "Go to Hell" by ghost of Mr. Brown
July 23	Words He Shouldn't Use Get Simple into the Dog House	S: ("A Word from 'Town & Country'")

Date	Title	Category and Subject
July 30	The Fascination of Harlem as Great as Ever, Despite the Heat	NF: LH's many visitors
Aug. 6	Old Ghost Appears before the Un-American Committee and Refuses to Remove His Hat	F: since Jackie Robinson's speech, Negroes have no spot on Committee's agenda; why not investigate KKK?
Aug. 13	Don't Spring a Surprise, Simple Advises, Unless You Can Take One	S: ("Surprise")
Aug. 20	Old Ghost Has No Appointment, but He Gets Heard Just the Same	F: Old Ghost meets the president on yacht
Aug. 27	Old Ghost Besports Himself in Cooling Waters in Spite of Jim Crow	F: ghost opens pool for blacks
Sept. 3	Simple Does Some Talking about Dogs, Cars, Houses and Lots	S: (line about people who let dogs curb them prefigures *Montage of a Dream Deferred*)
Sept. 10	Simple Gets a Letter that Brings Him Freedom and Changes His Life	S: Isabel writes to request uncontested divorce ("A Letter from Baltimore")
Sept. 17	Simple Tells a Tall Tale That Might or Not Be True	S: Old Sam Bucks and his talking mule and talking dog ("Get Over John," not published)
Sept. 24	World's Most Exciting Singer Poses Questions of Art, Politics, Race	NF: Paul Robeson
Oct. 1	From the Sky, the Lights of New York Symbolize the Goodness of Life	NF: If men can build sky-scrapers, they can alleviate hunger
Oct. 8	With the Crumbling of the Old Chain, Jim Crow Crumbles, Too	NF: travel—China

Continued on next page

Date	Title	Category and Subject
Oct. 15	American Citizens Should Not Have to Have Anyone to Front for Them, but We Do	NF: to rent property, to get insurance, to publish songs, blacks need a "front"
Oct. 22	Approaching Winter Time Brings Back Dreams of Sunnier Climes	NF: travel
Oct. 29	Simple Supposes What Would Happen if Our People Immune to Atom Bomb	S: then whites would do anything to marry blacks
Nov. 5	To Understand America, Nehru Should Visit Negro Ghettoes, Too	NF: injustice
Nov. 12	To Sleep, Perchance to Dream Is One of Life's Unfailing Dreams	NF: how soundly LH sleeps
Nov. 19	Simple Declares Be-Bop Music Comes from Bop! Bop! Bop! Mop!	S: ("Bop," *Wife*)
Nov. 26	Simple Says for Thanksgiving There Are Some Things Better than Turkey	S: pork—especially chitterlings
Dec. 3	An Exciting Young Negro Pianist Gives Meaning to Our Musical Heritage	NF: Margaret Bonds
Dec. 10	For a Gift That Lasts a Lifetime, Give a Book	NF: suggestions include *Annie Allen,* by Gwen Brooks
Dec. 17	Simple Wants to Be Santa Claus for Just One Day	S: fantasy which empowers Simple
Dec. 24	Simple Makes Up a Xmas Song about the Black Wise Man	S: refers to Aunt Lucy
Dec. 31	Langston Hughes Submits Roll of Honor for Last 50 Years	NF: tribute

Contents of *Simple Speaks His Mind*

THE FOLLOWING IS THE TABLE of contents of *Simple Speaks His Mind*, the first collection of Langston Hughes's Simple stories, with dates of the "Here to Yonder" columns used in them.

Bibliography

Selected Works by Langston Hughes

The Best of Simple. New York: Hill and Wang, 1961.

The Big Sea. [1940.] Reprint, New York: Hill and Wang, American Century Series, 1963.

"Down under in Harlem." *New Republic* 110 (March 27, 1944): 404-5.

"*Ebony*'s Nativity: An Evaluation from Birth." *Ebony* 21 (November 1965). Reprinted in *Ebony* 41 (November 1985): 148-56.

Fight for Freedom: The History of the N.A.A.C.P. New York: Berkley Medallion, 1962.

Five Plays by Langston Hughes: Tambourines to Glory, Soul Gone Home, Little Ham, Mulatto, Simply Heavenly. Ed. Webster Smalley. Bloomington: Indiana University Press, 1963.

"The Future of Black America." *Negro Digest* 2 (November 1943): 3-5. Reprinted from *New World* (Toronto, Canada [August 1943]).

Hughes Correspondence, Manuscripts. James Weldon Johnson Collection. Beinecke Rare Book and Manuscript Library, Yale University.

Hughes Correspondence, Manuscripts. Schomburg Center for Research in Black Culture. New York Public Library.

I Wonder as I Wander: An Autobiographical Journey. [1956.] Reprint, New York: Hill and Wang, American Century Series, 1964.

Introduction to *Bootsie and Others,* by Ollie Harrington. New York: Dodd, Mead, 1958.

The Langston Hughes Reader. New York: George Braziller, 1958.

Langston Hughes Reads from "Simple Speaks His Mind." Record album. Folkways. 1952. F P 90.

"Langston Hughes Speaks." *Crisis* 65 (May 1953): 279-80.

"The Need for Heroes." *Crisis* 48 (June 1941): 184-85, 206.

"The Negro Artist and the Racial Mountain." [*The Nation,* June 23, 1926.] In *On Being Black,* ed. Charles T. Davis and Daniel Walden (Greenwich, Conn.: Fawcett, 1970), 159-63.

Not without Laughter. 1930. New York: Knopf, 1971.

The Poetry of the Negro, 1746-1970. Ed. Langston Hughes and Arna Bontemps. New York: Doubleday, 1970.

The Return of Simple. Ed. [Donna] Akiba Sullivan Harper. New York: Hill and Wang, 1994.

Selected Poems of Langston Hughes. [1959.] Reprint, New York: Knopf, 1973.

"Simple Again" [or "Simple's Birth"]. *New York Post,* October 29, 1965.

"Simple and Me." *Phylon* 6 (1945): 349-53.

Simple Speaks His Mind. New York: Simon and Schuster, 1950. Reprint, London: Victor Gollancz, 1951.

Simple Stakes a Claim. New York: Rinehart, 1957.

"Simple's Long Trek to Broadway." Article on "Simply Heavenly" for the *New York Herald Tribune,* Yale, JWJ, Hughes MSS #3570.

Simple's Uncle Sam. New York: Hill and Wang, 1965.

Simple Takes a Wife. New York: Simon and Schuster, 1953.

Secondary Sources

Bakerman, Jane. "The Seams Can't Show: An Interview with Toni Morrison." *Black American Literature Forum* 12 (Summer 1978): 56-60.

Baldwin, James. Review of *Selected Poems. New York Times Book Review,* March 29, 1959.

Barksdale, Richard K. *Langston Hughes: The Poet and His Critics.* Chicago: American Library, 1977.

———. "Langston Hughes: His Times and His Humanistic Techniques." In *Black American Literature and Humanism,* edited by R. Baxter Miller (Lexington: University Press of Kentucky, 1981), 11-26. (Reprinted in Barksdale, *Praisesong of Survival,* and in Harold Bloom, ed., *Modern Critical Views.*)

———. *Praisesong of Survival: Lectures and Essays, 1957-1989.* Urbana: University of Illinois Press, 1992.

Bell, Derrick. *Faces at the Bottom of the Well: The Permanence of Racism.* New York: HarperCollins, Basic, 1992.

Bigsby, C. W. E., ed. *The Black American Writer.* Vol. 1, *Fiction.* Baltimore: Penguin, 1969.

Blackshire-Belay, Carol Aisha, ed. *Language and Literature in the African American Imagination.* Westport, Conn.: Greenwood, 1992.

Bloom, Harold, ed. *Modern Critical Views: Langston Hughes.* New York: Chelsea House, 1989.

Bourne, St. Clair, director. "Langston Hughes: The Dream Keeper." *Voices and Visions* Series, PBS, February 1988.

Brown, Soi-Daniel W. " 'Black Orpheus': Langston Hughes' Reception in German Translation (An Overview)." *Langston Hughes Review* 4.2 (Fall 1985): 30–38.

Bruck, Peter. "Black American Short Fiction in the Twentieth Century: Problems of Audience, and the Evolution of Artistic Stances and Themes." In *The Black American Short Story in the Twentieth Century: A Collection of Critical Essays,* edited by Peter Bruck (Amsterdam: B. R. Gruner, 1977), 1–19.

Carey, Julian C. "Jesse B. Semple Revisited and Revised." *Phylon* 32 (Summer 1971): 158–63.

Chandler, G. Lewis. "For Your Recreation and Reflection." *Phylon* 12 (Spring 1951): 94–95.

———. "Selfsameness and a Promise." *Phylon* 10 (Summer 1949): 189–91.

Clarke, John Henrik. "Langston Hughes and Jesse B. Semple." *Freedomways* 8 (Spring 1968): 167–69.

Cooke, Michael G. *Afro-American Literature in the Twentieth Century: The Achievement of Intimacy.* New Haven: Yale University Press, 1984.

Dandridge, Rita B. "The Black Woman as a Freedom Fighter in Langston Hughes' *Simple's Uncle Sam.*" *CLA Journal* 18 (December 1974): 273–83.

Davis, Arthur P. *From the Dark Tower: Afro-American Writers, 1900 to 1960.* Washington, D.C.: Howard University Press, 1974.

———. "Jesse B. Semple: Negro American." *Phylon* 15 (Spring 1954): 21–28.

Davis, Arthur P., and J. Saunders Redding, eds. *Cavalcade: Negro American Writing from 1760 to the Present.* Boston: Houghton Mifflin, 1971.

Davis, Arthur P., J. Saunders Redding, and Joyce Ann Joyce, eds. *The New Cavalcade: African American Writing from 1760 to the Present.* 2 vols. Washington, D.C.: Howard University Press, 1991.

Dee, Ruby. *My One Good Nerve: Rhythms, Rhymes, Reasons.* Chicago: Third World, 1987.

Dees, James Walter, Jr., and James S. Hadley. *Jim Crow.* Ann Arbor, Mich.: Ann Arbor, 1951.

Dickinson, Donald C. *A Bio-bibliography of Langston Hughes: 1902–1967.* 2d ed. Hamden, Conn.: Archon Books, 1972.

Drake, St. Clair, and Horace R. Cayton. *Black Metropolis.* Vol. 2. 1945. Reprint, New York: Harbinger/Harcourt, Brace, and World, 1962.

Dudden, Arthur Power. "The Record of Political Humor." *American Quarterly* 37 (Spring 1985): 50–70.

Emanuel, James A. "The Short Stories of Langston Hughes." Ph.D. diss., Columbia University, 1962.

Emanuel, James A., and Theodore L. Gross, eds. *Dark Symphony: Negro Literature in America.* New York: Free Press, Collier-Macmillan, 1968.

Fabre, Michel. "Hughes's Literary Reputation in France." *Langston Hughes Review* 6.1 (Spring 1987): 20–27.

Fanon, Frantz. *Black Skin, White Masks (Peau noire, masques blancs* [1952]). Translated by Charles Lam Markmann. New York: Grove, 1967.

———. *The Wretched of the Earth (Les Damnés de la terre* [1961]). Translated by Constance Farrington. New York: Grove, 1963.

Gates, Henry Louis, Jr. *Figures in Black: Words, Signs, and the "Racial" Self.* New York: Oxford University Press, 1987.

———. *Loose Canons: Notes on the Culture.* New York: Oxford University Press, 1992.

Gresson, Aaron D. "Beyond Selves Deferred: Langston Hughes' Style and the Psychology of Black Selfhood." *Langston Hughes Review* 4.1 (Spring 1985): 47–54.

———. *The Dialectics of Betrayal: Sacrifice, Violation, and the Oppressed.* Norwood, N.J.: Ablex, 1982.

Guzman, Jessie Parkhurst, ed. *Negro Year Book: A Review of Events Affecting Negro Life, 1941–1946.* Tuskegee Institute: Department of Records and Research, 1947.

Harper, Donna Akiba Sullivan. "The Complex Process of Crafting Langston Hughes's Simple, 1942-1949." Ph.D. diss., Emory University, 1988.

———. "Langston Hughes as Cultural Conservator: Women in the Life of a 'Negro Everyman.'" *Langston Hughes Review* 7.2 (Fall 1988): 15-21.

Hawthorne, Lucia Shelia. "A Rhetoric of Human Rights as Expressed in the 'Simple Columns' by Langston Hughes." Ph.D. diss., Pennsylvania State University, 1971.

Hernton, Calvin C. "The Poetic Consciousness of Langston Hughes: From Affirmation to Revolution." *Langston Hughes Review* 12.1 (Spring 1993): 2-9.

"History of Defender Related in New Book." Review of *They Seek a City,* by Arna Bontemps and Jack Conroy. *Chicago Defender,* June 23, 1945.

"International." *Langston Hughes Review* 6.1 (Spring 1987): 60.

Jackson, Blyden. "A Word about Simple." In *Langston Hughes: Black Genius,* edited by Therman B. O'Daniel, 110-19. (Reprinted in Jackson, *The Waiting Years: Essays on American Negro Literature* [Baton Rouge: Louisiana State University Press, 1976].)

Johnson, Abby Arthur, and Ronald Maberry Johnson. *Propaganda and Aesthetics: The Literary Politics of Afro-American Magazines in the Twentieth Century.* Amherst: University of Massachusetts Press, 1979.

Jones, Harry L. "Simple Speaks Danish." *Langston Hughes Review* 4.2 (Fall 1985): 24-26.

Kent, George E. *Blackness and the Adventure of Western Culture.* Chicago: Third World, 1972.

Klotman, Phyllis R. "Langston Hughes's Jess B. Semple and the Blues." *Phylon* 36 (Fall 1975): 68-77.

Labov, William. "The Logic of Nonstandard English." In *Black American English: Its Background and Its Usage in the Schools and in Literature,* edited by Paul Stoller, 89-131. New York: Delta, 1975.

Lewin, Leonard C., ed. Preface to *A Treasury of American Political Humor,* 15-20. New York: Delacorte/Dial, 1964.

Logan, Rayford, ed. *What the Negro Wants.* Chapel Hill: University of North Carolina Press, 1944.

Long, Richard A., and Eugenia W. Collier, eds. *Afro-American Writing: An Anthology of Prose and Poetry.* 2d ed. University Park: Pennsylvania State University Press, 1985.

Louis, Errol T. "The Life and Times of a College Buppie [Black Urban Professional]." *Essence* 16 (August 1985): 52, 102.

Marx, Gary T. *Protest and Prejudice: A Study of Belief in the Black Community.* New York: Harper, 1967.

Meltzer, Milton. *Langston Hughes: A Biography.* New York: Thomas Crowell, 1968.

Mikolyzk, Thomas A. *Langston Hughes: A Bio-Bibliography.* Westport, Conn.: Greenwood, 1990.

Miller, R. Baxter. *The Art and Imagination of Langston Hughes.* Lexington: University Press of Kentucky, 1989.

———. *Langston Hughes and Gwendolyn Brooks: A Reference Guide.* Boston: G. K. Hall, 1978.

Mullen, Edward J., ed. *Critical Essays on Langston Hughes.* Boston: G. K. Hall, 1986.

Myrdal, Gunnar. *An American Dilemma: The Negro Problem and Modern Democracy.* Twentieth Anniversary Edition. New York: Harper, 1962.

Nichols, Charles H., ed. *Arna Bontemps–Langston Hughes Letters, 1925–1967.* New York: Dodd, Mead, 1980.

Nielsen, Aldon L. *Writing between the Lines: Race and Intertextuality.* Athens: University of Georgia Press, 1994.

Oak, Vishnu V. *The Negro Newspaper.* Westport, Conn.: Negro University Press, 1948.

O'Daniel, Therman B., ed. *Langston Hughes: Black Genius.* New York: William Morrow, 1971.

Ostrom, Hans. *Langston Hughes: A Study of the Short Fiction.* New York: Twayne, 1993.

Presley, James. "The Birth of Jesse B. Semple." *Southwest Review* 58 (Summer 1973): 219–25.

Rampersad, Arnold. *The Life of Langston Hughes.* Vol. 1, *1902–1941: I, Too, Sing America.* New York and Oxford: Oxford University Press, 1986.

———. *The Life of Langston Hughes* . Vol. 2, *1941–1967: I Dream a World.* New York and Oxford: Oxford University Press, 1988.

Redding, J. Saunders. Review of *Simple's Uncle Sam,* by Langston Hughes. [1966.] Reprinted in *A Scholar's Conscience: Selected*

Writings of J. Saunders Redding, edited by Faith Berry (Lexington: University Press of Kentucky, 1992), 172-73.

———. "What It Means to Be Colored." Review of *Simple Speaks His Mind*. [1950.] Reprinted in *Critical Essays on Langston Hughes*, edited by Edward J. Mullen, 75-76.

Rose, Arnold M. *The Negro's Morale: Group Identification and Protest*. Minneapolis: University of Minnesota Press, 1949.

Rosenblatt, Roger. *Black Fiction*. Cambridge: Harvard University Press, 1974.

Sartre, Jean-Paul. "Black Orpheus." Trans. John MacCombie. [1964.] In *The Black American Writer*, vol. 2, *Poetry and Drama*, edited by C. W. E. Bigsby (Baltimore: Penguin, 1969), 5-40.

Sekoni, Oluropo. "Africanisms and the Post-Modernist Dimension of the Harlem Renaissance." Paper presented at "Langston Hughes: The Man and the Writer," Lincoln University, Pa., March 27, 1992. (Publication forthcoming.)

Smalley, Webster, ed. *Five Plays by Langston Hughes: Tambourines to Glory, Soul Gone Home, Little Ham, Mulatto, Simply Heavenly*. Bloomington: Indiana University Press, 1963.

Smith, William Gardner. "The Negro Writer: Pitfalls and Compensations." [1950.] In *The Black American Writer*, vol. 1, *Fiction*, edited by C. W. E. Bigsby, 71-78.

———. Review of *Simple Speaks His Mind*. *New Republic* 123 (September 4, 1950): 20.

Spradley, James P. *Participant Observation*. New York: Holt, Rinehart and Winston, 1980.

Thomas, H. Nigel. *From Folklore to Fiction: A Study of Folk Heroes and Rituals in the Black American Novel*. Westport, Conn.: Greenwood, 1988.

Tracy, Steven C. *Langston Hughes and the Blues*. Urbana and Chicago: University of Illinois Press, 1988.

Turner, Darwin T. "Hughes as Playwright." [1968.] In *Modern Critical Views*, edited by Harold Bloom, 5-15.

Turner, Darwin T., ed. *Black American Literature: Essays, Poetry, Fiction, Drama*. Columbus, Ohio: Charles E. Merrill, 1970.

Van Vechten, Carl. "Dialogues—But Barbed." Review of *Simple Speaks His Mind*. [1950.] In *Critical Essays on Langston Hughes*, edited by Edward J. Mullen, 74-75.

Watkins, Charles A. "Simple: The Alter Ego of Langston Hughes." *The Black Scholar* 2 (June 1971): 18–26.

West, John T., III. "A Fresh Look at Not-So-Simple Simple." Paper presented at the annual meeting of the College Language Association, Durham, N.C., April 15, 1994.

Whitlow, Roger. *Black American Literature: A Critical History.* Chicago: Neldon Hall, 1973.

Williams, Melvin G. "The Gospel according to Simple." *Black American Literature Forum* 11 (Summer 1977): 46–48.

———. "Langston Hughes's Jesse B. Semple: A Black Walter Mitty." *Negro American Literature Forum* 10 (Summer 1976): 66–69.

Wright, Richard. "Blueprint for Negro Writing." *New Challenge: A Literary Quarterly* 1 (Fall 1937): 53–65.

Index

Permissions

Published stories, unpublished stories, manuscripts, and letters used in this volume are reprinted with permission from the following: Harold Ober and Associates, in agreement with the Executors and Trustees of the Estate of Langston Hughes; the James Weldon Johnson Collection at the Beinecke Rare Book and Manuscript Library of Yale University; the Schomburg Center for Research in Black Culture at the New York Public Library; and Hill and Wang, a division of Farrar, Straus & Giroux, Inc. (for excerpts from *The Best of Simple,* by Langston Hughes, copyright © 1961 by Langston Hughes, copyright renewed © 1989 by George Houston Bass; excerpts from *The Return of Simple,* by Langston Hughes, edited by Akiba Sullivan Harper, copyright © 1994 by Ramona Bass and Arnold Rampersad; and excerpts from *Simple's Uncle Sam,* by Langston Hughes, copyright © 1965 by Langston Hughes, copyright renewed © 1993 by Ramona Bass and Arnold Rampersad). Excerpts from *My One Good Nerve* (Chicago: Third World Press, 1987), by Ruby Dee, are used by permission of Third World Press and Ms. Ruby Dee.

The author gratefully acknowledges the cooperation of all these publishers, institutions, and individuals in this effort.